State Collapse and Pos   **...rica**

State Collapse and Post-Conflict Development in Africa

The Case of Somalia (1960–2001)

Abdullah A. Mohamoud

Purdue University Press / West Lafayette, Indiana

Library of Congress Cataloging-in-Publication Data available.

I dedicate this book to my mother,
Fatuma Farah

Contents

List of Maps and Tables

Maps

Tables

List of Abbreviations

ASME	Historical Archive of the Italian Ministry of Foreign Office
BMA	British Military Administration
ELCA	United Nations Economic Commission for Latin America
GDP	Gross Domestic Product
GNP	Gross National Product
GSL	Greater Somalia League
HDMS	Hizbia Dastur Mustaqil Somali
IGAD	Inter-Governmental Authority for Development
IISS	International Institute for Strategic Studies
NFD	Northern Frontiers District
NSS	National Security Service
NUF	National United Front
OAU	Organisation of African Unity
SNL	Somali National League
SNM	Somali National Movement
SNS	Somaliland National Society
SOAS	School of Oriental and African Studies
SPM	Somali Patriotic Movement
SSDF	Somali Salvation Democratic Front
SYL	Somali Youth League
TNG	Transitional National Government
UN	United Nations
UNCHR	United Nations High Commission for Refugees
UNF	United National Front
UNITAF	Unified Task Force
UNOSO	United Nations Operation in Somalia
USC	United Somali Congress
USSR	Union of Soviet Socialist Republics

Map of Somalia

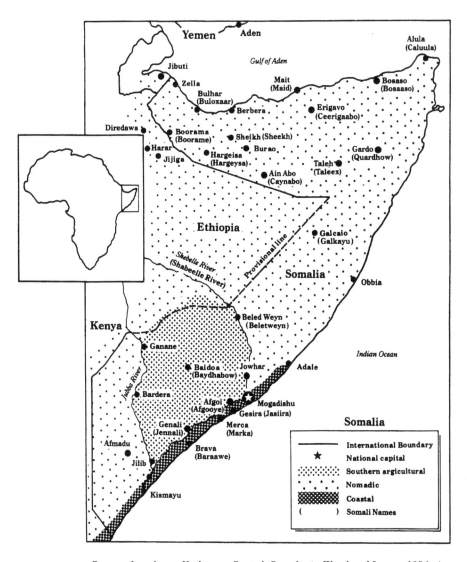

Source: Loughran, Katheryne S. et al. Somalia in Word and Image. 1986: 4

Preface and Acknowledgements

I started this research project in 1994 after the Somali state collapsed and the intervention of the international community was already in full gear in the country. During this period I often read and heard two explanations for the disintegration of the state, which were frequently reiterated in the writings emanating from conventional academic circles, journalists and occasional observers and broadcasted by the media. Firstly, the collapse of the state is presented as an event which happened suddenly, as no historical explanation is proffered. Secondly, primordial and violent clan politics are suggested to be the cause for the implosion of the state in Somalia. I found both explanations not only extremely shallow but also a-historical, static and idiosyncratic in nature. This dissatisfaction therefore is what motivated me to embark on writing this dissertation. Rather, I am of the opinion that the collapse of the Somali state must not be considered as a sudden event but as cumulative and incremental process over a long period of time. It is thus very important to search out the causes of the present in the past. Only in this way can we comprehend and delineate the significant forces that have been at work in the destruction of Somalia.

The purpose of the study is to probe below the simplistic headlines and examine the political economy of the collapsed state through a historically informed inquiry. Phrased in another way, the study discusses the collapse of the state within the dynamics of its own concrete historical reality and specific formation. In this respect, the study explores to what extent the constraints in the material environment and the misfortunes in the Somali history through time have contributed to the disintegration of the state. I will also consider, however, in brief the initiatives undertaken to restore a stable political order in Somalia and the obstacles, which are making it intractable. Since 1991, after the state collapsed, a post-conflict political development has been in process in Somalia. This ongoing political process merits a careful monitoring and, more importantly, further academic research. In short, this study is a modest contribution to the knowledge in the field of Somali studies and to the ongoing debates, which focus on the nature, construction, collapse and reconstitution of the contemporary states in Africa.

After the September 11, 2001 attacks on the World Trade Center and the Pentagon in the US, Somalia has once again captured the attention of the world media. This time Somalia was presented to the world not as a wretched place on earth, as was the case ten years ago but as an active collaborator to an international crime. Somalia was alleged to have camps run by al Qaeda militants who trained internationally operating terrorists. As a result, Somalia is now one of the top-listed countries that harbour terrorist groups and America is contemplating an attack on the country. This new development demonstrates how the absence of state authority and law and order and the enduring political anarchy in Somalia remain a threat not only to the Somalis living in the country but also can pose a threat to peace and security internationally.

Over the past ten years, power and authority have been the most highly contested issues in Somalia. Consequently, the political power in the country now is profoundly fragmented to nodes and myriads of rival powers organised along lines determined by locality, clans, militia factions, warlords, and religion. Each of these power groups is locked in a fight against the rest and also attempts to marshal external military and financial support to win the domestic war. It is in this way that the Somali protagonists in the country have been trying to regionalise and also internationalise their internal power struggles. And they have been getting assistance in one form or another from the neighbouring countries, Islamist groups and Somalis in the Diaspora. In this respect, the ongoing political conflict in Somalia is a good example of how a local conflict raging in a remote corner in the world can still entangle itself in wider regional and international power struggles.

The global political development after the September 11 attacks makes the conflict and post-conflict analysis in Somalia that I have discussed in the book significant in two respects.

Firstly, it is becoming very urgent now more than ever to thoroughly analyse and understand the root causes and dynamics of intra-state, interstate and regional conflicts wherever they take place. This is imperative if we want to prevent localised conflicts from escalating further and contain them in the zones where they have originated. Secondly, if certain localised and domestic conflicts are ignored or not dealt with constructively but allowed to drag on as in Somalia or Afghanistan, they are likely to have dangerous global ramifications. For instance, once again the domestic conflict in Somalia is becoming internationalised. In 1992, the international community led by the United States intervened in Somalia to restore order and stabilise the violent conflict raging in the country but that mission was withdrawn after a short while. Now after Afghanistan, America is planning to surgically bomb the suspected terrorist sites in Somalia. However, this kind of ad-hoc muscle flex is not a sensible strategy and will not succeed in subduing chronic conflicts like this in Somalia. In fact, conflicts like this in Somalia require a constant and long-time engagement in order to be managed and stabilised rather than ad-hoc interventions, a jolt of military muscle and prompt exit.

There are many people who contributed to the intellectual development in the preparation of this book over the past seven years. I should never have come so far without their support. I am grateful to them. Four people played a central role in the writing of this dissertation. First, I would like to thank to Prof. Gerd Junne, who agreed to be my principal supervisor of this doctoral research. I was extremely lucky to have Prof. Junne as a mentor. His kindness, patience and his confidence in me helped me to overcome my early inhibitions and insecurity. The perceptive mind and critical comments of my co-promotor Dr. Henk Overbeek helped clear the confusions of some of my concepts. Paul Aarts supported me in so many ways. He was not only a committed co-promotor but was a good friend who was always ready to help whenever I sought his assistance. I am glad to know such a wonderful human being. My external supervisor Prof. Ahmed Samatar was a source of encouragement. Despite his hectic schedule, Prof. Samatar read the entire first and second draft of the manuscript and his constructive critique and comments have provided me with the greatest stimulus to develop my ideas and research. He remains a source of intellectual inspiration to me. I will not forget the affection and the hospitality I received from him and his wife Marlene when I visited them in America. Each one of these four mentors has been of great help in commenting on the text and gradually improving it. From each of you I learned a great deal. Of course, I take full responsibility for how I presented the narrations in the book and the conclusions I have made.

There are also a number of colleagues and friends at the University of Amsterdam to whom I am very thankful since their presence in the department of political science made my life a pleasant one. Here, I thank Alex Fernandez, Jacqueline Vel, Marja Dreef, Leo Douw, Mehdi Amineh, Raymond Feddema, Henk Houweling, Nimako Kwame, and Marieke Riethof. My thanks also go to the staff in the library for their friendliness and prompt assistance, particularly Maike Sluijter.

I would like to express my sincerest gratitude to Azza Karam and Purnaka L. De Silva. These two people were in fact instrumental for me to undertake this research project. In the early stages of this research they contributed enormously to my intellectual development.

At some point in time the continuation of this research would not have been possible without the financial support of Stichting De Zaaier. For this, I am extremely grateful to Mia Berden.

Outside the academic world there are many others who stimulated me in the writing of this research. For this I thank Adri Nieuwhof, Christine van der Zee, Ingrid Jäger, Abdurahman Adam Samatar, Abdullahi Adam, and Zeinab Jumale. I am grateful to Anthea Hamaker for her help with editing the book and also Pim van Harten and Martin Sieperman for their support in the final stage of the thesis. And last but not least, a very special debt of gratitude to Juliette Verhoeven because of her love, support and patience.

To all those mentioned and to the many that quietly inspired, trusted and encouraged, my very warm thanks.

14

Chapter One

Overview of the Study

1. 1. Introduction

In this the twenty-first century, the state, the single most important political phenomenon, comes under tremendous pressure in some parts of the world. Yet, it is an indispensable political system without which no modern society can exist. In fact, as the current tragic events and experiences in certain countries clearly demonstrate, the breakdown of state amounts to nothing less than doom. Nonetheless, at this historic moment, the forces challenging the state are globally pervasive, and not confined only to a particular continent or country. The factors can be external, such as the impact of global economy driven by the logic of the market and maximisation of profit, or internal, arising from sectarian and particularistic tendencies, ethnic, religious, linguistic or cultural differences, or political and economic insecurities. However, the deleterious effects of these relentless pressures are more conspicuous amongst the states in the semi-periphery and periphery than those in the core regions. Acute examples of these deleterious effects are the state disintegration in the former Soviet Union, Yugoslavia and in certain African countries. Although the problem of failed states is historic and globally pervasive, the continent of Africa has the most examples of collapsed states among all of the continents (Zartman 1995). Since 1990s, more African states have suffered the worst of tragedies due to the strains emerging from these challenges. The effects among the different African countries have been varied. While some of them fragmented into enclaves of fiefdoms controlled by armed clan militias, ethnic groups and mercenary gangs like Liberia, Sierra Leone and Somalia, others like Algeria, Angola, Burundi and Congo are still in the midst of vicious power struggles that are waged according to sectarian pursuits, as well as along ethnic and religious lines.

With respect to the states in the Horn of Africa, among many dramatic events, the abrupt end of the Cold War era was the most crucial. In 1991, the two highly prized superpower client states of Ethiopia and Somalia in the Horn sub-region collapsed.[1] Consequently, Ethiopia embarked on experimenting with an alternative power arrangement. The old and overcentralised power of the state was radically deconstructed. The new statecraft, which lays emphasis on the division of the country into ethnic-based regions, is far-reaching since it gave birth to the emergence of a new state in the 1990s—Eritrea. Perhaps, this innovation of devising a new political society in the country was what ultimately saved the Ethiopian state from falling apart. Unfortunately, however, since May 1998 Ethiopia has been embroiled in a destructive border conflict with Eritrea over a disputed piece of barren desert, which has gravely destabilised both states. As a result, the peace dividend both countries enjoyed between 1991-1998 has been consigned to dust within a very short span of time. The war is now over but the political tension still remains.

---

[1] Despite the deeper internal fragmentation and power crises, the superpowers have helped both states to maintain a semblance of stability in decades. In fact, the high levels of superpower military involvement in both states is what earned the sub-region the nickname the "Horn of Conflict" as it is now known globally.

By contrast, in the case of Somalia with the termination of the Cold War the central government collapsed and the fragmentation process of the state was set on course. The combustions of this disintegration process further propelled the state of Somalia into its total demise with dire social consequences. Not one of the societies of the aforementioned states, no matter how crippled, has experienced such a total demise. The appalling situation in Somalia in the aftermath of the state collapse has been fittingly described by the Red Cross as "the worst humanitarian disaster in the world since 1945" (Geshekter 1997:81). The dire extent of the fragmentation process is what makes the situation in Somalia so exceptional. Somalia is the only country where the disintegration of the state is complete. In other words, the fragmentation of the state has totally ruined the infrastructure of the metropolis of what Migdal (1988) calls, "the state's home base", in this case, Mogadishu. In this respect, the case of Somalia represents an apocalyptic form of social disaster in this twenty-first century.[2]

In the spring of 1991, Somalia ceased to exist as a state, at least in the modern sense of a state system that functions as a mechanism for control and social organisation. After that time, the country disintegrated into fiefdoms that are controlled by clan-based rival factions led by predatory warlords. Even now after a decade, Somalia has had no effective central government, no foreign embassies, no national army or police force, no courts, no public services, no national health system and finally no schools. Everything in Somalia is now localised and extremely privatised, providing an environment in which only the fittest and the richest few can survive.

The central government of Somalia collapsed after clan-based politico-military armed groups violently unseated the long reign of the military regime of Siad Barre. The consequences of this event were dramatic as they led to total social disarray. For instance, the cohesion and collective consciousness of the Somali nation was fragmented into countless smaller units.

The power contestations of these units, who identified themselves along kin and blood-related lines, further escalated to sharp political divisions. With the absence of state authority and law and order, a protracted conflict ensued from these politicised divisions, which plunged the whole, of the Somali population into an unprecedented anarchy and into a deeper social catastrophe. The carnage which is unequalled in the history of Somalia, has resulted in the deaths of more than 30,000 Somalis in battlefields, while another 300,000 have died of starvation and famine-related diseases as a consequences of the civil war (Sahnoun 1994:11). The tragic disintegration of the state, along with its institutional apparatuses, has led to loss of security of life and property. The people are defenceless against external predators who cheaply plunder the country's tropical fruits, pillage marine resources in its territorial waters and dump hazardous waste. Furthermore, the proliferation and privatisation of the means of violence, which is unprecedented in the history of Somalia has created a serious security problems all over the country. In this calamitous state of affairs, only the vicious and best armed survive. As Terrence Lyons and Ahmed Samatar (1995:7) succinctly note, "with the state collapsed, the Somali people suffered the horrible brutality of living in a Hobbesian world without law or institutions to regulate relations among groups or to protect the most vulnerable from the most vicious."

---

[2] "The prolonged civil war and marauding warlordism that followed the collapse of the Siad Barre regime left most of the country in ruins and spawned widespread famine in the southern portion of the county. This descent into chaos was so profound that even a massive international intervention, replete with thirty thousand UN peacekeeping troops and a multibillion-dollar budget, was unable to promote national reconciliation and resuscitate the failed Somali state" (Menkhaus and Ortmayer 2000:211).

Along with the collapse of the state and the unleashing of unparalleled violence and rampant lawlessness, there have been hundreds of thousands of displaced persons and refugees. People fled their homes on a massive scale, in search of security and protection to other parts of the country or to stay in refugee camps in neighbouring countries where conditions were appalling. Some have sought refuge in far-flung places beyond the region and become stranded as unwanted refugees in many countries in Eastern Europe like Romania and Russia. Others, especially those well-to-do ones, made it by crossing the Atlantic into places like Canada and the United States. According to the report of Refugee Policy Group, displaced Somalis, classified either in the bracket of 'internally displaced persons' or 'across borders refugees' have been estimated to amount to between one and two million.[3] In short, the death of the state has forced the Somali people to be become *qaxootin* or exodus, dispersed all over the world as refugees and asylum seekers.[4]

The breakdown of political order in Somalia brought about a total disruption of production. This happened because the continuation and intensification of violence that followed the disintegration of state institutions prevented the people from working and producing for their sustenance. This is evidenced by the fact that factional fighting has taken place mostly in the fertile and productive southern region, which is the breadbasket of the country. Consequently, deaths from starvation and malnutrition rose to tens of thousands of people, mostly children.

In 1992, the international community, spearheaded by the United States, ostensibly intervened in Somalia so as to avert further tragedy, restore law and order and reconstitute a political authority in the country. Initially, the intervention saved the lives of many innocent civilians, brought temporary respite from the violence and achieved modest success. But after failing to end the political crisis, the United Nations Operation in Somalia (UNOSOM) was brought to an end on March 4, 1995. Regrettably, after spending more than US$4 billion, the UN left the country in a situation no better than that which had prompted its intervention (Geshekter, 1997:65).

Now nearly eleven years have passed and Somalia still remains without a state. Since 1991, in the aftermath of the collapse of the sate, a post-conflict political development has been in process in Somalia. Between 1991 and 1997 twelve political reconciliation conferences have been convened but all efforts came to nil—scuttled by one warlord or another. In May 2000, the Djibouti President Ismael Omar Guelleh put forward a Somali peace plan and called a political reconciliation conference in his country. Eventually, the peace talks resulted in the formation of a Transitional National Government (TNG) in Djibouti in August 2000. Yet, the authority of the new transitional government is still challenged by local and regionally based authorities, faction leaders as well as armed warlords. In this respect, the political problem in the country is far from over.[5] Analysing the baffling political problem in Somalia demands an innovative approach and a high level of creativity. *The main purpose of this research project*

---

[3] See further Refugee Policy Group, Hope Restored? Humanitarian Aid in Somalia 1990-1994, (Washington DC: Refugee Policy Group, 1994): 114.

[4] According to Ahmed Samatar, for the contemporary Somali people, this era is "the age of qaxootin or exodus" (Ahmed Samatar, 2001:v). See further, *Bildhaan, An International Journal of Somali Studies,* volume 1 (2001).

[5] According to The Economist, "Somalia has broken down into districts, mostly clan-based, which have evolved their own structures and systems. Many Somalis think the best way forward is for these clans and districts to meet as autonomous polities that might gradually agree to unify in a confederate system. Better, they say, than the present attempt to establish a top-down Mogadishu-based government, which could set off another war to decide who controls it" (56). See further, Somalia: Not Yet Reborn, *The Economist* (October 21, 2000).

is to explore to what extent the constraints in the material environment and the predicaments in the Somali history through time have contributed to the collapse of the state. This study also considers in brief the post-conflict development and initiatives undertaken to restore a stable political order in Somalia since 1991 and the obstacles, which are making it intractable.

1.2. A Brief Historical Backdrop

Pre-colonial Somalia was a stateless state.[6] Stateless state here means a political organisation where no formal centralised polity exists but which maintains the social order and stability through moral, material and social sanctions. This definition of stateless state concurs with what Adam and Mazrui call a society of rules without rulers or order without government (Hussein Adam 1997 and Ali Mazrui 1997). Throughout history, Somali people never developed a unified political authority and had no concept of a political order wider than kinship. They therefore existed as highly decentralised and fractionised society, lacking formal centralised political institutions. Never-theless they did develop a strong sense of cultural nationalism (Lewis 1994). Pre-colonial Somali society, as other societies in Africa, succeeded in establishing a relatively viable political system but not a formal system of government as existed in the Western world (Ellis 1999). Amongst the reasons why African societies failed to develop a formal and territorially based system of government are related to the constant migration of populations and absence of perpetual destructive wars as experienced by European societies in much of their history. In the case of Somalia, there was neither the economic means nor internal social dynamics that could have made the development of this formal system of authority possible.

Therefore, as had been the case of other stateless societies in Africa, the predominant principle of socio-political organisation of the Somali people in the pre-colonial era was that of kinship associated with communalism. In addition to kinship, Islam was also an important element in the superstructure of the pre-colonial Somali social formation. The kinship that Somalis forged constitutes two central components. The first element is blood ties, which define the position of the individual in relation to his/her mother's side and to his/her father's side. The second aspect is heer which the Somali lineages and clans worked out as constituting definite legal, and social contract implemented by a council of all adult males. In addition to blood ties and heer, Islam was the third element of the superstructure, which ordered the political organisation of the Somali people in the pre-colonial social formation. Islam played a significant role in helping the Somali people transcend the narrow boundaries of lineage and clan associations and promoted a Somali-wide political consciousness. In essence, the prevalence of the principle of kinship in the political arrangement of the traditional Somalis was due to the low level of the material environment primarily dominated by subsistence-based pastoral economy. Somali people had lived in this simple organisation

---

[6] As Evans-Pritchard explained (1940), stateless societies do not have centralised political organisations. On the contrary, these societies that are most often pastoral and nomadic organise their social order through lineage and kinship arrangements. In the Weberian sense, segmentary social groups are characterised by a (myth of) common lineage and bound together by linear loyalties. As Khazanov notes, "the segmentation system is characterised as 'stability-without government' i.e. primarily as a way of employing a specific mechanism to maintain internal order in conditions where social differentiation has not developed sufficiently" (Khazanov 1983:145).

of communalism and stateless condition until around 1860 which was when the colonial powers forcefully intruded into the country.

Colonialism terminated the stateless state in Somalia. Upon highly decentralised and kinship mediated political system, the colonial powers arbitrarily imposed a centralised authority. This foreign imperial domination installed in the country alien state structures, which neither the pre-existing social organisation nor the meagre means of the pastoral production in which the Somalis subsist, could support. This brief historical outline itself shows that the formal colonial government(s) in Somalia existed as a rootless institution divorced from the traditional and the organic political system of the Somali people.

The post-colonial state of Somalia, though the product of accumulated inconsistencies between pre-colonial and colonial social formations, has acquired its own right to existence. Furthermore, that existence clearly delineates the specific dynamics and duration of the post-colonial state. Unlike its precursors, the existence of the post-colonial state of Somalia was affirmed through the juridical recognition conferred by the international community[7] and by the domestically constituted power arrangements which made the concept of internal control a reality. For instance, as Jean-Francois Bayart asserts, "The State in Africa rests upon autochthonous foundations and a process of reappropriation of institutions of colonial origin which give it its own historicity; it can no longer be taken as a purely exogenous structure" (Bayart 1993:260). This affirmation allows us to consider the post-colonial state of Somalia not merely as an alien structure hovering above the society. Therefore, it seems appropriate to start the colonial setting as a point of a historical departure in order to understand the artificiality of the Somali state. Despite this, the causes for its current collapse must be partially sought in the modus operandi of the post-colonial political pursuits.

1.3. State and (Post)-State Literature on Somalia

During the life of the state (1960-1991), there was hardly any study which concurrently took into account the constraints in the material environment and the misfortunes in the history that have been shaping the process of the Somali social formation both across time and across space.[8] The limited studies that did exist considered the political economy of Somalia during different historical times, and focused on specific regions. Now there exists a whole body of historically based publications on Somalia undertaken during the post-colonial period which are mainly concerned with the social, political and economic development of specific regions in the country (Hess 1966; Cassanelli 1982; Geshekter 1983; Laitin and Samatar 1987; Lewis 1988;

---

[7] For a comprehensive overview on this aspect with respect to the newly created states in sub-Saharan Africa, see Robert H. Jackson, "Negative Sovereignty in Sub-Saharan Africa", *Review of International Studies* 12 (October 1986): 247-64.

[8] The exception is the seminal study undertaken by Ahmed I. Samatar before the state collapsed. Samatar, challenging the continuity and the uncritical endorsement of the clan-based analysis that dominated the scholarly literature on Somalia, embarked on a study which focused on the transformation of Somali society and its political economy both across time and across space. For a more elaborate account on this topic, see Ahmed I. Samatar, Socialist Somalia: Rhetoric and Reality (London: Zed Press, 1988). Another study, which to lesser extent also considers the process of the Somali social formation through time and space, is the recent dissertation by Alice Bettis Hashim, The Fallen State: Dictatorship, Social Cleavage and Dissonance in Somalia, University of Virginia (UMI Dissertation Services, 1995). Hashim attempts to explain the collapse of the state in Somalia as the result of cumulative tensions or what she calls "viruses" to which Somalia was exposed at different historical times.

Abdi Samatar 1989). These historical writings have greatly contributed to scant knowledge in the field of Somali studies, but they remain isolated, regional studies. The weakness of regional studies is that they fall to account for the coherence of the distinct historical processes of the diverse regions in the country. And, particularly as the current situation in Somalia makes clear, it is not possible to understand the problem of the collapse of the state through a specific regional analysis. In fact, considering the present situation in which the whole Somalia irrespective of regions is in a deep political turmoil, focusing on a countrywide historical approach is more appropriate in terms of explanatory power.

This study will consider the underlying causes for the breakdown of the state across both time and space. Time here is used in the sense of across the different triple history - pre-colonial, colonial and post-colonial processes. Space is used in the sense of taking the whole of Somalia as a unit of analysis. The point is that this approach enables us to unearth different structural crises over a period of time and also examine their cumulative effects on the current upheavals in Somalia. It is within this setting that this study considers how *the constraints in the harsh material environment, subsistence pastoral mode of existence, and the predicament in the Somali history - colonial intervention and its division of the land into five parts, Cold War geopolitics, decades of armed struggles and the post-colonial crisis of governance - have all set in motion the fragmentation process of the state in Somalia.*

Since 1991, after the state collapsed in Somalia, a growing body of post-state literature appeared: personal memoirs, autobiographies, journalistic, and academic publications. Each work presents and narrates its own version of why the state fragmented. Some of the publications present polemic and blame narration of the past while others record experiences and personal reminiscence or attempts to break new grounds (Ahmed 1995,1996; Dualeh 1994, Ghalib 1995, Omar 1992, Issa-Salwe 1994).[9] There exists, however, a scholarly literature on Somalia which critically analyses the disintegration of the state and the contemporary predicament of the Somali society. This literature is represented by two rival academic traditions - traditionalist versus transformationist. My focus here is to discuss the disintegration of the state within the debates between these two major schools of Somali studies since they advance historical lines and intelligible interpretations regarding the causes of the current crisis in Somalia. They also engage in fierce intellectual battles, which significantly advance the production of knowledge in the field of Somali studies.

The first school takes a traditionalist line of approach in explaining the implosion of the state. Scholars of this traditionalist paradigm argue that the continuity of clan politics has destroyed the state. They therefore presume that 'the causes' which have led to the demise of the state in Somalia are internal and lodged in the persistence of the primordial clan divisiveness and Somali cultural praxis (See, e.g., Lewis 1993, 1994; Said Samatar 1991; and Simons 1995). The second school presents an alternative transformationist line in accounting for the breakdown of the political system in Somalia. Scholars of this transformationist perspective offer external explanations and structural changes as the primary causes for the collapse of the

---

[9] See further an excellent overview by Alex de Waal on some of these publications. After critically assessing their shortcomings, de Waal then concludes that, "factual accounts have proved so inadequate, perhaps it should come as no surprise that the outstanding recent book on Somalia comes from an intermediate genre, of fictionalised contemporary history" (de Waal 1995:12). Here, de Waal refers to the novel of Ahmed Omar Askar, *Sharks and Soldiers (1992)*. de Waal reviewed publications that are all produced by Somalis. With respect to non-Somali authors, see the comprehensive overview by Ahmed Samatar *(2001)*, The Somali Catastrophe: Explanations and Implications. In Lilius, Muddle Suzanne (ed.) Variations of the Theme of Somaliness (Proceedings of the EASS/SSIA International Congress of Somali Studies). Turku: Centre for Continuing Education, Åbo Akademi University: 7-30.

state. They contend that the transformation of the political economy which gave rise to internal elite rivalries and clanised the national politics, was what ultimately fragmented the state (See, e.g., Abdi Samatar 1992, 1993; and Ahmed I. Samatar 1993, 1994). In a nutshell, while the traditionalist emphases continuity, the transformationist focuses on change as the underlying cause of fragmentation of the state in Somalia. Both approaches and their intellectual lineages, will be elaborated in detail in the next chapter.

I owe a great deal of intellectual debts to the scholars of both traditions since this study draws heavily on their work. For instance, it is their pioneering work in the field of Somali studies and their continuing heated academic debates, which steadily widens our horizons in understanding the past and present historical context of the Somali people and their polity. By tailoring the substantive analyses that both schools advance, this study examines to what extent the combined effects of the dynamics of *continuity* and *change* contributed to the disintegration of the state. Continuity and change bring together internal and external processes, which have been shaping the Somali social formation over a period of time. These processes are structural, historical, and momentary episodes. More concretely, they are the constraints in the material environment; perennial struggles against foreign aggressions and conquests; and series of external interventions and influences such as the colonial occupation and the impact of the Cold War geopolitics.

The secondary substantive premise that supports the central proposition of this dissertation that I have already advanced is how unresolved cumulative tensions of the triple history - pre-colonial, colonial and post-colonial processes - have led to the collapse of the Somali state. This study uncovers two reinforcing and yet contradictory tendencies, which have been shaping the Somali society in much of its history. Both the manifestations are the making of the constraints in the material environment and the predicament in the Somali history across time. The first is given rise to by the extreme poverty of the pastoral economy in the country and the second developed as a reaction against foreign threats, aggressions and conquests. Due to want of better terms, I refer to these perennial historical manifestations as *private and public pursuits*.[10] Throughout the recorded history of Somalia, the persistent tendency towards private pursuit has pushed the Somali people towards narrow and parochial interests, internal social cleavages and political fragmentation. By contrast, public pursuit has manifested as a tendency, in pulling the Somali people towards feelings of communality, of unity and of a deep sense of nationhood. The contradictory tendencies of both pursuits have been pushing and pulling the Somali society into opposing and irreconcilable directions. It is this push and pull effect that precisely explains how an unresolved structural problem of a duration can still have an immense impact on the next period, forming the bases of new tensions or crises. Indeed, as Putnam eloquently put it, "what comes first conditions what comes later" (Putnam 1993:8). *This is the hypothesis that this dissertation advances in order to explain the material environment and historical causes for the collapse of the state in Somalia.*

Placing the contradictory tendencies towards private and public pursuits in concrete historical processes will reveal more of their centrality in the dynamics of the Somali social formation across historical time. For instance, in the pre-colonial era, because of the meagre economic existence on the land, the tendency towards private pursuit is what pushed the Somali people to struggle fiercely along sectarian lines, primarily for subsistence and sheer survival. During that period the struggle for the private pursuit was waged as an enterprise of collective

---

[10] In a normal English usage private pursuit is understood as a pursuit for private gains and public pursuit as a pursuit for the common good. However, in this study the manner I will use both terms is more complex, broader and time specific as the subsequent three chapters demonstrate.

endeavour. The family and blood-related groups used to band together (in order to reduce individual liability) in search of bare livelihood. However, during the colonial and the post-colonial periods when the domestic production expanded due to the commercialisation of the livestock and the introduction of cash economy, the tendency towards private pursuit became altered as an enterprise of individualised private appropriation and aggrandisement. It cannot be overstated how important the persistence of the tendency of private pursuit across the triple history has to a large extent nurtured the post-colonial Somali elite to view the state as an instrument of private appropriation instead of an institution of collective polity.

The tendency towards private pursuit also affects the nature of the social and the political organisation of the Somali people as it causes the society to fragment into groupings or small nomadic bands. In the anthropological lexicon, these groupings are labeled as clans, primary lineage groups and sub-clans. However, the segmentation of the Somali society along those lines has an important economic function. It is the best rational strategy that any pastoral society can adopt to survive in a harsh material environment, which demands constant mobility in search of grazing land and water. Furthermore, the tendency towards private pursuit is what retards the Somali people from developing a political consciousness beyond that of the clan. This is due to the frequent mobility that the Somali pastoral nomads undertake, their dispersal in small groupings over a large area in search of livelihood and the scarcity of their livestock economy. The meagre existence of the pastoral economy is hardly sufficient for bare subsistence let alone generating a surplus to raise a political authority. The specific working of the tendency towards private pursuit on the economy, as well as the social and the political dynamics of the Somali society across time will be discussed in detail in the subsequent chapters.

By contrast, the tendency towards public pursuit has been nurturing the idea of Somali-wide identity, political unity and nationalism across historical time. Since the sixteenth century, as the written chronicles of the Somali history clearly indicate, the tendency towards public pursuit is what inspired the Somali-wide struggles against foreign aggressions and conquests. For instance, from 1540 to 1560, Somalis fought as a united cultural group against the invasion and expansion of the Coptic Christian Ethiopian kingdom, to defend their Somali oneness, religion and the integrity of their value system. Similarly, from 1900 to 1920, Somalis, as a united front, fought under the charismatic leader Sayyid Mohamed Abdulle Hassan against colonial occupation in order to liberate the country. Furthermore, since the 1960s onwards, after independence, when the Republic of Somalia was created from the unification of the British Somaliland and Italian Somalia, the paramount struggle of the Somali-wide public pursuit had been to unite all Somalis under one flag.

In the late nineteenth century, rival colonial powers partitioned the country into five imperial zones for their imperial designs. This unscrupulous division of the country fragmented and consigned the Somali population to demarcated frontiers and this unresolved colonial legacy has been the basis of persistent political problems since Somalia achieved statehood. In fact it is this bequeathed predicament that forced the successive post-colonial Somali political elite to embark on a policy of aggressive irredentism in order to regain the missing Somali inhabited territories. It is for this reason that the Somali-wide public pursuit has constantly retained the highest priority in the political and the economic decision-making processes of the government from 1960 until the debacle of the Ogaden war with Ethiopia in 1978.

As I illustrated here in brief, the workings of the contradictory tendencies towards private and public pursuits enable us to systematically unearth and explain concrete trajectories and deeper historical struggles that have been shaping the Somali society over a period of time. Both manifestations also advance better and fuller alternative explanations for the collapse of the state than those currently on offer. It is this explanatory power therefore that makes both frameworks paramount to this study because of their centrality for the purpose of clarifying the narratives of fragmentation of the state in Somalia.

The key questions addressed in this work are:

- What are the decisive historical tendencies that set the state on the collapsing course?
- How did the constraints in the material environment and the extreme poverty of the pastoral economy engender parochial interests, social schisms and political fragmentation in Somalia?
- How did the pitfalls of the colonial dismemberment of the country determine irredentism after Somalia achieved statehood?
- To what extent does the interplay of the critical episodes of the Cold War geopolitical imperatives, the military rule, the Ogaden war and the dissident challenges eventually disintegrate the state?
- Why did the intervention of the international community fail to resolve the political crisis in Somalia?

The rationale of this research study is to contribute to the understanding of why the Somali state collapsed, to contribute to the search for ways of rebuilding a viable political order in Somalia, to expand on the meagre scholarly publications in the field of Somali studies and, finally, to add to the debate which focuses on the nature, construction, collapse and reconstitution of the contemporary states in Africa. *This study is different from other studies undertaken since the Somali state collapsed. It not only retraces the historical process of state fragmentation retrospectively but also attempts to break a new ground by identifying decisive historical, tendencies (that have generated cumulative tensions across historical time) in the hope of advancing new insights into the present political predicament in Somalia.*

1.4. Methods of Inquiry

The approach of this study is to explore the political economy of the collapsed state in Somalia through a long historical approach. This *longue durée*[11] historical approach, as suggested by the French historian Fernand Braudel, equips us with the ability to cover different problems and their impacts over a period of time. In this research study I will seek to explore how cumulative structural crises of the triple history - pre-colonial, colonial and post-colonial processes - have led to the collapse of the state. In this study I shall particularly focus on a set of critical episodes in the Somali history since 1886, namely: the colonial incursions, the Cold War overlay, the military coup, the Ogaden war, the dissident challenges, and the fragmentation of the central authority in 1991.

In Africa, the significance of this *longue durée* concept in understanding the specific historical experiences and trajectories of African societies was recently introduced by Jean-Francois Bayart in his book: *'The State in Africa: The Politics of the Belly' (1993)*. In that

---

[11] According to Braudel (1980), the *longue durée* time span is a history which flows slowly and changes only very slowly as it is different from that of the *histoire événementielle*, or the history of short events.

23

book Bayart argues that both modernisation and dependency approaches, which dominated the academic literature on the state in Africa from the early 1960s until the late 1970s, have either been ignored or misread the true historicity of the continent. And now, since both perspectives have run their course, they are of little assistance in understanding the historical specificity of African states. Mahmood Mamdani, in a similar line of thinking, argues that the debates of both schools present the reality of African society not as a historical process, but rather as "a history by analogy". Accordingly, Mamdani suggests that instead of mirroring the historical experience of African states to an earlier history elsewhere, the historical legitimacy of African society must be taken as a unit of analysis (Mamdani 1996:8-13).

Bayart proposes that the trajectories of African states must be grounded and discussed in their social and historical roots since politics in Africa, as elsewhere, is largely produced internally. He further emphasises that in the present social reality of African society "the continuity of political movements from the beginning of the century to those of the 1950s or 1960s is widely acknowledged" (ibid: 33). On this point, Bayart concurs with Georges Balandier who affirms that "the present situation of African societies was the result of a triple history which has drawn together its constituent parts - pre-colonial, colonial and post-colonial history" (cited in Bayart 1993:33). Although Bayart presents his alternative historicity of the post-colonial state of Africa as it explains all the existing political trajectories of African states, he mainly deals with a few states like Cameroon, Nigeria, Togo and Zaire.[12] Thus, more case studies on other African states are what is now indeed needed. This study on the Somali state therefore is one of the case studies.

This study relies upon three sources of data: historical sources, archival work and elite-specialised interviewing. I will comment on each one of them very briefly.

(a) Historical Research: this is collected as secondary historical data. For instance, in Somalia, it was during the colonial period that the first serious historical research was conducted (Burton 1894; Lewis 1955). Afterwards, more historical studies on Somalia have been undertaken since the country achieved statehood; these are now available in the public libraries. In this study, both the colonial and the post-colonial historical writings are very important to: (i) provide a historical background; and (ii) to understand the underlying historical trajectories which have been shaping the Somali society across time.

(b) Archival Work: This is largely primary material. The archival data that I used in this study are mainly the recordings of the British and the Italian colonial Administration as well as the subsequent post-colonial publications. The colonial period is a central concern to this study as both Britain and Italy had each colonised part of Somalia. The British established colonial rule in northern Somaliland in 1885 and Italy carved up southern Somalia in 1889. Finally, the post-colonial state of Somalia came into being as the result of the unification of British Somaliland in the north and Italian Somalia in the south on the 1st July 1960.

The archives both in Britain and Italy store annual colonial reports, pamphlets and other documentation, which shed light on the modus operandi of the colonial state consolidation in

---

[12] For a well-elaborated critique against this generalised presentation by Bayart, see Chris Allen, 'Understanding African Politics', *Review of African Political Economy* 65 (1995): 301-320. Allen argues that the study of Bayart on the state in Africa "in the end tells us much more about states like Cameroon or Togo, and relatively little about Ghana before 1980 (or after), or Somalia, or indeed Angola and Mozambique. It is not therefore properly to be considered a general study on African politics, but instead a study of one crucial political process within African politics" (ibid: 316-317)

Somalia. The publications also cover diverse areas extending from politics, economics and trade to other administrative and social issues. In England, the places I found most published literature on Somalia are the School of Oriental and African Studies (SOAS), the British library, the Commonwealth and Foreign Office library, the London School of Economics Library. I also found some unpublished reports in the Public Record Office at Kew Gardens in London. In Italy, the places where most of the published materials on Somalia can be found are the Historical Archive of the Italian Ministry of Foreign Office (ASMAE), and the library of Institute Italo-Africano, which are in Rome. In the region, the two main archives where I found most of the published materials on Somalia are the Institute of Ethiopian studies, and the Institute of Nationalities in Addis Ababa. Both institutes store considerable historical and political records on Somalia before and during the colonial and post-colonial periods.

(c) Elite and specialised interviewing: this technique is essentially very useful for collecting data for this work. The method is specially used for interviewing the well-informed and key individuals in higher portfolios of state administration rather than with low ranking employees (Dexter 1970). Elite interviewing can be usefully combined with an informant technique.[13] Elite interviewing is very different from standardised interviewing. In standardised interviewing, "the investigator defines the question and the problem" and then searches for "answers within the bounds set by his presuppositions" (ibid: 5). By contrast, in elite interviewing, "the investigator is willing, and often eager to let the interviewee teach him what the problem, the question, the situation, is - to the limits, of course, of the interviewer's ability to perceive relationships to his basic problems, whatever these may be" (ibid).

Mostly, interviewing takes the form of elite interviewing. The significance of elite interviewing is that it recognises the position and the importance of the well-informed interviewee by granting him a VIP treatment. This enables the interviewee to narrate how he recollects the situation and state what he regards to be relevant. Furthermore, the procedure of elite interviewing means selectively identifying and choosing before-hand those individuals who can give not only insightful answers to the investigator but, more importantly, have the aptitude to articulate how important state policies and decisions are formulated and implemented.

Elite interviewing and informant technique can be usefully combined. The difference between the two methods is that the informants are often persons who have not participated in the decision-making of a government policy but because of their special knowledge become perceptive and well informed on the subject matter of the investigator. Thus, informants because of their erudition and scholarly knowledge on the situation are useful in helping to formulate latent assumptions about the development of political attitudes, and who else is to be interviewed. In this work, I utilised both the techniques as required by the central issues of the study, rather than the reverse. For instance, the persons who have a good deal of information both in depth and in detail about the critical episodes this work addresses are usually those who have held key government offices of the state as well as perceptive

---

[13] "An informant is distinguished from an elite interviewee by two factors: participation and time. The informant is regarded to some, often to a considerable extent as a sub-professional colleague or co-worker of the research of the research investigator" (Dexter 1970

informants. In fact, each of the critical episodes raises different questions. These questions can be adequately answered by persons who have been involved practically in the decision-making process of one or other particular policy or are intimately knowledgeable on the political development in Somalia.

With respect to perceptive informants, I conducted first exploratory investigations by interviewing an academic expert such as Professor Ahmed Ashkir Bootaan, who now lives in The Netherlands. Professor Bootaan was once a Minister of Education and later became a professor of law and the Rector of the Somali National University, a position he held until the central authority in Somalia broke down in 1991. Professor Bootaan was also a spokesperson and speech advisor for the former President of Somalia, Mohamed Siad Barre, for a long time. In Addis Ababa, I consulted with Dr. Omar Macalim Mohamed, a well-informed informant on the political development in the country since the 1950s. Dr. Mohamed was the first Ambassador of Somalia to America in 1961. Furthermore, in Ethiopia, I sought the ideas and recollections of another perceptive informant, Mohamed Mohamed Sheikh, the Director of the Somali Community Literacy Centre in Addis Ababa. The suggestions and the insights of these perceptive informants helped me to acquire a better picture of the subject matter of this study. It also allowed me to identify and choose certain key political figures that I have subsequently interviewed. Afterwards, using the elite interviewing technique, I interviewed such personalities like General Mohamed Abshir Muse, Colonel Abdullahi Yusuf and Major-General Abdullahi Ali Omar among others. I conducted most of the interviews in Addis Ababa and in London between 1996 and 1998.

1.5. Structure of the Research

The dramatic and the total collapse of the post-colonial state of Somalia is not an event that happened suddenly. But as I will argue strongly in this study, the disintegration of the state is an outcome of cumulative structural crises and incremental processes across the pre-colonial, colonial and post-colonial periods, which can only be grasped through a long historical approach.

Organisationally, the first chapters of the study, particularly 3 and 4, delineate the political economy crises of the state in the pre-colonial and post-colonial periods. Chapter 2 reviews the state debates proffered by the traditionalist and the transformationist schools of Somali studies, which are informed by the modernisation and the dependency perspectives respectively. Here emphasis is placed on the continuity and change explanations for the collapse of the state that both predominant schools of Somali studies alternatively stress. It is also in this chapter that I shall elaborate in detail on the alternative frameworks of the private and public pursuit that I use throughout this study. As I will show in the dissertation, both modes of analysis advance a more powerful explanation of collapse of the state. Chapter 3 considers the constraints in the material environment and the tendency towards private pursuit. Chapter 4 discusses the predicament of the colonial dismemberment of Somalia and the politics of the public pursuit.

Chapters 5, 6 and 7 situate the political economy problems of the state in the post-colonial period. In these chapters, I will examine a set of critical episodes and explain how their destructive interplay led to the implosion of the state. Chapter 5 extends the discussion in chapter 3 and examines further how the endemic structural poverty of the domestic economy exacerbated the tendency towards private pursuit and also condemned the post-colonial state of Somalia to subsist on foreign aid. Chapter 6 furthers the discussion in chapter 4 and probes how the politics towards public pursuit militarised the state during the Cold War era. Chapter 7 explains how the pitfalls of the politics of private and public pursuit have caused the state to collapse. Chapter 8 is an account of the events which took place in the aftermath of the state collapse in 1991. Chapter 9, in conclusion, summarises the alternative explanations that I have advanced for the collapse of the state and also briefly discusses the post-conflict development in the country.

1.6. Scheme of the Study

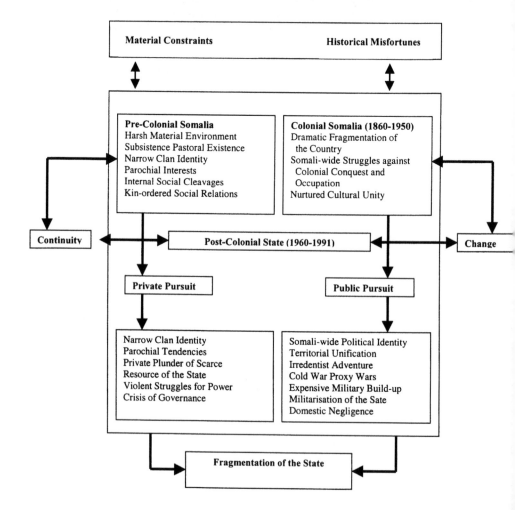

This scheme summaries the discussion of the study. It illustrates how the constraints in the material environment and the misfortunes in the Somali history across time have set in motion the destructive turn of events that fragmented the state. Particularly, the chart powerfully depicts the cumulated structural problems that the pre-colonial and colonial pitfalls had bequeathed to the post-colonial state of Somalia. The state inherited a poor and subsistence-based pastoral economy on the one hand and a colonially divided Somali ethnic population in fragmented territories on the other hand. In response, the political leadership of the post-colonial state of Somalia has set in motion two contradictory tendencies. On the one hand, since the meagre domestic economy cannot resolve their accumulation problems, the political elites resorted to private pursuit politics that resulted in the plunder of the scarce national resources, state bankruptcy and a violent struggle for power, which led to a crisis of governance. On the other hand, the political elite embarked on a policy of aggressive irredentism. to regain the missing Somali inhabited territories, and that became the primary political occupation of the state. In fact, this struggle for a public pursuit or for a Pan-Somali unity has retained an overriding position over the immense domestic social, economic and development problems since Somalia achieved statehood. Thanks to the Cold War geopolitics, the Somali political elite succeeded in building-up a large military might and arming the nation to the teeth. Somalia launched several irredentist wars against its neighbouring countries, particularly Ethiopia, but failed to regain the missing territories. Consequently, the militarisation of the state and the society also greatly contributed to the fragmentation of the state.[14] However, although the competition for private pursuit continues in an aggravated manner because of the accumulation crisis that the political elite endures, the struggle for a Somali-wide public pursuit has been abandoned since Somalia lost the Ogaden war against Ethiopia in 1978.

Continuity and change terms hanging outside the scheme represent the arguments advanced by the traditionalist and transformationist scholars of Somali studies in explaining the causes of the fragmentation of the state. This study thus attempts to broaden the continuity and change debates so as to transcend the limitation of the both schools of Somali studies. The continuity and change dynamics that the dominant schools of Somali studies advance have partially identified certain negative aspects which have been affecting the Somali social formation over a period of time but have left out many other decisive elements that this study attempts to address in a comprehensive manner.

---

[14] The Somali political elite militarised the state by diverting a significant portion of government resources from tackling the immense social and economic problems in the country to import arms and military hardware from abroad. In this respect, the Somali political elite invested heavy in the military sector without however building military industries in the country which would have created jobs and other social benefits for the nation. Eventually, the priority of this military policy bankrupted the state economically. Furthermore, the violent military culture that the Somali political elite has pursued in decades also militarised the society. For a discussion of how the militarisation of the governing apparatuses and the society resulted in the fragmentation of the state, see further in chapter 6 and 7 of the book.

Chapter Two

The Somali State in Academic Discourse

2.1. Introduction

The state is a political system, which has become an indispensable mechanism for social organisation in this present day world. This quintessential polity thus makes the state a central component of our contemporary social inquiry. Here I review the debates about the Somali state that the traditionalist and the transformationist schools of Somali studies have advanced. Emphasis is placed on the continuity of the primordial socio-cultural aspects in the society and change of the political economy explanations that both schools alternatively presented for the collapse of the state. The discussion also introduces the modernisation and dependency debates as a backdrop to the discourses of both schools of Somali studies that I have just mentioned above. It is important to appreciate these perspectives as they informed the logic and reasoning of both traditions. Furthermore, it is in this chapter that I shall elaborate in detail on the alternative frameworks of private and public pursuit that I use throughout this study. As I will show in this research study, both pursuits advance a more cogent explanation for the collapse of the state than hitherto available.

The post-colonial Somali state, like other African states, has been a subject of academic discourse[15] over the past four decades. More often than not, this academic debate has been conducted in reference to historical experiences and social realities that have taken place outside the continent of Africa. For instance, the historical trajectories of state formations in Europe and Latin America were the mirror reflections through which the African state was imagined, theorised over and also analysed. Or, as Stephen Ellis writes, the body of literature on the state in Africa is "derived from political theory rather than from close observation of African history or society" (Ellis 1996:2).

From the early 1960s until the late 1970s, the academic debate on the state in Africa has been conducted within the parameters of the modernisation and the dependency theories, which their respective proponents claim to possess a universal relevance. Indeed, both paradigms were presented as meta-perspectives, which could explain the social phenomena of every society around the globe. In fact, until the late 1980s, the prevailing academic perspectives of both the universalist perspectives have greatly influenced how we conceive the state in Africa in a theoretical sense. Consequently, the respective debates of both schools had strong bearings on the conceptual orientation of the Somalist scholars writing on the Somali state over the past four decades. In this chapter I will first present an exposé of the theoretical debates between the modernisation and the dependency schools as a backdrop and then pinpoint how they informed the dominant scholarship on the state in Somalia.

---

[15] For a more condensed overview on this debate see Martin R. Doornbos, "The African State in Academic Debate: Retrospect and Prospect", *Journal of Modern African Studies*, 28 no. 2(1990): 179-198; and Goran Hyden, Rethinking Theories of the State: An Africanist Perspective, *Africa Insight* 26 no. 1 (1996): 26-35.

2.2. The Modernisation Debate

The modernisation or political development perspective was a dominant intellectual tradition from the late 1950s until the late 1960s. The paradigm was the product of a search for a comparative approach to politics that was extended to the developing areas. It was formulated as a guiding framework for the social scientists, particularly American researchers at the time, who embarked on studying the problems of political transitions, democracy, institutional stability and economic development in the newly independent states of the Third World (Almond and Coleman 1960). In this sense, the blossoming of the modernisation school was very much linked to developments in American political science in the 1950s. During that time the policy imperative of the US government was to equip the country with regional expertise, which would be needed to bolster up its new role as a superpower. The United States emerged as the leading superpower from World War II and was determined to keep this hegemonic power by preventing the spread of communism from engulfing the newly decolonised states in Africa and Asia. Phrased in another way, what the US in essence wanted was to keep the expansion and the ideological influences of the rival Soviet-led communist bloc at bay away from the states in the Third World. It is this policy imperative therefore that compelled the social scientists, already attached to the rapidly expanding American academic establishment, to launch a new initiative to encompass research in the field of Third World studies. These researchers with active encouragement and generous financial support from the government then produced a considerable amount of literature. In practice, the study was aimed at developing a programme for the promotion of modernisation in the newly independent Third World countries that would lead towards a Western rather than an Eastern path of economic and political development. In this respect, the modernisation school was not only predominantly an American product but was also a study very much influenced by the Cold War Politics.[16]

Historically speaking, the modernisation paradigm was considerably informed both by evolutionary and functionalist perspectives. Evolutionary theory became popular in the aftermath of the Industrial and the French Revolutions, which heralded the emergence of a new social order in Europe. The perspective was dominant at the time because it helped explain the transition from traditional to modern society in Western Europe in the nineteenth century. The basic premise of the evolutionary theory was the belief that all mankind develops along a linear path from a primitive to an advanced state of civilisation.

The functionalist theory, on the other hand, distinguishes societies through the "pattern variables" as formulated by Talcott Parsons. In this categorisation, traditional societies are attributed with features, which are collectively oriented, particularistic, ascriptive and diffuse, while modern societies are perceived to have characteristics based on rational and universal values, meritocratic statuses, and specialised and differentiated social functions (Parsons 1952:58-67). Other features generally seen as characteristic of traditional societies include factors such a low level of division of labour, dependence on agriculture, low rates of growth of production and limited administrative competence. Modern societies achieve exactly the opposite.

---

[16] For an excellent explanation of how development theory is the product of American foreign policy that aimed to combat and contain the spread of communism, see Irene Gendzier, Managing Political Change: Social Scientists and the Third World (Boulder: Westview, 1985).

Heavily influenced by such basic parameters of the evolutionary and the functionalist theories, the modernisation scholars began to study the 'political development' of Africa and other developing countries. They therefore embarked on their research study with the predetermined notion that human society, irrespective of the point in time, goes through stages of an evolutionary process, which is unidirectional and irreversible. Such development is a lengthy process and proceeds in a slow, gradual and piecemeal way. Accordingly, the passing from traditional forms of society to modernity is positive and inevitably progressive since this transformation leads to an ultimate form of social advancement. Consequently, the societies in the newly independent Third World states must obliterate their outdated cultural traits, traditional values and belief system and instead establish a modern social system that would be participative, pluralistic and democratic. David Apter, one of the influential modernisation writers on Africa, explains modernisation as the importation of advanced ideas, values and practices originating from the developed world into traditional societies in the Third World (Apter 1965:42). This is indeed the central gist of the modernisation proponents who assume that the tradition-modernity dichotomy is universally applicable.

For the modernisation writers, the nature and the political role of the state was not a key concept in their analysis. It was left out as a sideline arena. However, the "reluctance to use the state concept stemmed rather from their interest in understanding the prospects for the political development of these societies along Western democratic lines" (Hyden 1996:27). As a result, the vast literature that the scholars of the modernisation school produced was mainly concerned with the study on political development.[17] Nonetheless, despite such limitation, the modernisation study had a very strong practical orientation, while its aim was to provide grounds for immediate action. Some of its programmes were presented to leaders and political elites of the newly independent states. These political leaders in the Third World were strongly encouraged to use the programmes as a recipe and a manual guide to act upon if they wanted to modernise their traditional societies within a short frame of time. It was presumed that implementing practically the recommendations from the study on political development would speed up the transition from traditional to 'modern' forms of social associations and political organisations of the backward pre-capitalist societies of the ex-colonies. More importantly, the proponents of the modernisation school argued, with conviction, that coping with these modernisation programmes would help the developing societies engineer stable political structures imbued with a sense of national unity, foster social reforms and nation-building and ensure a rapid economic development (Almond and Coleman 1960). Despite this, the modernisation theory as a practical policy approach was eventually a disaster, as it failed to yield rapid development results. According to Leys, "for over ten years (i.e. from late 1955 to the late 1960s) 'development theory'... progressed with only modest excitement. Then, partly due to disappointment with the results of policies based on 'development theory' (especially in Latin America and India), and partly to the general reaction of the 1960s against all 'official' values and ideas, the theoretical temperament rose" (Leys 1996:7). However, as an intellectual product and in orientation, the modernisation school had a wider impact on academic research as it opened up new academic areas in the field of Third World studies (Leys 1996: 10).

---

[17] See, for instance, Lucien W. Pye and Sidney Verba (eds.). Political Culture and Political Development (Princeton: Princeton University Press, 1965); David E. Apter, The Politics of Modernisation (Chicago: University of Chicago Press, 1965); Joseph La Palombara and Myron Weiner, (eds.). Political Parties and Political Development (Princeton: Princeton University Press, 1966); and Marion Levy, Modernisation and the Structure of Societies: A Setting for International Affairs (Princeton: Princeton University Press, 1966) among others.

Nonetheless, there were weaknesses in the conceptual orientation of the modernisation theory. Firstly, the modernisation writers are criticised for assuming the existence of a single, evolutionary path to modernity. This assumption therefore was what led them to claim that each country would progress unproblematically towards modernity. Secondly, the modernisation researchers are accused of having certain biases. Specifically, they are accused of having an inclination which favours domestic rather than external explanations for political occurrences as well as having socio-cultural rather than historical and structural factors in their political analysis. Thirdly, the modernisation exponents are criticised of treating traditional culture as something, which is pristine and static that condemns the Third World society to relative stagnation. Fourthly, the modernisation writers are attacked for saying nothing or little about the role of economic forces, the emergence patterns of class formation, and class conflict.[18] Lastly, the modernisation scholars are criticised for being 'a-historical' since they presented essentialist explanations in understanding the social conditions in the Third World countries (So 1990: 53-59).[19]

However, despite this theoretical limitation, the modernisation study has considerably informed the traditionalist scholarship of Somali studies in two respects. First of all, like the modernisation theorists, the traditionalist writers on Somalia favour domestic explanations for political occurrences. They therefore put more emphasis on internal dynamics in the analysis of the politics in Somalia. Second, like the modernisation writers, the traditionalist scholars on Somalia advance socio-cultural rather than historical and structural explanations as the causes for the domestic political problems and the predicament of the Somali society. I will return later to this discussion of the traditionalist school of Somali studies. I shall now turn to the dependency theory, which to some extent informed the transformationist literature in the field of Somali studies.

2.3. The Dependency Debate

The dependency school emerged in the late 1960s as a critique of the mainstream modernisation school. In contrast to the modernisation perspective, which was developed in the West, the dependency theory was formulated in the Third World. As Blomstrom and Hettne put it, the dependency school speaks of "the voices from the periphery" that aim to challenge and deconstruct the intellectual hegemony of the American modernisation school.[20] According to So, "just as the modernisation school can be said to examine development from the point of view of the United States and other Western countries, the dependency school can be said to view development from a Third World perspective" (So 1990:91). As I will show later, the dependency theory turned many of the assumptions of the modernisation perspective upside down.

The dependency school originated in Latin America. The concept developed as a reaction to the great disappointment concerning the programme of the UN Economic Commission for

---

[18] However, an exception is that of Walt W Rostow. The Stages of Economic Growth (Cambridge: Cambridge University Press, 1967).

[19] With respect to Africa, see Richard Sandbrook, "The Crisis in Political Development Theory," *The Journal of Development Studies* 12, no. 2 (1976): 165-185.

[20] See further, Magnus Blomstrom and Bjorn Hettne, Development Theory in Transition: The Dependency Debate and Beyond - Third World Responses (London: Zed, 1984).

Latin America (ECLA). The programme had been based on the policies informed by modernisation theory (Dos Santos 1973). The failure to generate rapid economic growth and establish political stability through this modernisation path of development had dashed the high expectations of many populist regimes in Latin America as well as many Latin American researchers in academia. The social researchers particularly, were disillusioned by the inability of modernisation theory to explain the problems of the economic stagnation and political crises that faced the nations not only in Latin America but also in other Third World countries. To put it differently, they were concerned with the problem of explaining why Latin America and other Third World regions were not developing as predicted by the modernisation thesis.

Heavily influenced by radical neo-Marxist theories, the dependency exponents devised a way to popularise and spread this alternative perspective beyond Latin America. And Andre Gunder Frank was, so to speak, the right scholar in the right place at the right time to formulate and deploy the concepts of dependency and underdevelopment against modernisation theory. Frank was in Latin America in the early 1960s during the time when the dependency debate was evolving as a serious intellectual orientation. Consequently, it was Frank who disseminated the ideas and the theoretical contention of the dependency school to the rest of the world through his seminal publications.[21] Other exponents of the dependency and underdevelopment orientations for Latin America include Fernando Henrique Cardoso, Enzo Faletto and James Petras.

Dependency theory overturned many premises of the modernisation approach. First, in stark contrast to the modernisation perspective, dependency theory focused not on the process of development but on the root causes of underdevelopment. Second, the dependency writers offer external rather than internal explanations for the underdevelopment of Third World countries. They stress that the experience of colonialism and neo-colonialism is what perpetuates the economic backwardness of Third World countries. On this point, they drastically shifted the focus of political analyses from the domestic to the international and from the idiosyncratic to the structural. Third, the units of analysis of the dependency researchers were not the individual and the domestic national systems but classes and/or the global system. Fourth, the dependency writers placed more emphasis on economic factors such as modes of production, social formations and class conflict. Finally, the dependency theorists uphold the view that the linkages between Third World countries and Western countries are harmful since they are exploitative and retard the development of the former.[22] As a result, some of the radical exponents of the dependency school even advocated that Third World countries must break the linkages with the dominant capitalist Western world and embark on an autonomous and independent path of development.[23]

---

[21] The most influential writings of Andre Gunder Frank include, Capitalism and Underdevelopment in Latin America, (New York: Monthly Review Press, 1967); Latin America: Underdevelopment or Revolution, (New York: Monthly Review Press, 1969); and On Capitalist Underdevelopment, (Bombay: Oxford University Press, 1975).

[22] For a comprehensive elaboration of how these external linkages work, see., T. Smith, 'Requiem or New Agenda for Third World Studies?' in World Politics, 1985:532-561. Smith explains how the convergence of interests between local petty bourgeoisie and modern state elite of the underdeveloped and foreign capital of the developed countries destroys the subsistence economy of the marginalised domestic forces.

[23] For this radical stance, see Walter Rodney, How Europe Underdeveloped Africa (Dar es Salaam: Tanzania Publishing House, 1972); and Samir Amin, Unequal Development (Sussex: Harvester, 1976). Both writers powerfully argue that it is the logic and the dynamics of capitalism, which do not permit Third World countries to develop and thus the only option they have is to turn to socialism.

Although the dependency theory first emerged in Latin America as the result of economic and political problems specific to that continent, it was later transferred to Africa like the modernisation concept before it. In this respect, the conceptual development of the dependency theory was not born out by the specific historical experience or by concrete economic and political conditions within Africa. Nonetheless, in Africa, the dependency and underdevelopment perspectives were deployed by Africanists and African social scientists, who wanted to address and explain the process of development and the economic backwardness of the continent In relation to the West.[24] These researchers adopted the notion of the state as viewed by the dependency scholarship. The dependency approach considers the state to be an instrument of power and domination rather than a tool to solve societal problems as argued by the modernisation writers. Thus, the African state is viewed as an instrument used by minority elites in power to serve their own and foreign interests at the expense of the majority of the population. Since the 1970s, it was this instrumentalist nature of the state that the dependency researchers on Africa have been attempting to explain in many of their academic writings (Hyden 1996:28). However, in the late 1980s, when the dependency debate on the state in Africa became unable to explain the political and economic predicaments in the continent such as the rise of ethnic tensions, military coups, personal rule and declining growth rate, the dependency concept was abandoned.[25] Thereafter, the academic discourse on the state in Africa has shifted to that of statist theory. Here is not a place to review the statist debate in detail since it is not the central concern of this research study. Suffice to note that the statist approach sees the state as a primary motor force behind social and economic occurrences, and power holders are held accountable for the political and economic crises in the continent.[26]

The dependency school like the modernisation school which preceded it also came under severe criticism in the early 1970s. Firstly, the dependency writers were charged with being economy deterministic and failing to consider the social and cultural aspects that also affect the process of the development in Third World countries. Secondly, the dependency proponents were accused of over-emphasising external factors in explaining underdevelopment and neglecting the role and impact of internal dynamics such as social classes, the state and other forms of political struggles. Thirdly, the dependency writers were criticised for presenting vague policy conclusions and for failing to spell out concrete guidelines for action in local arenas, which would help the newly independent states to realise their national goals. Fourthly, the dependency researchers were attacked for sacrificing close empirical studies on domestic processes in favour of debates over theory. Finally, the dependency perspective was accused of being highly abstract, particularly in so far as it delineated a general or a universal pattern of dependency perceived applicable to any country

---

[24] See Colin Leys, Underdevelopment in Kenya: The Political Economy of Neo-Colonialism (London: Heinemann, 1975) and Issa Shivji, Class Struggles in Tanzania (London: Heinemann Educational Books, 1975). For a good review, see further Leys, Colin. 1980: Kenya: What Does 'Dependency' Explain?, *Review of African Political Economy*. Vol. 17 (January-April): 108-113.

[25] See further, Naomi Chazan, Robert Mortimer, John Ravenhill and Donald Rothchild, Politics and Society in contemporary Africa, 2 edition (Boulder: Lynne Rienner Publishers, 1992).

[26] For a succinct analysis in this approach, see Thomas M. Callaghy, The State-Society Struggle: Zaire in Comparative Perspective (New York: Columbia University Press, 1984). Also see Christopher Clapham, Third World Politics: An Introduction (Madison: University of Wisconsin Press, 1985), and Richard Sandbrook, The Politics of Africa's Economic Stagnation, (Cambridge: Cambridge University Press, 1985).

in the periphery but neglected the historically specific development of each particular Third World state.[27]

Yet despite its shortcomings, the dependency school has largely informed the writings of the transformationist scholarship of Somali studies in two respects. Firstly, like the dependency scholars, the transformationist writers put greater emphasis on the impact of external factors rather than internal dynamics while examining the process of economic underdevelopment in Somalia. Secondly, like the dependency proponents, the transformationist scholars focus on the state class which they blame for the political disintegration of Somalia. Let me now first turn to the traditionalist debate of Somali studies.

2.4. The Traditionalist Debate of Somali Studies

The traditionalist paradigm of Somali studies is informed by three intellectual sources. These are the historical writings of the British colonial explorers,[28] notably the adventurer Richard Burton, the anthropological diachronic recordings of Evans-Pritchard and the modernisation theory noted earlier. Richard Burton was the first to write in length, in English, the history of the Somali people, albeit in the way he saw it. In his book titled 'First Footsteps in East Africa', Burton writes an account of the cultural, social and political institutions of the Somali people at the time, which was indeed tainted by his ethnocentrism (Burton, 1894). Nonetheless, since there was no written Somali language and there were hardly any other publications on Somali society and culture except for the few recordings of the journals of few Arab travelers,[29] Burton deserves credit for this initiative. The Evans-Pritchard's formulation of the Nuer lineage segmentation in the Sudan has also considerably informed the traditionalist scholarship on Somalia.[30] However, a more comprehensive scholarly study on the Somali society, culture and institutions has developed very recently. This began when Ioan M. Lewis as a young postgraduate student at the Institute of Social Anthropology at Oxford University became interested in doing research on the social and the political structure of the Somali nomads in the late 1950s. Lewis, in his own words, justified his research

---

[27] For a good critique, see Tony Smith, "The Underdevelopment of Development Literature", *World Politics* 31, no. 2 (1979): 245-288.

[28] Apart from Richard Burton, the writings of other colonial explorers worth notable include Ralph E. Drake-Brockman, British Somaliland (London: Hurst & Blackett, Ltd., 1912); Angus Hamilton, Somaliland (Westport, Conn.: Negro Universities Press, 1911/1970); F.L. James, The Unknown Horn of Africa (London: George Philip & Son, 1888); Douglas Jardine, The Mad Mullah of Somaliland (New York: Negro Universities Press, 1926/1969); Major H. Rayne, Sun, Sand and Somalis: Leaves from the Notebook of a District Commissioner in British Somaliland (London: H.F. & G. Witherby, 1921); Major H.G.C. Swayne, Seventeen Trips Through Somaliland and a Visit to Abyssinia (London: Rowland Ward, Ltd., 1900); F. Adam, Handbook of Somaliland (London, 1900); A.H.E. Morse, My Somali Book (London, 1913); JR. Rodd, Social and Diplomatic Memories (London, 1923). All these recordings contain narrations of personal experiences mixed with accounts of Somali society and culture coloured by the writer's own perceptions of them.

[29] The most important of those few Arab travelers who documented facts about Somalia was the North African Ibn Battuta. See further Ibn Batuta, Ibn Batuta in Black Africa: Selections Translated by Said Hamdun and Noel King (London: Collings, 1975).

[30] The lineage segmentation model developed by Evans-Pritchard is adopted by the traditionalist writers to describe and analyse the Somali social structure, albeit in a more flexible application. See further E.E. Evans-Pritchard, The Nuer: A Description of the Modes of Livelihood and Political Institutions of a Nilotic People (New York: Oxford University Press, 1940/1978).

interest in Somalia as "my romantic ambition to go and study the nomads" (Lewis 1994:2). Lewis undertook this research project when Somalia was still under colonial rule. Understandably, the Colonial Social Science Research Council had sponsored the anthropological fieldwork of Lewis in the country. Nonetheless, the exotic and romantic ambition of Lewis to study the Somali nomads gradually developed into an important academic discourse on Somalia. From 1955 to 1960, Lewis published a series of works on the Somali people, their lineage segmentation, kinship system, religion and their modern political associations.[31] And it was through these early writings that Lewis laid down the groundwork of an intellectual foundation in the traditional field of Somali studies. However, the major intellectual breakthrough came when Lewis published his classical book entitled: *A Pastoral Democracy: A Study of Pastoralism and Politics Among the Northern Somali of the Horn of Africa (1961)*. It was in this book that Lewis outlined the thesis of the traditionalist school of Somali studies he expounded. According to Lewis, the social structure of the Somali pastoral nomads has the following key characteristics. First, the Somalis are highly egalitarian because of the absence of exploitation and domination in their power relations. Second, the Somali society is stateless, lacking centralised institutions and formalised authority. Third, the primary social networks of the Somali people are regulated by a web of lineage segmentation, which provides the fundamental basis for identity-formation. Accordingly, the persistence of this primordial kinship segmentation has been what prevented Somali society from developing a single political unit during the pre-colonial period. Even in the contemporary post-colonial era, the tenacity of this lineage segmentation is what perpetuates social divisiveness and political fragmentation among the Somali population. Thus, lineage segmentation remains central to the thesis of the traditionalist scholars of Somali studies, since according to them it provides the most sophisticated explanatory power in understanding the social and the political behaviour of Somali society.[32]

Since then, this traditionalist thesis pioneered by Lewis has received for wider currency and emulation. Many subsequent studies were tailored to fit the centrality of Lewis' thesis, as a crucial point of departure in analysing the social and the political structure of the Somali people. For instance, Lewis and his disciples have been repeatedly arguing over the past four decades that the continuity of the law of lineage segmentation system is what informs and also explains the nature of the political dynamics in Somalia. To concur with Lewis and confirm his thesis, David Laitin and Said Samatar wrote that:

"For years the eminent European anthropologists Enrico Cerulli and I. M. Lewis have been telling us that to understand Somali politics, it is necessary to understand Somali clanship and

---

[31] The publications of these diverse topics about the Somali people include, see I.M. Lewis, Peoples of the Horn of Africa: Somali Afar and Saho (London: International African Institute, 1955/1969); "Sufism in Somaliland: A Study in Tribal Islam," Bulletin of the School of Oriental and African Studies, XVII 581-602; XVIII, 146-60 (1955-6); The Somali Lineage System and the Total Genealogy: A General Introduction to Basic Principles of Somali Political Institutions (Somaliland: Hargeisa, 1957); Modern Political Movements in Somaliland, International African Institute, Memorandum xxx, (Oxford: Oxford University Press, 1958); "Clanship and Contract in Northern Somaliland", Africa, xxix (1959:274-293); "The Somali Conquest of the Horn of Africa", Journal of African History I (1960:213-30). However, as can be seen in the titles, most of Lewis's study in the country concentrated on the Somali pastoral nomads in the Somaliland.

[32] For instance, Said Samatar argues that "lineage segmentation produces a society of extreme individualism, in which each man is his own sultan with no one endowed, legally or morally, to exercise centralised national authority. Fragmentation is the norm in such societies. Thus.... anarchic factionalism is in fact endemic in Somali society" (S. Samatar 1993:16). See also Said Samatar, Somalia: A Nation in Turmoil (London: Minority Rights Group, 199 1).

kinship ties... The political history of independent Somalia, however, makes the relevance of Lewis and Cerulli's argument painfully clear. One can scarcely think of a significant domestic or foreign development in Somali politics since independence that was not influenced to a large degree by an underlying clan consideration" (Laitin and Samatar 1987:155).

For the traditionalist writers, as the quotation makes clear, clanship is the bedrock of Somali politics, while the clan ties are the real political stuff through which the wheeling and dealings in Somalia from local to national are instrumentally used. They therefore posited that the primacy of clanship relations over national unity is indeed the crux of the social and political problems in Somalia. This last point has currency. That is to say, it provides a convincing explanation as to why the modernised state elites attempt to obliterate the nomadic clanship influence and culture in the society. Guided by this traditionalist informed policy orientation, the state elites in Somalia embarked on modernisation projects aimed to sedentarise the pastoral nomads and to eradicate their cultural value systems, norms and traditional institutions. Eventually, although the attempt did not weaken the primacy of the clanship relations, the sedentarisation policy negatively affected the productive capacity of the pastoral nomads[33] and also emasculated their traditional techniques of managing conflicts. The Somali state elites were with the view that the traditional conflict settlement mechanisms were an outdated practice that challenge and undermine to the desirability of modern laws, court institutions and government authority.

After the state collapsed in 1991, the traditionalist proponents proclaimed the triumph of their internally oriented socio-cultural thesis. This is what their eminent foreman has to say. According to Lewis, the collapse of the colonially created state is a reaffirmation of the supremacy of the segmentary lineage system and kinship in action in the Somali politics. As I shall quote in length, this is how this perception was summed up by Lewis:

"At a more abstract level, the collapse of the colonially created state represents technically a triumph for the segmentary lineage system and the political power of kinship. For better or worse, clanship has certainly prevailed, and the assertions of some Somali and non-Somali ideologues that clanship was an atavistic force doomed to oblivion in the modern world seem rather dated. Given then, that like nationalism, clanship is a human invention, is it in the 1990s basically the same phenomenon that it was in the 1890s? Linguistically the answer must be "yes", since the same terminology has been employed throughout the recorded history of the Somalis. Sociologically, the evidence also supports this view. Indeed, the argument of this book is that clanship is and was essentially a multipurpose, culturally constructed resource of compelling power because of its ostensibly inherent character "bred in the bone" and running "in the blood", as Somalis conceptualise it" (Lewis 1994:233).

Since then, a lot has been published which unequivocally endorses the thesis of Lewis.[34] Most of these writers often cite passages from the work of Lewis in order to affirm the validity of their explanations. Thus, in a nutshell, the theoretical orientation of the traditionalist

---

[33] For an excellent critique of these modernisation programmes see Gerald Braun, The Somali Development Concept in Crisis, *Northeast African Studies* 11, no.3 (1989): 1-12.

[34] For a few samples, see Walter Clarke and Jeffrey Herbst, eds., Learning from Somalia: The Lessons of Armed Humanitarian Intervention (Boulder: Westview, 1997); Virginia Luling, "Come Back Somalia? Questioning a Collapsed State", in *Third World Quarterly* 18, no.2 (1997): 287-300; Jonathan Stevenson, Losing Mogadishu: Testing U.S. Policy in Somalia

scholarship of Somali studies (especially the continuity of primordial clan politics) still remains pervasive and is what largely informs the conventional academic circles, the popular media as well as influencing the decisions and policy making procedures of countries and international organisations currently involved in Somalia.[35] I will now turn to the transformationist school of Somali studies.

2.5. The Transformationist Debate of Somali Studies

The transformationist perspective of Somali studies arose as a major intellectual challenge to the traditionalist scholarship in the 1980s. This transformationist school has been pioneered by the brothers Abdi and Ahmed Ismail Samatar. And like the traditionalist writers, who were informed by modernisation theory, the transformationist scholars were influenced by the dependency discourse. In a collective publication by both brothers, this is how they affirmed their theoretical orientation:

"We suggest that the materialist literature more accurately depicts both the general global milieu within which Africa's submerged classes continue to struggle, and the nature and role of the post-colonial state" (Samatar and Samatar 1987:673).

Ahmed Samatar goes on to explain the significance of deploying the analytical tools of critical political economy to delineate the historical changes in the material production and socio-political transformation of the Somali society over a period of time. According to Ahmed Samatar:

"This paradigm concerns itself with the production and accumulation, distribution of economic surplus, social reproduction, political arrangements and the impingement of the global order" (Ahmed Samatar 1989:8).

Furthermore, like the dependency scholars, the transformationist writers focus more on external factors in the making of the contemporary social and economic conditions in Somalia. For instance, the transformationist researchers advance that the penetration of the global market economy and the imposition of the colonial state impacted fundamental structural changes on the pre-colonial mode of production and social relations of the Somali society. However, before they outline the core of their thesis, the transformationist scholars first challenge the epistemological grid of the traditionalist approach which they consider to be an outdated anthropological concept that lacks the grasp of capturing the dynamics of the moment. This is how Abdi Samatar formulated the attack:

"The first task in this effort is to deconstruct the ghettoization of Somali studies as a

---

(Annapolis: Naval Institute Press, 1995); and Anna Simons, Network of Dissolution: Somalia Undone (Boulder: Westview Press, 1995).

[35] For example, since the civil war broke out in the country, the regional organisations such as Intergovernmental Authority for Development (IGAD), states and the United Nations bodies involved in the peace process in Somalia have been enlisting traditionalist scholars as political advisors, commissioning them to write reports and policy oriented research papers, consulting their academic works and also basing the interventions they undertake in the country on the policy recommendations of these traditionalist consultants.

backwater area in African studies. In spite of the revolutionary theoretical advances in the latter field in the last twenty years, which was stimulated by the crisis of peripheral capitalist development in the continent, Somali studies seem marooned to the earlier phases of modernisation theory. It is therefore high time that the theoretical and methodological innovation in the study of African underdevelopment penetrate and inform the Somali condition" (Abdi Samatar 1989:4).

Firstly, the transformationist writers charge the traditionalist approach with lacking specificity, with being static and a-historical. Secondly, the traditionalist proponents are accused of confusing the explanations of key concepts such as pastoralism, tribalism and the state in the process of the Somali social formations. Thirdly, the traditionalist scholars are criticised for lacking the insight to grasp the difference between clanism and kinship since they often confuse both terms by using them as if they had the same meaning.

After these scathing critiques of the traditionalist scholarship, the transformationist proponents then present their thesis, which according to them is guided by historicity and specificity (Abdi Samatar 1992). Firstly, the transformationist writers argue that the pre-colonial process of Somali social formation did not remain static. Instead, it continued, albeit in a decomposed form because of its incorporation into the global economy as a periphery, the impact of violent imperial incursions, the commercialisation of its subsistence pastoral production, and finally its subordination to a centralised state (both colonial and post-colonial). Thus, the impact of all these historical episodes attests not to a static but to a far-reaching process of transformation of the structure of Somali society. Secondly, the transformationist scholars attempt to proffer a historical context as well as social meanings in order to make plain the distinction between kinship and clanism. This is how Ahmed Samatar clarifies the misconception:

"Kinship denotes a central relationship buttressed by both blood-ties and deeply revered tradition and custom *(xeer)* - one which mediates among individuals or groups. This is part of the dominant ideology in some pre-capitalist social formations. Clanism, on the other hand, is the transformation of kinship by detaching blood-ties from tradition and custom. This bifurcation results from the forceful intrusion of an alien type of social and economic organisation and its concomitant norms and values" (Ahmed Samatar, 1989:8).

Finally, the transformationist writers contend that the process of the transformation of the Somali society, which has been going on well over one hundred years, has resulted in the emergence of social stratification in Somalia. These new social strata can be classified as pastoral producers, merchants, petty bourgeoisie and intelligentsia. However, these new social forces have emerged in an environment of acute material deprivation, economic crisis and underdevelopment, which is the result of Somalia's peripherisation in the global capitalist system. Consequently, the tensions that have been simmering from the struggles of these new social forces since then, have created a deeper domestic social disorder that eventually led to the disintegration of the state.

Therefore, focusing on the dynamics of social struggles in the society, the transformationist critics, unlike the traditionalist writers, contend that in Somalia, it is the rivalry between the new social strata, which hampers economic development and perpetuates the political problems in the country. To be more specific, the transformationist writers argue that it is the internal tussles of the ruling state class, the petty bourgeoisie and the intelligentsia, over power and appropriation of the surplus produced by peasants and pastoral nomads which is the core of the problem in Somalia (Ahmed Samatar and Abdi Samatar 1987:669-690). In a nutshell, for the transformationist scholars, the major culprits to be blamed for the collapse of the state are these dominant class fractions who used perverse clan politics as an instrument to advance their narrow material interests. In this respect, the transformationist writers put more emphasis on intra-class competition at the level of the state, although they are careful not to subscribe the Somali society to the rigid classification of classical Marxism. Nonetheless, for the transformationist proponents, class conflict is the most appropriate level of analysis in understanding and explaining why the Somali state collapsed. However, the recent writings of the transformationist scholars shifted the focus of the class analysis to the nature of the state and the leadership in Africa.[36]

2.6. The Continuity and Change Debate

To recap the substantive arguments of the debate, both major discourses of Somali studies draw on the conflicting theories of modernisation and dependency schools. The traditionalist writers claim that it is the continuity of the primordial socio-cultural idiosyncrasies in the Somali society, which is the core of the political problems in Somalia. By contrast, the transformationist critics severely repudiate this premise and instead argue that the externally impacted dynamics of change in the field of production and power relations put on course the present political crisis in the country. Put simply, both approaches view the causes of the collapse of the state either as the result of the continuity of segmentary lineage system or the change of the political economy brought about by external dynamics. This study attempts to bring together the substantive aspects of the continuity and change explanations both schools advance. Nonetheless, the continuity and change explanations this study will offer are more comprehensive than from those argued by both schools of Somali studies.

However before sketching in detail the outlines of my alternative explanations, let me first clarify my theoretical point of departure. The theoretical orientation of this study is guided by the longue durée perspective of Braudel and by the distinct historicity of Bayart or what Mamdani calls a historically specific social reality of Africa - which must be established as a unit of analysis (see chapter 1). The longue durée perspective enables us to examine the political economy trajectories of present societies in Africa in terms of their own distinct histories. The concept of historicity as Bayart argues, informs us that politics must always be viewed as a moment in a complex and very long-term history. Accordingly, this long-term political history must therefore bring together the influences of external and internal dynamics, which are specific to the country under study. Bayart holds the view that the contemporary political reality in Africa is shaped by the concurrent effects of a 'triple history' – the pre-colonial, the colonial and the post-colonial dynamics. In Africa the colonial and postcolonial periods are relatively short periods in which the continuity of the pre-colonial cultural processes and historical dynamics have certainly not yet ceased. Consequently, without insight into these pre-colonial and colonial past dynamics, the contemporary politics in Africa cannot be understood.[37] Similarly, Mamdani suggests to us that we should study the social reality in Africa as a specific historical process rather than as a history by analogy. For instance, Mamdani writes, "Africanist debates tend to focus on whether contemporary African reality most

---

[36] See Abdi Samatar, An African Miracle: State and Class Leadership and Colonial Legacy in Botswana Development, (Portsmouth: Heinemann, 1999).

[37] See further, Jean-Francois Bayart, " Finishing with the Idea of the Third World: The Concept of the Political Trajectory", in James Manor (ed.) Rethinking Third World Politics (London: Longman, 1991): 51-7 1.

closely resemble the transition to capitalism under seventeen-century European Absolutism or that under other Third World experiences, or whether the postcolonial state in Africa should be labeled Bonapartist or absolutist. Whatever their differences, both sides agree that African reality has meaning only insofar as it can be seen to reflect a particular stage in the development of an earlier history" (Mamdani 1996:12).[38] Thus, both scholars concur that each concrete case taken as a unit of analysis, be it a given country or Africa as a continent for that matter, must be examined against its own distinct historical trajectory. This approach enables us to restore the specificity and the legitimate historical reality of the state in Africa.

This study takes its point of departure from this historically informed theoretical orientation. In doing so, it transcends the now sterile debates between modernisation and dependency theories that have shaped the academic discourse concerning the state of Somalia over the past four decades. It also challenges the principal thrust of the debates between the traditionalist and transformationist Somali scholarship that have been conducted to hold a mirror to the historical and social reality in Somalia to experiences that have taken place elsewhere. In short, this study seeks to establish the historical specificity of Somalia as a unit of analysis. Put simply, it attempts to examine the current political problems and the collapse of the state in the country against each distinct historical conjuncture and crisis through which the Somali political institutions have evolved over a long period of time.

After critically reading about the history and the political economy of the Somali society across a historical time, I have come to this conclusion - that the dire constraints in the material environment and the predicaments in the history of Somalia have been determining the process of the Somali social formation across the triple history--that is the pre-colonial, the colonial and the post-colonial periods. The deleterious effects of both misfortunes--enduring poverty of the domestic economy on the one hand and the pitfalls of the colonial intervention and fragmentation of the country on the other have produced contradictory tendencies of private and public pursuits which I outlined in the introductory chapter. As I explained, both tendencies systematically unearth concrete trajectories, which have been shaping the social and political life of the Somali society over a long period of time. Moreover, the identification of the contradictory tendencies towards private and public pursuits enables us to read and interpret the underlying historical dynamics of the Somali society as a coherent process. This remains so without however losing the focus as Braudel advises us that, "research is question of endlessly proceeding from the social reality to the model, and then back again, and so on, in a series of readjustments and patiently renewed trips" (Braudel 1980:45). Furthermore, the dynamics of both private and public pursuits offer better explanations in the synthesis of analysis of continuity and change discussions than those which the major schools of Somali studies respectively advance.

On this point, though this study builds on the insight of these Somalist scholars and follows their lead, it seeks in a modest way to construct a mode of analysis and interpretation in the hope of advancing better and fuller alternative explanations into the contemporary political crisis in Somalia.

As I previously mentioned, the emphasis on the continuity versus the change explanations as to why the state collapsed, advanced by the two dominant schools of Somali studies has a significance. Yet, my purpose in this study is to problematise both contentions through a critical

---

[38] For an excellent and devastating critique of all these forms of "contemporary unilinear evolutionism", see Mahmood Mamdani, Citizen and Subject: Contemporary Africa and The Legacy of Late Colonialism, (Princeton: Princeton University Press, 1996).

analysis. To begin with, the gist of my critique of the traditionalist thesis is that it stresses that the persistence of clan atavistic loyalty *is the* core of the political disaster in Somalia. In fact, the subscribers to these traditionalist schools argue that the primordial clan tendency is a factor in continuity across time, and this single variable powerfully explains Somali politics throughout history. This socio-cultural proposition posits an essentialist line of argument, precisely because the traditionalist focus on this single clan analysis overlooks the impact of the limited development of productive forces in the country that actually perpetuates the survival of kin ties in the Somali society. It also neglects significant concrete variables that the historical dimensions of the tendency towards private pursuit powerfully illustrate. More objectionable, the traditionalist writers read the contemporary historical process of the Somali society incorrectly since they claim the current resurgence of clan atavistic tendency to be the cause of the political predicament in Somalia though in reality it is the consequence. For instance, the power struggles of the political elite are what reproduce the clan schisms as they deliberately exploit the clan differences and use them as sources of political instrument for their private pursuits.

The theoretical proposition of this study in contrast to the traditionalist thesis is that internally the continuity of the tendency towards concrete private pursuit rather than innate clan animosity is what largely determined the collapse of the state in Somalia. As I will illustrate in this study, the continuity of the tendency towards private pursuit, which is given rise to by the extreme material deprivation in the country, explains in a concrete way why different groupings in Somali society still pursue sectarian interests, remain organised along kinship lines, exercise fragmented politics and fail to establish a single political unit. Put simply, the continuity of the tendency towards private pursuit can be observed in the social, economic and political spheres of contemporary Somali society. In this sense, the tendency towards private pursuit is not only confined to the embezzlement of public resources for parochial gains; its influence also affects other structures in the society. The explanatory power of this alternative mode of analysis is that it reads the political economy of the society not in a piecemeal way as in the case of the traditionalist writer's approach but in its historical totality. In a way, traditionalist proponents resolutely detach politics from economics and say virtually nothing about the relation between them. More significantly, this alternative framework brings together both the causes and the consequences of the Somali predicament, which are largely wrought by the constraints in the material environment which most of the Somali people still endure.

This study also contests the thesis of the transformationist scholars who argue that the change brought about by the colonial economic and political intervention is what fundamentally accounts for the destructive turn of events in Somalia today. The colonial occupation not only transformed the political economy of the Somali society as the transformationists emphasise, but more deleteriously it gravely dismembered the Somali people and their territorial habitat. In this respect, the division of the country was the most dramatic change that the Somali people have ever endured. For instance, the colonial imperial designs ruthlessly wounded the very psyche of Somali cultural nationalism, as it fragmented the ethnic Somalis under different foreign political powers. Since then, the healing of this wound by struggling to bring together the ethnic Somalis in one place is what has given rise to the primacy of the public pursuit in the Somali politics. Thus, as I will explain in this study, the history of Somali-wide politics since colonialism has largely been the history of this public pursuit. The other related history at the sub-national level that manifested as sectarian politics is that of private pursuit. In this respect, both dynamics are not separate phenomena but are interacting tendencies in a complex whole of historical processes that have been shaping the Somali society through the ages. Nonetheless, each tendency has impacted on the Somali social formation in its own distinctive ways. But ultimately, the positive and negative impulses of both private and public pursuits have largely determined the social and political realities in contemporary Somalia.

In a nutshell, my alternative proposition to the continuity and change explanations is that of the private and public pursuit since both tendencies identify comprehensive historical processes --internal and external--at work in Somalia. Private and public pursuits uncover aspects which advance continuity and change explanations that offer different interpretations for the collapse of the state than those hitherto available. Furthermore, the comprehensive aspects that the private and public pursuits underline include the elements that have been already addressed by the traditionalist and transformationist scholars of the Somali studies. Therefore, I will argue in this study that the manifestations of both of these historical processes are indeed the *key* or dominant determinants over all other variables that are put forward to explain the causes for the collapse of the state in Somalia. Throughout this study I will also use both terms as guiding frameworks. In the following two chapters, the constraints in the material environment and the misfortunes in the Somali history, which wrought the conditions that have engendered the tendencies towards private and public pursuit will be discussed.

2.7. Conclusion

In this chapter, I attempted to review the debates on the post-colonial Somali state since the late 1950s. The main body of this chapter discusses how the debates on the Somali state, as other states in Africa, was largely conducted in reference to historical and social experiences that have taken place either in the West or in Latin America. Modernisation proponents who first conceptualised the society and the state in Africa viewed the continent to be in a process of a pre-modern and pre-industrial stage of development that Europe has already passed. Accordingly, it was felt that with a rapid economic development and social transformation along that linear path already taken by Western society, society in Africa will arrive at a modern and industrial capitalist transition in a foreseeable time frame. Similarly, the dependency theory that followed up the modernisation perspective also debated the African state and society in the light of social and political experiences which had taken place in Latin America. More problematically, the dependency scholars treated the countries in the Third World as if they had similar political economy problems since they seldom conducted a close empirical study of specific cases. In this respect, both the grand theories have ignored or misread the specific historical experiences of African states since they failed to guide our understanding of the problems facing the continent. Despite this, both universal perspectives have influenced the debates between the traditionalist and transformationist proponents of Somali studies. Take, for instance, the explanations of the domestic socio-cultural continuity as argued by the traditionalist writers versus the externally induced political economy change as encountered by the transformationist scholars, which they respectively advance to be the genesis of the contemporary political predicament in Somalia.

Since the late 1980s a new research agenda was initiated in response to the failure of the modernisation and the dependency perspectives. The tendency now is to examine each concrete case against its own historical conjuncture instead of mirroring to a historical experience elsewhere. To put it simply, this means that we should study each African state in the context of its distinctive historical trajectories, rather than in terms of highly abstract perspectives, which are flawed or outdated.[39] In this study, taking a point of departure that is based on a historically informed theory, I will analyse the collapsed state in Somalia in the light of its own long-term trajectories through which the political institutions of the Somali society have evolved. In other words, I will attempt to seek out the causes of the contemporary collapse of the state within the context of the past economic and political history of the Somali people.

---

[39] I am however very much aware that rejecting the determinism of modernisation and of dependency should not lead to an historical historicism, but to a more dialectical approach. This is why in the context of Somalia the dialectic towards private and public pursuits in the historical process plays the centrality of this study.

Chapter Three

Environmental Constraints and Private Pursuit

3.1. Introduction

This chapter discusses how the constraints in the harsh material environment vigorously perpetuate the continuity of the tendency towards private pursuit in Somalia. Moreover, the chapter delineates several decisive facets of the tendency towards private pursuit, notably the competition for livelihood survival, narrow identity and parochial social and political arrangements. In doing so, I will depart from the traditionalist line of reasoning. That school takes an essentialist line of argument and claims that primordial clan animosity (which is indeed a single variable of the tendency towards private pursuit) is the only factor of continuity. However, the proponents of this traditionalist thesis fail to consider the underlying material deprivation, which maintains the persistence of clan structure in the social relationship of the Somali society. Furthermore, the traditionalist writers neglect other particularistic aspects of the tendency towards private pursuit in the economy and the political sphere that are also of continuity.

In Somalia, the continuity of the tendency towards private pursuit is sustained by the limited development of productive forces in the country, while the low and insufficient level of productive forces is largely conditioned by the constraints in the material environment such as the cycles of extreme climatic conditions and the extensive exploitation of the land required in rearing the livestock. As I outlined in the introductory chapter, Somalis waged the struggles for private pursuit for different motives during the pre-colonial, colonial and post-colonial periods. For instance, during the pre-colonial period when the communal mode of production was dominant, the tendency towards private pursuit was what pushed the lineages and family related groups to aid mutually and cooperate economically, socially and politically. Thus, in the early communal formation of the Somali people, the tendency towards private pursuit worked to encourage collectivism and communal survival. By contrast, since the colonial state was imposed on Somalia and the peripheral capitalist mode of production became prevalent, the tendency towards private pursuit was profoundly altered, so that individualistic economic and power interests predominated. The reason is that in the communal mode the relations of production are regulated by kinship relations, while in the peripheral capitalist mode the relations of production are mediated by capitalist market relations.

3.2. The Communal Mode of Production

In pre-colonial Somalia, pastoral nomadism was the primary communal mode of production. The pastoral mode of production can be appropriately understood as one of variable communal modes of production. In other words, pastoral economic activity is one sort of the various sets of the communal modes. For the purpose of this study, pastoral nomadism is an economic existence based on extensive use of pasture in a condition where the level of technology is still simple (Max 1981; Moghadam 1988). In early Somalia, pastoral production, which was the livelihood of the majority of the population, coexisted with other modes of economic activity - such as agriculture and trade. Yet, both economic activities were marginal and remained subordinated to the dominance of the pastoral mode of production. Thus, in pre-capitalist communal Somalia, it was the pastoral mode of production which prevailed over other modes of economic existence.

However, in Somalia, the dominance of this meagre pastoral economy is conditioned by the constraints in the material environment. The nature of the ecology in the country is semi-arid where the rain is very scarce and climate is extremely harsh. Therefore, the only economic existence this poor environment can sustain is that of animal husbandry. According to David D. Laitin and Said S. Samatar:

> "In this land of hardy vegetation, steaming sand dunes, and sun-baked coastal plains, the Somalis have evolved during the centuries a way of life peculiarly suited to their demanding environment: on the one hand, a transhumant pastoralism designed to maximise the meagre resources of water wells and pasturelands for the pastoralists and their herds and, on the other hand, a social organization that encourages collective action and mutual aid" (Laitin and Samatar 1987:22).

The animals the Somali nomads rear in this demanding environment are goats, sheep, camels, and less commonly cattle. As cattle need frequent watering, raising them on this waterless environment with low scrub bush is hardly possible. It is the smaller pockets in the river area, south of the country which are conducive to cattle husbandry. However, even rearing other animals such as camels, sheep and goats in this dreadful environment is not an easy occupation since that itself demands a constant mobility. The scarcity and the uneven distribution of the rainfall push the pastoral nomads to move frequently with their livestock in search of water and pasture. This constant migration however is the best rational strategy and the best 'tactical adaptability' to assure that the pastoral nomads in Somalia can survive despite the constraints in the material environment (Braun 1989; Doornbos 1993:104).

Among the livestock that the Somali pastoral nomads raise, camels because of their greater material value remain the mainstay of livelihood. Camels have a strong capacity to endure harsh conditions and unique stamina and ability compared with the sheep and goats. On top of this superior quality for endurance and resistance to drought, camels also give prestige to the owner since they constitute a symbol of wealth and richness. This accords camels therefore the highest esteem among the Somali pastoral nomads.[40] The following classical Somali poetry testifies to the significance of the possession of camels:

> "He who does not own camels lives under the protection of others. At a place where camels did not calve I will not stay. For a man who owns no camels, the event of his death will pass unnoticed" (Rirash 1988:64-65).

---

[40] The status of camels in the eyes of the Somali nomads can be compared to the horses of the nomads in Central Asia. The Central Asian nomads accord horses high esteem because of their usefulness as a means of transport and for herding the livestock. For example, the Central Asian nomads venerate in numerous proverbs and poems the horses in a similar manner as that of the Somali pastoral nomads with respect to camels (Leeuwen, Emeljanebko, and Popova 1994).

For the livestock economic production in Somalia, the grazing land is not owned privately but is owned or controlled collectively. This collective ownership of the pastureland provides the kin-related groups inhabiting the area with a certain priority right for the use of the pasture resources. This arrangement however will not deny access to others from the distant lineage groups as long as there are sufficient pasture resources for all (Swift, 1977). By contrast, the animals are privately owned. Each household, which is the basic social unit of production, possesses its own herds. Furthermore, this household-based livestock production was an occupation engaged in by all adult members of the nuclear family. In other worlds, each able-bodied individual participated in the production of the scarce livestock economy for the survival of the whole family. Consequently, this limited development of productive forces in the subsistence pastoral economy is what in fact prevented the emergence of individualised private pursuit in the early communal formation of the Somali people.[41]

In Africa today, Somalia is the only country where pastoral nomads still form the majority of the population. About 65% of the Somali people still lead a nomadic life and practise pastoral economic production, which is in fact the highest percentage of any country in the world (Geshekter 1997:68).

Also, compared to the rest of Africa, Somalia is a country in which the livestock production remains the backbone of the economy even today.[42] According to Marx, transhumant pastoral nomadism has been the first form of maintaining human existence. Marx then writes in the Pre-Capitalist Economic Formations that:

> "We take it for granted that pastoralism or more generally a migratory life, is the first form of maintaining existence, the tribe not settling in a fixed place but using up what it finds locally and passing on" (Marx 1964:68).

Yet, for the pastoral nomads in Somalia, generations after generations are still preoccupied with this mode of living of what Marx again refers to as a "given natural instrument of production" (Marx 1970:68). Likewise, Karl Polanyi (1966) concurs with Marx and terms this simple pastoral mode of production a "natural economy" as it is largely the consequence of the climatic environment. However, most discussions on the residues of natural economy and on the types of communal modes of production that existed in the precapitalist formations are limited to hunting and gathering and settled cultivation as if pastoral nomadism does not exist as a means of economic livelihood. The reason perhaps may be that, in the West, the pastoral mode of production has been insignificant historically and in the process of economic transformation has totally disappeared. For instance, when Cox lists the residue of communal modes of production of pre-capitalist formations, he notes only four modes as if they are the only existing forms of economic activities. Cox writers that:

> "Four modes of social relations of production, all originating in the precapitalist era of simple reproduction, survive in social formations characterised by dynamic development, whether of the capitalist or redistributive types. These are

---

[41] The reason was that the means of the production were too limited and the productive forces of the family members owned it collectively.

[42] For instance in 1990, of the entire livestock population in the continent of Africa, Somalia owned 43% of camels, 2% of cattle, 10% of goats and 5% of sheep. This recent statistics was compiled by the Department of Planning and Statistics of the Ministry of Livestock, Forestry and Range in cooperation with GTZ (Damooei 1997:275).

subsistence agriculture, peasant-lord agriculture, the primitive labour market, and household production" (Cox 1987:35)

In the list what is missing is pastoral nomadism, which is the oldest form of social production and human existence. Pastoral nomadism is not only an ancient form of simple reproduction, but it is still an economic mainstay of several minor societies in the peripheral areas like Somalia, where it has survived despite its subordination to the capitalist world economy.

Pastoral production is an economic activity, which does not produce surplus. In fact, it is an economy of simple subsistence, which is not at all self-sufficient. And this lack has been the main reason, which forced the pre-capitalist Somali pastoral nomads to establish barter relations with the outside world (Abdi Samatar 1989). Somali nomads bartered their livestock and livestock products for grain and clothing brought in by long-distance traders. However, a more structural problem is that pastoral economic activity hardly grows beyond bare subsistence level. And even if it is compared with other economic activities it becomes obvious that nomads everywhere are faced with the same problems of resource deprivation (Khazanov 1983). Everywhere, the salient feature of the pastoral economy is essentially non-autarkic.[43] Alluding to rich historical data regarding the nomads in Central Asia, Khazanov argues that this material deprivation historically forced many traditional pastoral nomads to wage frequent wars in order to conquer sedentary agricultural and urban societies mainly for economic gains.

Early Somali pastoral nomads did in reality wage frequent wars to conquer the sedentary farmers inhabiting the fertile pockets located in the south of the country. But the number of the pastoral nomads from the semi-arid zones in the north who migrated to the agriculturally productive areas in the south were in fact very small. The nature of the conquests and the historical process of this migration have been already extensively documented elsewhere and thus further repetition is not necessary here.[44] What I am interested in exploring here is: How the majority of the pastoral nomads who are still the largest part of the Somali population survived in the challenging environment of the country for centuries? And how the coping mechanisms they adopted to subsist in the meagre pastoral existence affected their economic, social and political outlook? Among other coping strategies that the Somali nomads have opted for, two are worth noting because of their far-reaching ramifications. The first survival strategy that the traditional Somali pastoral nomads have adopted has been to organise the pastoral production on the basis of small primary units. Central to this coping mechanism is the making of the nuclear family the basic unit of production. In Somalia, the clan, which is the highest political unit, occupies and controls a specified grazing territory but it lacks both the capacity and the power to organise the pastoral production. This function is therefore left

---

[43] Khazanov uses the term non-autarkic to denote that all kinds of pastoral production not only lack surplus but also do not at all generate a self-sufficient means of living. More on this discussion, see further Khazanov (1983). According to Moghadam, "the highly specialised nature of pastoral production does not allow nomads to be autarkic and requires that they enter into a socio-political and economic relation with the sedentary people" (Moghadam 1988:397). A better explanation perhaps is that since pastoral nomads everywhere repeatedly face frequent draughts because of the constraints in the environment, establishing trade and economic relations with the outside world is indeed needed for sheer survival.

[44] See further I.M. Lewis, "From Nomadism to Cultivation: The Expansion of Political Solidarity in Southern Somalia", in M. Douglas and P. Kaberry (eds.), Man in Africa, (London: Tavistock, 1969); 59-78.

50

to the units at lower levels of the clan segmentation to pursue it privately and independently. These units can be a single household, clusters of households, 'dia-paying groups'[45] etc.

The second survival strategy that the Somali nomads adopted has been to disperse as widely as possible in order to utilise effectively the marginal pasture resources on the land. As the productive capacity of the land is very limited, this method of extensive pastoralism permits the nomads to cope with the ordinary environmental hazards. In this pattern of organising the production, the primary agnatic units are allowed to move freely in the areas which the clans to which they belong control. Accordingly, these agnatic units who fragment further into smaller close-knit groupings wander around and appropriate whatever pasture resources they can get on the land, be it water or grass. Thus, both of the coping mechanisms that the traditional Somali nomads have adopted were suggested to be highly rational and environmentally sound. According to Abdi Samatar:

> "Pastoral production required mobility and flexibility in order to adequately utilise marginal ecological conditions. Given the precarious environment and precapitalist technology, units of pastoral production were small and widely dispersed to avoid resource depletion" (Abdi Samatar 1989:23).

This is true. Somali pastoral nomads could not have survived living in this harsh environment in the country for centuries if they had not organised the production of their pastoral livelihood skilfully. However, the marginal environment that conditioned the household to be the basic unit of production and forced the pastoral nomads to disperse as thinly as possible have also wrought characteristics specific to the Somali society. And although these salient features emerged in the distant past of pre-colonial traditional Somalia they still influence the contemporary dynamics of the society. First, the regular mobility that the organisation of the pastoral production requires still prevents the Somali nomads from settling and remaining in a fixed place permanently. Second, specified clan-inhabited geographical zones developed very early before the establishment of the nation-state in 1960. See the clan-based territories on Map 2. Even now a certain Somali clan is claiming that on the basis of that early traditional clan-inhabited zones, it should be recognised as a clan-based state.[46] Third, the limited development of productive forces in the subsistence pastoral economy still remains a factor, which perpetuates the continuity and the primacy of the kinship ties in the social organisation of the Somali people. It is in this last instance that I am challenging the thesis of the traditionalist writers who claim that it is the primordial blood ties which perpetuate the clan dominance in the social organisation of the Somali society. This argument of the traditionalist proponents can be refuted as it is common everywhere that pastoral nomads organise their social relations of production through a kinship system.[47] Thus, the prevalence and the

---

[45] Dia-paying group or *Jilib* in Somali is the smallest unit, which is also the most stable and fundamental political structure of the Somali clan system. Members of the dia-paying group are closely related families who are united by the sheer necessity of mutual aid and cooperation without which survival in this harsh environment is hardly possible. They therefore enter a joint contract (*heer*), which pledges the contracted kinsmen to act in concert and help each other when individually or collectively they face a threat from members of other distant dia-paying groups.

[46] The Somali Isaaq clan inhabiting in the northern Somalia or Somaliland as it is now call, use in addition the argument that the area was colonised separately by the British as a fundamental reason that must entitle them the international recognition as a new and independent nation state. See further, Hussein Adam, 'Formation and Recognition of New States: Somaliland in Contrast to Eritrea', in: *Review of African Political Economy*, vol.21 (1994), no. 59.

apparent manifestation of kinship relations are neither unique nor specific only to the Somali society. In fact, everywhere, it is the level of the productive forces of the pastoral economy, which gives rise to and maintains such finite social relations and not primordial consciousness as claimed by the traditionalist scholars.[48] Fourth, because of the lack of an institutionalised hierarchy, pre-colonial traditional Somali society was stateless, for the simple reason that the prevalence of the lower technology of pastoral production in Somalia reproduces its simple kin-ordered political organisations. Ibn Khaldun[49] was the first who brilliantly analysed the relationship between the precarious material existence of the pastoral nomads and its corresponding rudimentary political organisation in North Africa in the fourteenth century. And in his thesis, Ibn Khaldun locates the absence of a higher level of political superstructure among the pastoral nomads in the extremely rudimentary nature of their productive activities.[50] Fredrik Barth (1973) concurs with the argument of Ibn Khaldun. Barth writes that the dearth of political structure beyond lineage and kinship relations among the pastoral nomads is conditioned by their meagre material basis that neither needs nor can maintain it.

In this study what I am trying to explain without sounding an ecological determinist is how the constraints in the material environment impinged on and determined the mode of livelihood and the social organisation of the Somali society throughout time. As Evans-Pritchard explicates: "in a general sense, modes of livelihood, together with environmental conditions, which always impose effective limits on modes of livelihood, determine the dominant values of the peoples and strongly influence their social organisations, including their political systems" (Evans-Pritchard 1940:8). In a nutshell, in Somalia, the ecology has given rise to a society, which organises along clan and lineages lines and pursues its economic survival in smaller groups. Thus, in pre-colonial Somalia, due to the constraints of the material environment, there was no sustained collective solidarity and cooperation beyond the lower levels of lineage. Put differently, there was no Somali-wide collective pursuit but a parochial kin-oriented private pursuit. In times of peace, this was largely the case. However, in times of war, be it internal or for that matter, external foreign invasions across borders, a temporary realignment and cooperation at clan or a Somali-wide level was possible. But this collective solidarity was often short-lived as it withered away as soon as the threat of war disappeared. In this respect, what was constant was the cooperation of the smallest units of the clan such as the nuclear family or a number of families related in blood in organising the production of the livestock, well-digging, physical protection, occasional ritual ceremonies and other similar functions in these narrowest spheres (Sahlins 1968). And the reason as Wolf

---

[47] As Samatar explains, "social theorists argue that blood-ties in the old tradition were part and parcel of communitarian social relations whose primary purpose was to ensure the production of necessities in the pastoral range" (Abdi Samtar 1992b: 630).

[48] For an excellent analysis of how the subsistence pastoral mode of livelihood creates and perpetuates vertical communities of clans, see Fatemeh E. Moghadam, Nomadic Invasions and the Development of Productive Forces: An Historical Study of Iran (1000-1800), *Science & Society* 52, 4 (Winter 1988): 389-412.

[49] Ibn Khaldun was a fourteenth century North African statesman, jurist, historian, and scholar.

[50] For further elaboration, see the classical book of Ibn Khaldun, The Muqaddimah: An Introduction to History (London: RKP, 1967); particularly chapter 2; see also Yves Lacoste, Ibn Khaldun: The Birth of History and the Past of the Third World (London: Verso, 1984). Lacoste commenting on Ibn Khaldun writes, " if a privileged minority is to emerge and exercise something more than a moral influence over the tribe, there must be surplus available for appropriation. No such surplus exists in these poverty-striken groups" (1984:112). With respect to the Somali clans, I.M Lewis has recorded how some Somali pastoral nomads who migrated from the arid dissert in the north and settled in the agriculturally rich areas south of the country after adopting farming have developed a hierarchical and a formalised authority of leadership (Lewis 1955).

suggests is that "the ties of kinship set limits to the amount of social labour that can be mobilised for collective purposes" (Wolf 1982:99). Perhaps it maybe argued that the dominance of the ties of kinship is what perpetuates the tendency to clan and lineage rather than a Somali-wide solidarity in Somalia even now. Here, a theoretical interest worth consideration is how the workings of the tendency towards private pursuit provide positive impulses at sub-national or sub-sate levels in terms of security, communal solidarity and group survival but negatively affect at the national and state levels of the Somali social formation. [51]

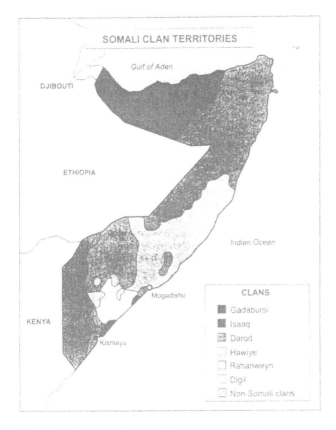

Source: Ricciuti, Edward R. Somalia A Crisis of Famine and War. 1995:10

---

[51] A seminal analysis of the how the positive impulses of the tendency towards private pursuit guarantees the physical, social and economic security of the Somali population at the sub-national and sub-state levels is recently provided by Maria Brons in her book: Society, Security, Sovereignty and the state in Somalia: From Statelessness to statelessness? (Utrecht: International Books, 2001).

3.3. The Dominance of Kinship Relations

In Marxian historical materialism, a mode of production corresponds to a single dominant set of social relations, which has arisen from a finite level of development of the productive forces. In the Somali context, it is the pastoral communal mode of production that creates and recreates the dominance of kinship relations, for the simple reason that pastoral economic activity has a very low development of productive forces which cannot afford or permit the development of a social structure beyond the kinship system. Therefore, in the communal formation of Somalia it was the kinship relations which regulated the productive forces of the pastoral economy. As Samir Amin explains:

> "It seems obvious that the low level of development is inextricably linked with lineage, clan, and tribal relations.... Thus, wherever we find these relations, the level of the productive forces is necessarily low, and where we do not find them, it is necessarily high. The existence of these relations is furthermore the expression of the dominance of kinship (and the absence of the state)" (Amin 1980:48-9).

For the Somali pastoral nomads the kinship system not only regulated the production of the livestock economy but also governed all aspect of the cultural, social and political life of society. There is now an ongoing fierce debate between the two dominant schools of Somali studies about the elements of which kinship is constituted. For instance, traditionalist writers explain kinship simply as that of "blood and bone" as epitomised by I.M. Lewis, while transformationist contenders understand it as an institution or an ideology on the other hand.[52] Ahmed Samatar debating with the traditionalist scholars spelled out what kinship system in essence embodies. According to Samatar, the kinship system in pre-colonial communal Somali society was partly blood-ties and partly a customary law. It was partly blood-ties reckoned through patrilineal lines. Somalis trace their close or distant family relations through male ancestry. Normally, those closely related groups are expected to enter into a joint contract for mutual aid and cooperation in order to survive in the harsh environment. Thus, the blood descent element of the kinship system was significant because it served as the basis of bond and solidarity that guaranteed the physical and economic security of the smallest units of the lineage segments. The kinship system was partly a customary law or heer. This other component of the kinship ideology served to regulate the wider social relations of the clans and the clan-families at the highest political apex. Heer is a secular and unwritten social contract. Somali pastoral nomads used heer norms, rules and regulations to maintain the social order of the whole community at different political levels. For instance, lineage segmented groups enter into heer social contract for different needs such as not making use of each other's pasture zones and bore wells without prior permission. Also, neighbouring clans enter into heer treaty for a peaceful coexistence. Moreover, heer sanctions are used as conflict settlement mechanisms when tension arises between groups and lineages for the access to the meagre resources such as water and pasture. Furthermore, heer rules are applied to instances of homicide,

---

[52] For example, kinship as blood versus ideology, see the ongoing debate between I.M. Lewis and Ahmed I. Samatar. See particularly the book by Lewis, Blood and Bone: The Call of Kinship in Somali Society (Lawrenceville, N.J.: The Red Sea Press, 1994); and Samatar, 'The Curse of Allah: Civic Disembowelment and the Collapse of the State in Somalia', in The Somali Challenge From Catastrophe to Renewal? ed. Ahmed I. Samatar (Boulder: Lynne Rienner, 1994).

injury, robbery etc. The men who specialise in the procedures of heer laws are known as 'wisemen'.[53] For instance, since the Somali language was oral, it was the successive aged elders of the pastoral nomads who were the repositories of the heer laws. And it was in this way that every generation transmitted heer constitution to the next generation.

Samatar carries the debate further. He explains that this secular kinship system spelled out above was not the only value which regulated the social relations of communal Somalia. Religious dictates of the Islamic sharia also played a complementary role, albeit a secondary one. For instance, sharia laws were infused with the secular heer rules in order to enhance the effectiveness for the mechanisms of the political mediation. Islam came to Somalia around the tenth century when Arab proselytisers first arrived at the coastal towns of the country. Accordingly, as the Islam belief system widely spread in the country, native religious men (wadaado), specialising in sharia laws had emerged. They stood alongside the wisemen specialising in secular heer rules. Thereafter, both heer and sharia scholars worked together as a judiciary team in order to prevent, manage and resolve the political tensions within the community at large. This is how they conducted the reconciliation process as conflict arose. First, the men versed in secular heer rules sit in shir[54] and deliberate the grievances and the issues to the conflict. After they reach a decision and pronounce the final verdict, the men of sharia step in to complete the matter. The men of sharia solemnise the verdict by reading verses in the holy Quran and praying that such conflict shall not occur again in the community. The mediating role of the men of Islamic sharia was to provide deeper spiritual bindings which the parties involved are expected to abide by. In a nutshell, "together, heer and Islam, in particular, gave the stateless Somalis a rightful political centre of gravity capable of controlling capriciousness, managing intersubjectivity, and offering order and continuity" (Ahmed Samatar 1994:111). Thus, in pre-colonial communal Somalia, this is how effective social stability and political order were maintained. More significantly, the blending of the values and the laws of Islam with that of the native kinship ideology is what gradually matured to "a moral commonwealth or Umma",[55] the superstructure of the old Somali order in communal Somalia. Ahmed Samatar concludes the debate on how the moral commonwealth governed the social relations of pre-colonial Somali by drawing the following scheme. The charter illustrates the make-up of the constitution of the old Somali order.

---

[53] In Somalia, wisemen are those who embody the great wisdom and excellent erudition of the traditional mechanisms of conflict settlements and whose advice in heer matters is highly regarded.

[54] Shir is a Somali word, which literally means assembly. Shir assembly is a forum in which the men of the community gather in order to resolve the burning conflicts.

[55] For an interesting and a broad historical account of how the constitution of Umma developed and ordered the social relations of pre-colonial Somali society, see Ahmed Samatar (1994).

Figure 1.1 Basic Elements of Somali Traditional Moral Order

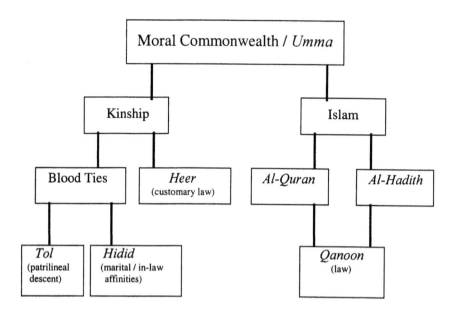

Source: *Adapted from Ahmed I. Samatar, The Somali Challenge: From Catastrophe to Renewal? (1994).*

Indeed, the analysis here of the dominance of the kinship system in pre-colonial Somalia demonstrates that communal or traditional Somali society does not lack public order but formalised political institutions, simply because "the kin-ordered mode inhibits the institutionalisation of political power, resting essentially upon the management of consensus among clusters of participants" (Wolf 1982:99). However, it was in the absence of this authoritarian structure that the public order was not coercive but essentially moral. As elsewhere, communal Somalia was not without conflicts due to the constraints in the material environment on the land. The frequent droughts, the scarcity of rain, and the competition for the meagre pasture resources such as water and grass were bones of contention and the source of occasional clashes. Particularly, during the periods of drought and dry seasons such tensions were more acute. Fortunately, the moral public order was an effective mechanism of social control for the simple reason that the pastoral production was a communal activity. Put simply, it was a communal activity embedded in social relations of production in which the economic production, political life and culture were all intermeshed (Lyons and Samatar 1995:10). Thus, in pre-colonial Somalia, the prevalence of the communitarian social relations of production is what regulated the competition for the sparse resources and kept in check its concomitant conflicts. In fact, no individual or group dared not to conform to this communitarian social relations of production since the system guaranteed the orderly and the stable production of the pastoral moral economy that was the mainstay of the whole community. More significantly, the economic production was part and parcel of much wider social relationships.[56]

In brief, throughout the pre-colonial Somali history, the communitarian social order in which individualism has no place is what reigned supreme. Polanyi explains better the nature of this communitarian ethos when he writes that "...man's economy, as a rule, is submerged in his social relationships. He does not act so as to safeguard his individual interest in the possession of material goods; he acts so as to safeguard his social standing, his social claims, his social assets" (Polanyi 1944:46). However, in the Somali society, this pre-capitalist communalism did not last forever. As I will explain below, the penetration of the market relations of peripheral capitalism into the subsistence pastoral production has deleteriously transformed the communitarian social order of the Somali society.

3.4. Peripheral Capitalism

The pastoral communal mode of production in Somalia was submerged under the peripheral capitalism in the late 19th century when the powerful forces of the international market and European imperialism intruded. To put it simply, the imposition of the peripheral capitalism on Somalia has put to an end the dominance of the pre-capitalist communal mode of production. For instance, the impact of the capitalist intrusion changed the subsistence pastoral production from a community-oriented production into a market-oriented commodity.

Britain was the first colonial power to impose its political authority on Somalia in 1886. Initially, British imperial power took over northern Somalia with the objective of appropriating livestock meat to supply its military garrison stationed in the Aden desert. However, in no time, this overseas economic interest considerably commercialised the livestock production in Somalia. From then onwards, the occupation of trade and its attending demands by external markets have become more valuable than that of the meagre subsistence production. For example, the needs of the British colonial state opened up external markets, which stimulated the export of large numbers of herds for the first time in the history of Somalia. And the surplus derived from this expanding livestock trade had deeper impacts on the productive forces of the communal pastoral mode of production, which was the material basis of the kinship system. This is how Ahmed I. Samatar summed up the new age in which the communal pastoral Somali nomads was ushered:

> "The precolonial Somali tradition has been blown asunder by its incorporation into the world capitalist system. Livestock and pastoral production, which originally was principally geared for domestic use, has been commoditized, qualitatively transforming precolonial nonexploitive social relations into peripheral capitalist relations" (Ahmed Samatar 1989:154).

---

[56] Karl Polanyi speaking of the moral economy of communitarian societies like that of early traditional Somali explains that "the individual's economic interest is rarely paramount, for the community keeps all its members from starving unless it is itself borne down by catastrophe, in which case interests are again threatened collectively, not individually. The maintenance of social ties, on the other hand, is crucial. First, because by disregarding the accepted code of honour, or generosity, the individual cuts himself off from the community and becomes an outcast; second, because, in the long run, all social obligations are reciprocal, and their fulfilment serves also the individual's give-and-take interests best"(Polanyi 1944:46).

The commercialisation of livestock production not only heralded the transition to a new mode of production but also to the making of a new social order. Transformationist critics often accuse the traditionalist proponents of failing to grasp the unfolding dynamics of change taking place in the society. According to the transformationist critics, traditionalists often discuss contemporary Somali society as if nothing qualitatively had changed since European imperialism and global market forces penetrated. But the truth of the matter was that the pre-colonial communitarian Somali social relations did not remain unscathed. As Abdi Samatar explains:

> "The imposition of colonial rule on stateless societies, the new dynamics of social relations, and the transformation of the pastoral economy are all deemed to be mere quantitative alterations in Somali society rather than fundamental modifications of pre-colonial tradition. By evading the qualitative nature of the changes experienced, the traditionalists are able to avoid systematic analysis of any mutations of the social structures and the governing ethos that might have taken place in the last century" (Abdi Samatar 1992b: 627).[57]

Before the colonial state intervened in Somalia there were hardly any significant internal or external markets for the livestock production.[58] The demands of both the domestic and Arabian markets were too small. This was confirmed by the available recorded data of the pre-colonial trade in Somalia (Burton 1894; Richard Pankhurst 1965; Abdi Samatar 1989b). Furthermore, the pre-colonial trade pattern in Somalia was not monetised and conducted largely on barter basis. Therefore, it was due to this barter basis that the pre-colonial communitarian production had use-values and not exchange-values. And it was only later and precisely in the era of peripheral capitalism that the logic of the market economy stimulated the Somali pastoral nomads to rear the livestock not only for sustenance but also for external trade. Gradually the livestock trade had become an internal component of the global capitalist economy.

As the livestock trade to external markets increased, commercial transactions between the pastoral nomads in the countryside and the merchants in the coastal towns had intensified. This trading activity was facilitated by the existence of such Somali middlemen as that of *Abbaans* and *Dilaals* (guides and brokers). These intermediary natives did not emerge suddenly due to the demands of the global trade; they were already there. The early inception of the Middle Eastern traders in the region had already created such domestic social agents though they remained incipient in nature. Their initial emergence however had a heavy impact upon the pre-existing communitarian (egalitarian) pastoralism as it set in motion a rudimentary social differentiation and individualised private pursuits. According to Ahmed Samatar,

---

[57] See also Abdi Samatar, "Somali Tradition, Peripheral Capitalism, and the Politics of Development", *Northeast African Studies* 11, 1(1989): 39-52.

[58] However the immediate impact of the colonial economy on the austere life of the Somali pastoral nomads was deplorable. This is what a British consular in Somalia at the time observed: "in a civilized country, with a settled population employed in the agricultural arts and manufactures, the standard of material comfort is associated with advancement, but in a nomadic society it denotes deterioration and a disintegration of those austere qualities requisite for enduring a hard and precarious existence" (quoted in Geshekter 1993:6).

"this new element in Somali society, which encouraged the dilution of kin loyalty and ushered in an attachment to a foreign source of power, would seem to presage latter-day politics of clientalism; and moreover, a modern analyst would probably argue that the Abbaans were the precursors of the links that chain peripheral states of Africa to the 'tributary system'" (Ahmed Samatar 1988:14-15).

Gradually, the complete induction of the Somali pastoral society into global trade (in the late 19th century) had greatly enhanced the economic power of these intermediate social groups. They also blossomed and matured under colonialism. Thus, in this respect, Ahmed Samatar suggests that *Abbaans* and *Dilaals* must be seen to be the precursors of the later *petite bourgeoisie*. No detailed treatment of how the livestock is commoditised and the pastoral Somali nomads are inducted into the global system is necessary here since it is already widely discussed by the transformationist writers of Somali studies.[59] However, two aspects are worth noting here: (a) the transition from communal moral economy to peripheral capitalism in Somalia had created new interest groups, which could no longer be regulated by kinship relations; and (b) the new fortunes generated through the profits of trade and the benefits from the colonial state resources have undermined the old tradition of collective social obligations and reciprocity (the basis of the communal moral economy of the Somali society) to more individualistic interests and private pursuit. Thus, under peripheral capitalism the rules of merchant capital encouraged competition and individual accumulation and as a result submerged the kinship regulated communitarian production. Furthermore and more importantly the continuity of the tendency towards private pursuit in the economic sphere became altered from communal to individualistic interests. In this respect, the tendency towards private pursuit is time specific as it manifests differently during the pre-colonial and colonial periods.

3.5. The Dominance of the Colonial State

As is evident in the discussion above, the kinship system was dominant when the mode of production was based on use value and the level of development of the Somali pastoral productive forces was very low, hardly beyond subsistence. However when the mode of production expanded as more herds were sold on the international market and the exchange value became prevalent under the era of peripheral capitalism, new productive forces crystallised which necessitated corresponding social relations of production. In this respect, the impact of the colonial state economy reproduced a Somali clan system of a different nature due to the transformation resulting from the traditional economic base.

Initially, these social relations were benign mercantilism. Consequently, the physical imposition of the colonial state as an institution of regulation ended the domination of the kinship system. Yet, kinship relations did not disappear altogether but remained a

---

[59]Transformationist scholars have extensively discussed in numerous publications how the global capitalist system predicated the commoditisation of the subsistence livestock economy, decomposed the pre-colonial social relations of the Somali society and made Somalia a peripheral capitalism. For some important groundbreaking literature of this school see, Ahmed I. Samatar, Socialist Somalia: Rhetoric & Reality, (London: Zed Books, 1988); Abdi Ismail Samatar, The State and Rural Transformation in Northern Somalia 1884-1986, (Madison: The University of Wisconsin Press, 1989).

subordinate form of regulation. Although the colonial state was dominant in peripheral capitalism, its control and organisation were more effective in the urban than in the rural areas. For instance, towns and coastal residents were under the regimes and the direct rule of the colonial state, while in the rest of the country, the kinship system known as "native authority" prevailed.[60]

Under mercantilism, the task of the colonial state administration was to ensure the subordinate induction of the livestock economy into global trade. Therefore, maintaining peace and order in the colony[61] was the utmost priority of the colonial state. Particularly, the security issues were what largely preoccupied the British colonial administration in the northern part of Somalia.[62] In this respect, the British Administration undertook two chief functions essential to the material benefits of the colonial government. One was to keep peaceful the coastal towns through which the livestock was shipped to external markets; and the second was to prevent any disturbances that might jeopardise the safety of the caravan routes which link the hinterland to the coastal enclaves. Beyond these two instances that could directly endanger the immediate material needs of the Administration if it was left unprotected the security problems in the rest of the country was not its concern.

Yet there is a widely held claim that colonialism ushered in a period of peace and political stability in Africa. Henry Wilson notes that, "the prime justification for the European partition of Africa had been to maintain pax - peace and stability - where the precolonial rules of Africa were deemed to have failed" (Wilson 1994:16). Some others have also suggested similar viewpoints (see Oliver and Atmore 1977). However, ample evidence in colonial Somalia contradicts this claim. In Somalia, the presence of the colonial state(s) did not only increase conflicts among the Somali clans but also helped its configurations at least in three respects. First, the colonial state played the clans and lineages against each other, perfecting its policy of divide and rule. For example, at any point of time, the loyal headmen and their lineages were armed to defend themselves, to the disadvantage of other lineages that resisted the cooperation with the colonial Administration. And it was through this buying tactic that Somali clans acquired for the first time sophisticated and modern weapons which replaced their simple traditional swords and daggers. More damaging was the easy availability of firearms which had increased raiding as well as the intensity of the violent clashes among the pastoral

---

[60]This bifurcated and Janus-faced colonial state in which direct rule is enforced as "centralised despotism" and indirect rule as "decentralised despotism" is creatively treated by Mamdani (1996).

[61] Somalia and the Somali people had been parcelled by different imperial powers. The northern part of the country came under the British colonial state while Italy colonised the southern part of Somalia. The French colonial state occupied the tiny coastal city of Djibouti. However, this study focuses on British Somaliland in the north and Italian Somaliland in the south of the country. In this section the discussion of the pastoral economic activity that is still the dominant mode of production countrywide, northern Somalia, (the home of animal husbandry) and its occupation by the British colonial state will be central. Southern Somalia is equally important but its agricultural production is small and remains subordinate to animal husbandry.

[62] Northern Somalia was a protectorate since it was a territory under British domination but not of settlement. By contrast, southern Somalia was a colony because it was carved to become a proper settlement of Italian population. Robert Hess noted that the Italians residing in Somalia were fewer than one thousand in 1923 (Hess 1966:180). However, in 1931, there were 1,600 settlers which afterwards rose to 8,000 by 1941. Subsequently, nearly two –thirds returned to Italy. And since Somalia fell under the United Nations trusteeship and Italy was a mandated as an administering authority, the number of the Italians in the country has again increased to over 5,000 in 1953. However, since then, as many of them repatriated back to Italy, this number was in a process of a gradual decline. See further, *The Economy of the Trust Territory of Somaliland* (1957:5).

nomads in the hinterlands far removed from the peaceful enclaves under the colonial state. Furthermore, the competition for access to the colonial state fortunes in the towns and for the provision of more firearms had presented new kind of rivalries between the clans.[63]

Second, the very presence of the colonial state ignited a new and a different sort of conflict among the Somalis. The colonial Administration was determined to eliminate any group that could challenge its supremacy in the country. In Somalia, the Muslim resistance movement was the only group at the time that resisted the presence of the colonial state. Consequently, in order to subdue and crush the power of the Muslim resistance movement, the colonial Administration armed the loyal clans and lineages to fight against their own Somali countrymen. The intention of this strategy was to use the loyal clans and lineages as buffers, which would protect the security of the tiny colonial Administration against the invasion of the Muslim resistance movement. However, it created a situation in which for the first time in Somali history closely related lineage groups fought against each other on secular and religious lines. In other words, the Somalis started fighting each other in defence of foreign colonial versus national interests. This divide and rule policy served very well the interests of the colonial Administration.

Third and most critical was the war between the Dervish Muslim resistance movement and the colonial state. The long struggles of the Dervish movement (1900-1920) against the colonial domination have been extensively documented so further repetition is not necessary.[64] This conflict in Somalia however ushered in decades of destructive militarism and the result was a high human cost for the Somali population. As Charles Geshekter notes, "during the first 36 years of colonial rule (1884-1920), British imperial armies resorted to unprecedented violence and military force (especially after 1899) in efforts to subdue the Somali Dervish movement" (Geshekter 1993:4).

The Italian colonial state in southern Somalia was even more savage because of its fascist practices.[65] It was in this way that the colonial state(s) deliberately militarised the Somali clans and plunged them into a situation in which turmoil, instability and destruction prevailed. The point I want to make clear here is that the imposition of the colonial state(s) on Somalia did not bring peace and social stability but on the contrary, it escalated the local conflict by widening the warring configurations. As everywhere in Africa, the rule of the colonial state was based on force despite its variation in degrees. In this case, Somalia was not an exception. However the colonial manpower in Somalia was very small in number and could hardly exert more than a skeletal authority even in towns and coastal enclaves under their direct control let alone the vast hinterland of the

---

[63] "Clans, which until then had regulated access to the means of rural production (land, water, and livestock), now vied for control of resources controlled by others [colonial state]: export licenses; dhow licenses; the right to collect zariba dues and other tolls; and the rights to dig permanent, privately owned wells, buy trucks, open shops, and so forth" (Kapteijns 1994:220-221).

[64] For an extensive historical account of Dervishe's struggles against the colonial Administration in Somalia, see Lawrence L. James, The Savage Wars: British Campaigns in Africa, 1870-1920 (London: Robert Hale, 1985); Ray Beachy, The Warrior Mullah: The Horn Aflame, 1892-1920 (London: Bellew Publishing, 1990).

[65] For a comprehensive account of the Italian colonial practice in southern Somalia, see Robert Hess, Italian Colonialism in Somalia (Chicago, 1966); Sylvia E. Pankhurst, Ex-Italian Somaliland (London, 1951).

country.[66] Confronted with such manpower scarcity and security problems in the countryside, the colonial Administration created rural authority or what Mamdani calls "Customary Native Authority in the local state".[67] The colonial Administration in Somalia nominated or hand picked chiefs, lineage headmen and clan elders and was empowered to extend and enforce the degree of the colonial authority in the countryside.[68] Yet their appointment was hazardous. According to Lidwien Kapteijns, "the colonial administration, in its desperate search for community leaders, supported one self-styled leader after another---whoever at any point in time either commanded some local authority or could persuade the colonial state that he did" (Kapteijns 1994:221). Indeed, what the colonial administration wanted was a new alternative authority in the interior that could regulate the political economy changes brought about by merchant capital.

In Somalia, the transition of the pre-colonial moral economy[69] to peripheral capitalism commoditised the livestock production but it did not transform its basic organisation. In other words, the scarce structural conditions of the pastoral production remained the same. Yet, the profits gained from the external markets and the resources of the colonial administration created greater inequality, which was in great contrast to the egalitarian ethos that prevailed in the pre-colonial moral economy.[70] As a consequence, the emerging inequality sharpened the rivalries between clans, lineages and individuals for access to the new wealth and power accumulated in the urban areas. Charles Geshekter relates how some strategically placed lineages benefited from the colonially boosted urban economy. He noted that:

> "As an external institution, the colonial state concentrated economic opportunities and material resources in places [urban locations] that Somalis feared and despised. The historical basis for the Somali national state was opposite to that of Europe where capitalism first emerged through civic social institutions and where centralised government became a legal instrument to correct inequalities and imbalances. Throughout the colonial period, some sub-clans benefited from the colonial presence because they were better positioned by pre-colonial social arrangements to take advantage of opportunities afforded

---

[66] For instance, as late as 1940, General Sir Archibald Wavell credits the military garrison in British Somaliland with only 14 British officers, 400 African Askaris and 150 African Reservists. See further *Supplement to The London Gazette*, (5 June 1946)

[67] A detailed analysis of the native power at the local state and its contrast with civil power at the center in general in colonial Africa, is documented by Mamdani (1996).

[68] "The colonialists saw themselves as paternalist, bureaucratic dictators, yet they relied on creating a class of intermediaries who could effectively intervene in the daily lives of Africans. This meant, in the countryside, the recognition (or creation) of the colonial chiefs whose primary function was to collect taxes and to preserve administrative control" (Freund 1984:137).

[69]In Somalia, pre-colonial moral economy was a livelihood activity submerged in communitarian social relations of production.

[70] "Differential allocation of shares of social labour can favour the emergence of influential managers; at the same time, contact with other groups can lend importance to persons able to deal with differences of interest and with possible conflict. These tendencies toward inequalities in function are greatly enhanced when kin-ordered groups enter into relationships with tributary or capitalist societies. Such relationships afford opportunities for the seizure and transfer of surpluses beyond those available within the kin-ordered mode" (Wolf 1982:96).

62

by collaboration" (Geshekter 1997:71).[71]

Also, well-placed individuals have gained a great deal from the urban economy that existed beyond the sphere of the kin-ordered traditional mode of production and the control of the clans. Particularly livestock merchants colonially paid native authority (aaqils), interpreters, seamen, drivers, cooks, subordinate civil servants, etc. In a nutshell, the political economy of the peripheral capitalism not only resulted in social inequality, fierce competition for access to the economy of the colonial state but more than that it eroded the effectiveness of the rules of kinship.[72]

3.6. Conclusion

In this chapter I showed how the constraints in the material environment conditioned pastoral nomadism as the primary means of livelihood in Somalia. I also delineated the variable manifestations of the tendency towards private pursuit which advance comprehensive explanations than those hitherto available. As I demonstrated in this chapter, the continuity of these manifestations can be discerned in the social, economic and political spheres of pre-colonial and colonial Somali society. For instance, both schools of Somali studies selectively identify certain elements among the variables of the tendency towards private pursuit. Moreover, I discussed how the several facets of the tendency towards private pursuit are decisive historical processes shaping the Somali social formation in different ways through the ages. Furthermore, I explained how the prevalence of this kin-ordered mode of production perpetuates the survival of clan relations in the Somali society. For this proposition, I challenge the thesis of the traditionalist scholars of Somali studies which claims that primordial blood-ties maintain clan relations in the contemporary Somali society.

In pre-colonial Somalia, the production of the livestock economy was a collective communal enterprise. It was also a subsistence-based economy in which use-value prevailed. This communitarian pastoral economy is embedded in social relations of kinship. Accordingly, the ethos and norms of that kin-ordered system provided mechanisms and social sanctions which have been effective in resolving conflicts among the lineages and clans and also ensured the reproduction of a stable social order.[73] Moreover, in pre-colonial Somalia, the constraints in the material environment created a society with a limited development of productive forces and a de-centralised polity. The reason proffered for the lack of advanced social transformation in the Somali society is that the subsistence pastoral existence cannot sustain any social relations of production beyond the kinship system. Or to put it differently, the prevalence of the kin-ordered mode prevents the institutionalisation of political power.

---

[71] For further discussion on this point, see Charles Geshekter (1997).

[72] According to Bradbury, " as new forms of wealth accumulated in the [colonial] state, the mandate of political leadership altered from regulating kin relations and entitlement to pastoral resources, to regulating access to the political and economic benefits of the state, thus sowing seeds of disunity and conflict" (Bradbury 1997:5).

[73] As Samatar writes, " the household, Islam and the kinship-based political-economic and moral order of pre-colonial Somalia did not prevent conflict between communities, but certainly precluded prolonged hostilities driven by genealogical differences" (Abdi Samatar 1997:694).

By contrast, in colonial Somalia, consequent to the intrusion of the global capitalist system, the mercantilist colonial state replaced kinship order as a mechanism for regulating the social relations of production. Also, the transition from the communal moral economy to the peripheral capitalist mode of production resulted in the domination of the market relations and exchange values. Gradually, the impact of the peripheral capitalism and the market economy transformed the traditional pastoral mode of production and slowly made redundant its corresponding communitarian social order. Moreover, the economy of the colonial state created rivalry and fierce competition between the clans, lineages and interest groups and individuals for its access. This relentless competition then slowly undermined the communal reciprocity and obligations of the Somali society as it reproduced a new social strata not hinged into the traditional pastoral economy. Furthermore, the colonial state policy, which was based on divide and rule added new fuel to of old animosities between the clans and lineages and further militarised the society by providing them with modern firearms. In short, the penetration of colonialism and capitalism in Somalia negatively impacted traditional pastoral socio-political institutions of the society and set the trends for social disunity and individualised private pursuit for the future. The discussion in this chapter will be further continued in chapter five. In that chapter I will discusses how the endemic structural poverty of the domestic economy condemned the post-colonial state of Somalia to subsist on foreign aid and also exacerbated the tendency of individualised private pursuit among the political elite.

Chapter four

The Pitfalls of Colonialism and Public Pursuit

4.1. Introduction

This chapter traces how the change brought about by the colonial imposition led to the primacy of the public pursuit in Somali politics over a century. The colonial occupation of Somalia not only transformed the political economy of Somali society as transformationists emphasize but also split the Somali people and their territories.[74] Therefore, as I will argue in this study, the multiple partitioning of the country is one of the key determinants that fundamentally account for the destructive turn of events in Somalia at present. The competing colonial powers partitioned Somalia into: (a) the British Somaliland Protectorate; (b) Italian Somalia; (c) French Somaliland or Djibouti; (d) Ogaden under Ethiopia; and (e) the Somali inhabited territory of Northern Kenya (also under British rule). In this study, the policy of the public pursuit is understood as a Pan-Somali aspiration and a dream of attaining a single united Somalia one day. The strategies that the Somalis adopted to wage the politics of the public pursuit alternated between militancy, passive and irredentist expansion. In this chapter, militant and passive public pursuit is examined while irredentism is discussed in chapter six which deals with the foreign politics of post-colonial Somalia.

However, as I demonstrate in this chapter, the efforts of the tendency towards public pursuit were constantly frustrated by the particularistic impulses towards private pursuit. In this context, the two pursuits are not separate but are inter-linked dynamics as they are parts in a complex whole of historical processes that shape the Somali society. Throughout the Somali history, the contradictory impulses of the tendencies towards private and public pursuits have been interacting at different levels in the society. Private pursuit manifested as a factor that has pulled the Somali social formation towards narrow clan identity and parochial social and political arrangements. By contrast, public pursuit crystallized as a tendency that has pushed the Somali social formation towards wider political identity, unity and nationhood. Consequently, the contradictory tendencies have produced tensions that indeed became sharpened as the colonial period was coming to its end.

4.2. The Nature of the Partitioning

Somalia was partitioned into five political entities for different colonial objectives and interests. In the late nineteenth century, Britain was the first colonial power, which established a protectorate in the north of the country. This took place around 1885 when the British authority had succeeded in signing formal commercial 'treaties' with Somali clan-heads in the territory. The option of running northern Somaliland as a protectorate was the cheapest way of controlling the area. And the interest of the British Empire in carving up northern Somaliland was mainly commerce and livestock trade. The British involvement in Somaliland was

---

[74] For more background information, see the booklet, The Somali Peoples' Quest for Unity: An explanation of the issues involved in the Somali/Ethiopian, Somali/Kenyan disputes and the liberation of French Somaliland (Mogadiscio: Ministry of Foreign Affairs, 1965).

indirectly determined by its possession of rich India (Jewel in the Crown) as a colony. In 1839 the British Empire established a military station in Aden in order to protect its trade interests with India. Aden was located on an important short sea route to India. However, Aden, apart from its strategic maritime communication links, had no other benefits. Aden had no economic resources, yet the British military personnel stationed there had to be fed. Britain easily resolved this problem by taking over Somaliland, which was not only the closest area to Aden but was also rich with livestock. In other words, it was the abundant livestock in the area and the urgent demand of meat supply to Aden that primarily brought this part of Somalia under the protectorate of the British government of India. At the time, Britain also had another overriding motive to take over Somalia and that was to prevent other competing European powers from occupying it.

Somaliland remained a protectorate as long as this arrangement served the economic and political needs of the British authority. This was how the British government of India explained its initial interest in annexing Somaliland:

> "The primary objectives of Government are to secure a supply market, to check the traffic in slaves, and to exclude the interference of foreign powers. It is consistent with these objectives, and with the protectorate which the India Government has assumed to interfere as little as possible with the customs of the people, and to have them administer their own internal affairs" (quoted in Samtar 1989:31).

The British Foreign Office was the authority which ran Somaliland when it was a protectorate. However in 1905 when the protectorate system of rule was abrogated and Somaliland became a proper British colony, the Colonial Office took over the control of the territory. Rescinding its protectorate status and making Somaliland a proper colony was in fact necessitated by the emergence of the militant Dervish movement in the countryside in 1900. The British authority, becoming anxious that such uprising could disturb trading routes in the countryside and the free flow of the supply of the livestock, imposed its military power throughout the territory.

During that period, a rival imperial power competing with Britain in the region was France. Both imperial powers were vying for the control of the Nile waters and their rivalry was further heightened when the Suez Canal was opened in November 1869. Britain, having already occupied Aden, was determined to prevent France (considered as a hostile power) from conquering the nearby Somali coast. However, France, in contrast to Britain, had bigger imperial ambitions in the Horn of Africa. Firstly, France had trade ambitions in Ethiopia and in 1881 the Franco-Ethiopian trading company was established in that country. Secondly, France had already acquired colonial possessions in Indochina as well as Madagascar and was in great need of a base and coaling station in the Horn of Africa for its ships plying the long sea-route. Thirdly, France was aware of the prestige of possessing a piece of land in Africa in the eyes of other ambitious rival colonial powers. In other words, at the time, possessing a colony was also a matter of prestige. Eventually, as politics in the region dictated, the French authority signed an Anglo-French treaty, which officially defined the possession and the border of the French colony in Somalia in 1888. In that treaty, France possessed French Somaliland, which is now called Djibouti.

In the race of scrambling Somalia, Italy later followed the British and the French. Italians searching for a place under the sun in Africa arrived late in Somalia. In this respect, they were latecomers to the orgy of slicing Somalia, yet Italians with the tacit consent of the British carved southern Somalia (Italian Somaliland) in 1893. The interest of Italy in Somalia actually grew after it possessed the port of Assab at the southern tip of the Red Sea. In southern Somalia, the Italians adopted a different colonial policy from that of the British in northern Somaliland. Unlike the British, the Italians planned from the beginning to create a proper colony for entire southern Somalia both at the coast and in the productive agricultural hinterland. According to Robert Hess (1966) at least two factors were critical. First, Italy was urgently seeking to acquire a settlement for the poor Italian farmers in the best and most fertile part of the agricultural land in the country where fruit plantations could be established. For an immediate practical purpose, the settlement of the poor Italians in Somalia was intended to reduce the population surplus Italy was then enduring. However, as the footnote in (see chapter 3) demonstrates, this ambitious plan to settle Italian population in Somalia failed. Second, Italy was looking for secure overseas markets for its industrial goods that hitherto had been threatened by England and the United States protectionist policies in the international trade at the time. Thus, both population pressure and economic interests were the main underlying factors, which urged Italy to establish a proper colony in southern Somalia. In fact, what the Italians wanted was to create a lasting colony in southern Somalia. Accordingly, with this long-term objective in mind, the Italians had adopted coercive measures in appropriating the fertile land in the upcountry and also subjected the sedentary farmers in the area to forced labour.[75] Indeed, these coercive measures were commensurate with the modus operandi of the fascist rule in Italy since 1923. Lisa Anderson (1986), in her study on the Italian rule in Libya, also noted harsh subjugations similar to that meted out to the Somali subjects in southern Somalia.

In addition to the European imperial powers, Ethiopia also participated in the dismembering and sharing out of Somalia. Imperial Ethiopia in the Horn of Africa was an important rival power, which could not be ignored. The Ethiopian empire having defeated Italy at the battle of Adowa in 1896 also had colonial ambitions in Somalia. After that military victory against Italy, the Ethiopian empire demonstrated itself to be a power that could not be subdued with force but one to be recognised and seriously negotiated with for peace and stability in the region. And it was this position of strength which led to the Anglo-Ethiopian treaty that ceded western Somaliland (Ogaden) to Ethiopia in 1897 (Lewis 1988). In the negotiation of this treaty, Menelik, the emperor of Ethiopia, not only got a share of Somalia, but was also accorded other concessions. For example, Britain permitted the Ethiopian emperor to import arms through its north Somaliland ports. Britain also exempted Ethiopia from customs duties for the goods imported for the household use of the emperor (Samatar 1989). Thus, the Ethiopian empire took part in the radical partitioning and sharing out of the land of the Somali people.

During World War II, Britain defeated Italy in East Africa. The defeat shattered Italy's dream of imperial grandeur in the Horn of Africa. In the war, Italy lost southern Somalia (which it

---

[75] Sylvia E. Pankhurst recorded in detail the ruthlessness of the modus operandi of Italian colonialism in southern Somalia. For example, Pankhurst noted that: "under the colonial system men, women and children had been taken by force from remote places and condemned to an indefinite period of servitude on Italian farms.... Punishment, inflicted by the resident on the ex-parte representations of the employer, was brutal and excessive. For a first offence of disobedience or indiscipline fifty lashes with a hippopotamus-hide whip was a common award, and for a second offence the victim was strung up for several hours on a gallows, with his toes just clear of the ground, suspended by chains attached to wooden billets under his armpits, and with his hands handcuffed behind his back" (139). See further her Ex- Italian Somaliland (London, 1951); See also, The First to be Freed: The Record of British Military Administration in Eritrea and Somalia 1941-1943; Issued by the Ministry of Information (London: His Majesty's Stationery Office, 1944)

ruled from 1893 to 1941) along with its East African Empire. This therefore ended the Italian occupation in southern Somalia. Consequently, the Italian defeat paved the way for the British military Administration to occupy southern Somalia in addition to the other areas in the country it already possessed. Britain already had under its control north Somaliland, Ogaden[76], and the Northern Frontier District (NFD) in Kenya, inhabited by Somali pastoral nomads. This means that in 1941 Britain controlled 90 per cent of the land inhabited by the Somali people except for the tiny French colony of Djibouti, which was only 10 percent of the country (Omar 1992). Eventually, the British military rule of Somalia lasted from 1941 to 1950.

In 1946, Britain tabled a proposal, which recommended that the best way for the wandering Somali pastoral nomads to survive in the marginal environment of Somalia was to let the country unite and remain under British Administration. However, this proposal, known as the Bevin[77] Plan was swiftly rejected by Ethiopia as well as by the other three big powers (France, USA, and the USSR) because they were suspicious of the British intentions. They also thought that accepting such a proposal could undermine their influence and political interests in Somalia. As a result, Somalia was partitioned once again. Southern Somalia was given back to the defeated Italy in 1950 to administer for a period of ten years under United Nations Trusteeship. Ogaden and its adjoining Somali areas were handed over to Ethiopia in 1948 and 1954 respectively. Northern British Somaliland reverted to its former protectorate system of rule; while the British Administration decided to give the Northern Frontier District (NFD), inhabited by Somali nationals, to Kenya in 1963. In a passing remark that sounds remorseful, this is what Lord Renell Rodd had to say on the slicing of Somalia decades later:

> "if we had been interested enough ... (and if the world had been sensible enough), all the Somalis ... might have remained under our administration. But the world was not sensible enough and we were not interested enough, and so the only part of Africa which is radically homogenous has been split into such parts as made Caesar's Gaul the problem and cockpit of Europe for the last two thousand years. And Somaliland will probably become a cockpit of East Africa" (quoted in Laitin and Said Samatar 1987:53-54).

---

[76] Ogaden is the name of a Somali inhabited region that is controlled by Ethiopia.

[77] Ernst Bevin was the Foreign Secretary of Britain at the time. Bevin was also the architect and staunch advocate of the unification of the Somali inhabited territories. Bevin is in fact the authority of the concept of a 'Greater Somalia'. This clarification is important because Greater Somalia is not a notion conceptualised by the Somalis. In the Big Four Power conference (Britian, France, USA and the USSR) in Paris 1946, Bevin pleaded that: " in all innocence, therefore, we proposed that British Somaliland, Italian Somaliland, and the adjacent part of Ethiopia, if Ethiopia agreed, should be lumped together as a trust territory, so that the nomads should lead their frugal existence with the least possible hindrance and there might be a real chance of a decent economic life" (quoted in Touval 1963:79).

In a nutshell, this was how Somalia was partitioned in the 1880s and again repartitioned in the 1950s. See beneath the colonial map of Somalia.

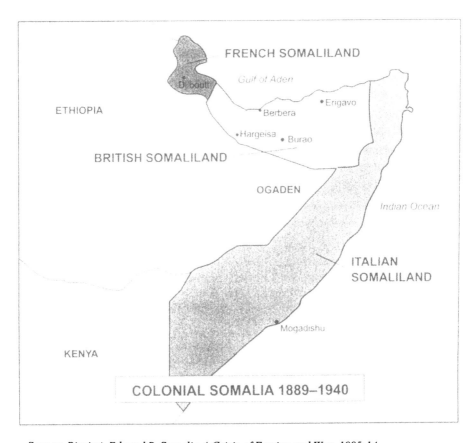

COLONIAL SOMALIA 1889–1940

Source: Ricciuti, Edward R. Somalia A Crisis of Famine and War. 1995:14

4.3. Dervishes and Militant Public Pursuit (1892-1920)

The first strategy that the Somalis adopted to resist the foreign conquests and colonial occupation was a militant one. This militant public pursuit was launched with religious fervour as Islam was used as a uniting factor of the segmented Somali lineages. The Muslim brotherhood led by a charismatic sheikh, Sayyid Mohamed Abdulle Hasan, was the domestic social spearhead of this militant Somali-wide public pursuit. The history and the colonial struggles of Sayyid Mohamed and his militant Dervishes are already recorded elsewhere and there is no need to repeat them here.[78] A significant aspect worth noting here is that the emergence of this Dervish movement heralded the first modern nationalist Somali resistance against foreign subjugation.

Colonial incursion in Somalia caused both fear and indignation as alien and predatory authorities were established in the country. First, the centralised system of governance of the colonial state was a great leap from the decentralised and egalitarian political system of the Somali people. Second, the colonisers were people of another faith and that created fear and suspicion in the minds of the Somali people about their intentions. Third, the Somali pastoral nomads felt the squeeze and the pressure on their grazing land, particularly by the expansion of the Ethiopian colonial army. It was a normal practice for the troops of emperor Menelik of Ethiopia to send expeditions into Somalia to raid and plunder the herds of the pastoral nomads.

In this respect, the intervention and partitioning of the country among foreign predators, snatching the pastureland, and raiding the livestock, was a momentous event and the turning point of the Somali people at the time. During that period, a Somali poet described the situation in the country in the following lines:

> "The British, the Ethiopians, and the Italians are squabbling,
> The country is snatched and divided by whosoever is stronger,
> The country is sold piece by piece without our knowledge,
> And for me, all this is the Teeth of the Last Days"![79]

For instance, the 'Teeth of the last Days!' understood in a concrete worldly sense meant the end of united Somalia and Somali people instead of the abstract and metaphysical imagination of the poet. Nevertheless, the poem signified the intolerable conditions of the Somali pastoral nomads at the time. Eventually, the oppression of the colonial subjugation sparked a militant uprising. The Somalis took up arms to drive the colonisers out of the country and to ensure that the Somali people remain united as one nation. This last point is important because although the Somali people did not develop a united political entity, they did nevertheless have a strong sense of cultural nationalism. Despite their lineage segmentation, they had the

---

[78] For an excellent historical accounts, see Said S. Samatar, Oral Poetry and Somali Nationalism: The Case of Sayyid Mohammed' Abdille Hassan (Cambridge: Cambridge University Press, 1982); see also Abdi Sheik-Abdi, Divine Madness: Mohammed Abdulle Hassan (1856-1920) (London: Zed, 1993).

[79] The poem is from the poet Faarax Nuur, quoted in B.W. Andrzejewski and I.M. Lewis, Somali Poetry: An Introduction (Oxford: Clarendon Press, 1964): 57.

feeling that they belong to one ethnic group, which shares the same language, history, religion, and memories of a common past.[80]

This first militant public pursuit, which lasted from 1892 to 1920, was waged by armed Dervishes[81] whom Ahmed Samatar referred to as "the proto-nationalists" in the early Somali struggles against foreign domination (Ahmed Samatar 1988:24). Sayyid Mohamed and his Dervish fighters had an uncompromising attitude towards the colonialist presence in the country as they determined to drive all of them from the Somali soil.

With this objective in mind, in 1899, Sayyid Mohamed called on all the young Somali men irrespective of their clan affiliations to join his Dervish army. He appealed to the clans in the spirit of their Islamic religious ties. Phrased differently, the message of the Sayyid was: let us unite in the name of our religion and confront the occupying foreigner infidels in order to save our land and our Islamic faith. Within a short period of time, the Sayyid had raised a fighting army of about 5000 men (Samatar 1989:38). At the same time, he started importing weapons and arming his militant Dervishes. Sayyid Mohamed financed his Dervish army, military campaign and weapon purchases through money and livestock donations he received mostly from the rural Somalis who were supportive to his cause.

In 1900, after raising enough young fighting men (numbered at round 6,000) across clans, and acquiring sufficient firearms, the Sayyid started engaging first the Ethiopian army at Jigjiga in Ethiopia. This military engagement against the Ethiopian expansion in Somalia was indeed the first test of the militant public pursuit. After the Ethiopian army, the next target of the Dervish movement was the British Colonial Administration. The movement declared war on the British presence in the country and as a direct warning raided several clans who were collaborating with the colonial Administration. As a reaction against this action, British troops, in collaboration with the Ethiopian army, mounted a punitive attack in order to root out the Dervish resistance.

Eventually, the British military action resulted in the defeat of the Dervish forces but it did not succeed in uprooting them. For instance, when the Dervishes were defeated several times in direct confrontation with the superior colonial troops, they changed their military tactics and resorted to guerrilla warfare. This militant public pursuit of the Dervish resistance continued unabated despite frequent military setbacks for years, until, finally, the British launched a massive and coordinated sea, land, and air offensive against the headquarters of the Dervish movement, which was known as the *Taleh* forts in 1920.[82] The combined massive offensive was a tremendous blow to the Dervish resistance as it decimated its military ranks. After this heavy loss, Sayyid Mohmed and few of his Dervish survivors escaped to the Ogaden region where he died of malaria in 1921. Eventually, the death of the leader ended the existence of the Dervish movement along with its militant strategy against the colonial occupation in Somalia.

Within established Somali scholarship, the underlying reasons for the emergence of the Dervish resistance in the country at the time have been presented in different interpretations.

---

[80] As Saadia Touval writes, "Somali nationalism stems from a feeling of national consciousness in the sense of 'we' as opposed to 'they' which has existed among the Somalis for many centuries. It was nurtured by tribal genealogies and traditions, by the Islamic religious ties, and by conflicts with foreign peoples" (Touval 1963:84).

[81] According to Beachey, the word Dervish that originates "from Turkish dervis or Persian darvesh and refers to those valiant and ardent fighters for Islam vowed to a life of poverty and austerity" (Beachey 1990:25).

[82] Somalia was the first African country in which air attacks were used by a colonial power.

Traditionalist scholars view religion as the main factor behind the appearance of the Dervish movement (Lewis 1988; Said Samatar 1982). Transformationist proponents like Abdi Samatar on the other hand contend that it was the crisis in the material life of the pastoral nomads brought about by the colonial predation, which led to the uprising of the Dervish movement (Samatar 1989). Modernisation writers represented by Saadia Touval, explain that it was the combination of both religious and nationalist motivations that resulted in the emergence of the Dervish resistance. According to Touval:

> "It would seem, therefore, that characterising the Mullah's movement as primarily a religious one, coupled with nationalistic corollaries, would be more appropriate than attempting to constrain it into a purely 'religious' or 'nationalist' mold" (Touval 1963:56).

There is no denying that all the above noted elements have played more or less a crucial role in the emergence of the Dervish movement in Somalia at the time. Yet, I believe that the liberation of the country from the colonial occupation was the overriding factor. For example, the country was taken away and was divided in pieces among different colonial powers and that was the most dramatic experience that the Somali people have ever endured. It was the most dramatic in three respects. Firstly, the division of the country resulted in the separation of family members into different colonial administrations. Secondly, the seasonal movements of the pastoral nomads was hindered as they could no longer cross from one pastureland to another as easily as was the case before because of the foreign manned border controls. Thirdly, the modus operandi of the colonial military in the country was oppressive, violent and cruel in nature. Thus, in my view, the occupation and the parcelling of the country was the key factor, which led to the emergence of the Dervish resistance. It also powerfully explains why since then the overriding political struggles of the Somali political elite have been for achieving independence from the colonial yoke and a Somali-wide territorial unification. This was indeed in the line with the core objective of the tendency towards public pursuit during the post-colonial period, namely the creation of a wider political identity, unity and a Somali-wide statehood. In the subsequent discussions in this study I will explain how the struggle to reunify the colonially dismembered territories inhabited by ethnic Somali populations has been the most important national project for the Somali political elites since Somalia achieved independence.

4.4. Political Parties and Passive Public Pursuit (1941-1960)

For almost two decades the crusades for the Somali-wide public pursuit waned not only as the result of the terrible military defeat of the militant Dervish forces, but also because of the physical occupation and control in the countryside of the colonial troops whose punitive expeditions wiped out any fickle uprising against their presence. Consequently, over twenty years, the struggles for liberation, freedom and for a pan-Somali public pursuit were temporary halted until the outbreak of the Second World War. However, the political outcome of the war presented an opportunity for the Somalis to revive the aspirations of their public pursuit against the foreign domination albeit through passive tactics. The military victory of the Allies in the war against the Axis was in fact the winning of the ideology of the universal emancipation over the fascist worldview. In Somalia, the colonial state of Italy, which represented the Axis in the region, was routed out by Britain, one of the Allied powers.

Fortunately, this momentous victory of the Allied powers presented a turning point for the political history of the Somali people as for many colonised societies around the globe.

After the war ended, Britain as the sole colonial power assumed the political control of both northern and southern Somalia from 1941 to 1950. Under the British Military Administration (BMA) the Somalis started organising themselves as political parties for the first time. The political parties were free to campaign for Somali-wide political freedom and the unification of all Somali inhabited territories by peaceful means. In this respect, political independence and territorial unity were the twin aspirations of the public pursuit that the Somali political elites have campaigned for since the end of the Second World War.

In northern Somalia, the important political party during that period was the Somaliland National Society (SNS) established in 1935. Later in 1947, SNS was renamed the Somali National League (SNL). In southern Somalia, the dominant political parties at the time were the Somali Youth Club, formed at Mogadishu on 15 May 1943 and the Hizbia Digil-Mirifle, created on 25 March 1947. Both political parties later changed their names. In 1947, the Somali Youth Club became the Somali Youth League (SYL), and the Hizbia Digil-Mirifle was transformed into Hizbia Dastur Mustaqil Somali (HDMS). During that period it was the "*benevolent paternalism*" of the ruling British Military Administration (BMA), which helped these newly emerged political parties to consolidate and flourish around the country (Lewis 1993:28). Others even suggested that the Somali Youth League, the leading political party in Somalia (before and after the independence) was in fact nurtured in the cradle of the local British Administration (Collins 1960; Touval 1963). It was perhaps for this reason that the political parties were less militant towards the colonial Administration and opted to achieve their independence and territorial unification of Somalia through peaceful means.

Yet, the passive public pursuit of the political parties in the aftermath of the Second World War was in great contrast to the militant Dervish movement in the early decades of the twenty- century. The early Dervish movement was conservative and primarily a religious-inspired uprising. Dervishes were adamantly against the presence of foreign infidels on the Somali soil as they were fearful that the missionary education of the Christian colonisers and its resultant influence would destroy their religion and pollute their spiritual purity. This is how Sayyid Mohamed, the spiritual-political leader of the Dervish movement orated:

> "Unbelieving men of religion have assaulted our country from their remote homelands. They wish to corrupt our religion, to force us to accept Christianity, supported by the armed forces of their governments, their weapons, their numbers. You have only your determination. Do not be frightened by their soldiers or armies; God is mightier than they. Be patient and steadfast in hardship. Our aim is to cleanse the land of Unbelievers" (Martin 1976:182).

Nonetheless, the freedom struggle of the Dervish movement was a source of great inspiration for the Pan-Somali pursuit of the later political parties (Lewis 1980). However, in the 1940s all the existent political parties in contrast to the Dervish movement had more or less exhibited a secular world-view. And despite their opposing political views, all parties were willing to achieve the aspirations of their political struggles without antagonising the ruling colonial Administration. Also, compared with the Dervish movement, the new political parties were open to the influence of the progressive ideals such as freedom, liberty, fraternity, democracy and self-determination that the Allies fought in the Second World War and were then spreading all over the world. In Somalia, some of the British officials working for the local colonial Administration were in fact the advocates of such universalised values.[83] Undoubtedly, it was these ideals, which inspired the Somali political parties in the 1940s to seek secular education, progress, political freedom and national unification.

It is important to note here that Somalia was the only country in sub-Saharan Africa where the Second World War was literally fought. As I noted earlier it was the place where the Allied forces defeated the Italian colonial army and ended Italy's East Africa Empire. During the war, many Somalis were recruited as a fighting army alongside the Allied forces. Gradually, the close contacts with the serving military men and the constant media broadcasting of the progressive ideals of the Allies waged the war in the country largely awakened the nationalist consciousness of the Somalis at the time. In other words, in contrast to many colonies in Africa, it was principally the global war and its political consequences, which provided a great impetus to the emergence of modern nationalism in Somalia.

Although all the newly created political movements agreed to operate within the laws and the policy restrictions laid down by the British Military Administration, and to pursue their political goals peacefully, they nonetheless failed to develop a collective national strategy. And this shortcoming had dire repercussions on their shared aspiration of the Pan-Somali pursuit. The fundamental problem was that most parties had different political agendas and contradictory aspirations. Moreover, they represented national, regional, socio-economic, and clan interests. For example, while the Somali Youth League was advocating broader national aspirations, the Hizbia Dastur Mustaqil Somali party was campaigning for particularistic clan interests.

During that early period, the HDMS was a clanist party, as it was not concerned with the interest of the nation as a whole. Among all the Somali political parties in the 1940s, the Somali Youth League (SYL) was the only party which had a national outlook. Also, the SYL. was the largest, best organised, and most widely represented party. Yet, it was considered by other rival political parties to be either a southern movement or a party dominated by northern pastoral nomads.[84] Unfortunately, it was this mistrust, suspicion, and narrow regional, socio-economic, and clanist interests, which prevented the political parties from collectively

---

[83] Some liberal minded British officers who fought on the Somali soil against the fascist Italians were sympathetic to the political aspirations of the Somali people. One of those officers who were supportive to the Somali cause was Douglas Collins. In his request to join the local British Administration in Somalia, Collins wrote that: "I am interested in the Somalis. I feel sympathetic to their aspirations, feel that I understand them, their problems, their way of life, and as an Administrative Officers I am sure that I can get closer to them" (Collins 1960:162). Collins wrote a book on the general condition and the political situation in Somalia during the rule of the British Military Administration in 1940-1950. The book that Collins dedicated to his beloved Somali mistress Amiina, who tragically died in a capsized dhow in the Indian Ocean of Somalia, was entitled "A Tear for Somalia". In the foreword of the book, another British military officer, Lieut-Colonel Humphrey French, who also served in Somalia at the time, noted his concern for the future of Somalia. French wrote in the foreword: "1960 sees the arrival of independence for Somalia. Let us hope that those countries who have brought her to independence will stand by to see that she survives in this difficult modern world without being made the plaything of international politics". This ominous forecast predicated what actually happened and the Somali state indeed became the plaything of the Cold War politics.

[84] For example, while the Somali National League in the north saw the SYL. as a southern party; the Hizbia Dastur Mustaqil Somali of the sedentary agricultural clans viewed it as a party for the pastoral nomads on the other hand.

74

struggling and campaigning for their overriding public pursuit - the unification of all Somali territories.

For instance, as I discussed earlier, in 1941, after Italy was defeated, all the territories of Somalia, with the exception of Djibouti, came under the control of British Military Administration. And for the Pan-Somali public pursuit, this was a godsend especially since Ernest Bevin, the British Foreign Secretary at the time was a supporter of the territorial unification of all the areas inhabited by the wandering Somali pastoral nomads. Bevin tabled a proposal to the Council of Foreign Ministers in which he pleaded for the preservation of a single united Somalia administered by the British under United Nations Trusteeship. Accordingly, in 1948, a United Nations Four-Power Commission comprising Britain, France, USA and the USSR came to Somalia to ascertain the aspirations of the Somali people. This was a golden occasion for the Somali political parties to put behind them their parochial differences and personal rivalries and collectively endorse the Bevin proposal of a single united Somalia since this was exactly what they wanted. For example, the president of the Somali Youth League, Haji Mohamed Hussien, while answering a question asked by a member of the Commission, replied:

> "Mr Bevin advocates the establishment of a Greater Somalia. That point appeared in English as well as Arabic newspapers. When we saw this being uttered by a Foreign Minister of a Greater Power we were very happy indeed because it is one of our great aims." (Four-Power Commission Reports, 1959:15; see also Collins, 1960:164).

Yet, the leaders of the political parties who presented the fate of the country to the Commission failed to convince the mission of the good sense of uniting the whole of the Somali-inhabited territories. According to Omar:

> "Keeping the territories together depended entirely on the wisdom and skill of those of our politicians who were meeting the Commission. Their ability in arguing the case would be crucial in deciding the fate of the people"(Omar 1992:20).

Even the leaders of the SYL who were the staunch advocates of the Pan-Somali aspirations and violently protested against the return of defeated Italy to Somalia failed to convince the Commission of the need to place Somalia under British Military Administration. The leaders of other rival parties, like Hizbia Dastur Mustaqil Somali in the south and splinter groupings had no inkling of the nation-wide aspirations and did not show any interest at all in the fate of the country as a whole. They were concerned only with their narrow clanist and individualistic interests. In opposition to the nation-wide policy of the SYL, the rival groupings formed an alliance named *"The Conference"* and made demands to the Commission that only the southern part of the country should become the Trusteeship of United Nations under Italian Administration. Italy colonised that part of Somalia from 1889 to 1941. Particularly the Hizbia Dastur Mustaqil Somali, the party of the southern agricultural clans, was staunchly in favour of Italy returning back to Somalia. The leaders of that political party had the belief that if Italy returned to the area, its presence would protect their clanist interests which they felt were being threatened by the numerically strong and dominant party (SYL) of the pastoral nomads from the north. Eventually, it was the lack of forceful articulation, internal rivalry, and particularistic instead of national interests, which made the Somali political parties allow this golden opportunity to pass.

As I explained earlier, the European powers (with the exception of Great Britain) as well as Ethiopia were totally against the proposal of the Bevin Plan – the unity of all the Somali-inhabited territories. Nonetheless, if the political parties had collectively supported the proposal, Bevin would have argued the case much more seriously in the Council of Foreign Ministers at the Paris Conference. And perhaps, at the time of gaining independence, the Somali political leaders would have inherited a single united Somalia (with the exception of Djibouti) from the British Military Administration. Unfortunately, Somalia was once again balkanised and this repetition was what Bevin was against. On 1 April 1950, only southern Somalia became a United Nations Trusteeship, with Italy as the administering authority.[85]

4.5. Public Versus Parochial Pursuit

During the early uprising of the Dervish movement, the struggles for a Somali-wide public pursuit, was subdued by the military aggression of the colonial powers. This was understandable since the colonial powers were defending their imperial domination. But this time it was the Somalis whose parochial concerns superseded the aspiration of Pan-Somali pursuits. For example, accepting Italy to administer only southern Somalia, a small portion of the country, was indeed a great setback to the goal of the Somali-wide territorial unification. More deleterious was the victory of parochial clanist and regionalist interests over the ideals of nation-wide aspirations.

In short, it was the victory for the forces of fragmentation over the forces of unity in Somalia. Or, to put it differently, it was the victory of private over public pursuit. The mission of the *Four Power Commission* to Somalia was a good litmus test to ascertain how far the political parties could transcend parochial identities, conflicts and particularistic interests. However, it soon became apparent that most of the political parties, which emerged in the 1940s, were primarily established to serve only narrow objectives. First and foremost, they were established to promote the interest of specific clans and lineages despite the affixed "Somali" associated with their respective party names. Some of the party leaders did not campaign for the interest of the Somali people as a whole since they did not comprehend the existence of Somalia either as a nation or as a state. A good example of this point was that a member of the Commission asked the president of the Hizbia Dighil e Mirifle party, Sheikh Abdullah, two questions.
The first question was whether:

> "He is not interested in the political activities of the country", and his answer was: "I have only interest in the Dighil Mirifle." The second question was whether "he is not concerned about the trusteeship of Somaliland", and his answer to this enquiry was: "when we asked for the trusteeship, we only meant for the country where the Dighil Mirifle live, not the rest of the country. We do not mean the rest of Somalia" (Four-Power Commission Reports, 1959:3).

---

[85] As Omar recently lamented: "if only Britain had been nominated by the Somali politicians of the time as the administering power, most of the Somali territories could even then have been brought together, united as one, with a good chance in due course of ultimately regaining our brothers who were then under French rule" (Omar 1992: 25-26).

76

The narrow vision of such an important party leader confirms the sectarian clan-based outlook of the leaders of most political parties at that time. Between 1940-1950s, the only political party, which to some extent achieved a political maturity enough to transcend parochial interests and which developed a sense of national outlook, was that of the Somali Youth League (SYL). However, during the 1950s, the worldview of the most localised political parties changed.[86] They manifested a nationalist spirit at least in their public slogans as announcing support for aspirations of the Somali-wide public pursuit. Even the Hizbia Dastur Mustaqil Somali which was a clanist party in the 1940s, adopted a nationalistic outlook. Encouraged by this new nationalistic political climate, new political parties were formed. One of these political parties was the National United Front (NUF) that was formed in the British Somaliland in 1955. This new political party was particularly created to struggle for the return of the Haud and the Reserved Area to British Somaliland in the north. The British surrendered the area to Ethiopia in 1954 under the pretext of honouring the treaty of 1897 between the two imperial powers.[87] The return of the area to Ethiopia angered the leaders of the Somali political parties both in the north and in the south of the country. Thus, the National United Front party was established to provide a platform for political parties and other organisations engaged in the struggle for independence and territorial unification of all Somalia. Another important political party, which was formed in the late 1950s, was the Greater Somalia League (GSL). This party emerged after a split in Somali Youth League ranks in 1958 and was led by Haji Mohamed Hussien. The GSL criticised the SYL for being moderate, pro-Italian, and less committed to pursuing the aspirations of a Somali-wide unity. Accordingly, the GSL party took a more militant stand in its advocacy for the unification of all the Somali-inhabited territories. Gradually, the militant view of this new political party influenced the policy agenda of the dominant SYL party. For example, in 1956, Somalia was granted an internal self-rule under Italian Administration and Abdullahi Isse, the leader of the SYL was appointed as Prime Minister. Accordingly:

"Abdullahi Isse in explaining his government's programme to the Somalia Assembly had given first place to the unification of the Somali territories. The Somali he told the assembly form a single race, practise the same religion and speak a single language. They inhabit a vast territory, which, in its turn constitutes a well-defined geographic unit. All must know that the government of Somalia will strive its uttermost, with the legal and peaceful means which are its democratic prerogative to attain this end: the union of Somalis, until all Somalis form a single Greater Somalia" (Lewis 1988:161).

This new Somali government in order to ensure that the aspirations of the Somali-wide public pursuit remain alive in the minds of successive generations invented a sky-blue national flag with a five-pointed star. Symbolically, the five-point star represents the five different political entities into which the land of the Somali people was divided.

---

[86] Among other developments, the impending independence of the country was the most silent political factor that awakened the nationalist consciousness of the most locally oriented political parties in the country. The leaders of these political parties then proclaimed a compromise with their old political stances and integrated their specific clan or regional interests with a Somali-wide nationalist cause – the struggle for the territorial independence of Somalia and for the unification of all the Somali inhabited territories (Touval 1963:95).

[87] As I noted earlier, the old Anglo-Ethiopian treaty of 1897 ceded the area to Ethiopia but in 1941 as the result of the Second World War, the whole of Somalia including Ogaden came under British Military Administration. The defeat of the Italian colony in the war, that had occupied Ethiopia since 1936 had paved the way for the British to rule over the entire country except for French Somaliland (Djibouti).

4.6. Public Pursuit Versus Domestic Matters

The aspirations to unify all the Somali-inhabited territories was not only frustrated by the parochial interests of the political parties but was also hampered by domestic preoccupations such as the tasks of running the local administration of government, the race for private spoils and the problem of choosing an official language for the country. In fact, both facets one after another superseded the primacy of the nation-wide public pursuit with detrimental consequences. For instance, while the pursuit of parochial interests undermined the collective project of the Somali nation and thereby indirectly aided in dividing the country once again, the preoccupation with domestic matters on the other hand led to a temporary abandonment of the Somali cause.

After the country was divided again, northern Somalia had remained under the British Administration. The Administration took the responsibility for running that part of the country separately and for the preparation for its independence when that time came. With this objective in mind, the Administration introduced a simple form of local government by the enactment of the Local Authorities Ordinance, and by the formation of advisory bodies at a district level to be known as District Councils.[88] This initiative gave the natives a greater share in running the local government. And even some Somali individuals gradually acquired senior posts in the Administration, Agriculture, Education, Police, Information, Prisons and Public Works Departments.[89]

Southern Somalia on the other hand was brought under the United Nations Trusteeship and Italy was mandated to prepare the area for its independence within ten year's time (1950-60). Yet the time frame was very short while the task needed to be accomplished was daunting. The Italian Administration had to develop everything in this political entity within the country very rapidly, from a parliamentary system of government to local municipality. They had to train Somali administrative cadre, draft a constitution, design political programmes, establish government institutions, and give Somalis the opportunity to participate in running the administration of the territory. This means that the existing Somali political parties had to get involved in the domestic affairs of the area. And the domestic matters to be attended to were overwhelming whether public or for private pursuits as these absorbed the time, energy and the activities of the political parties at the expense of the Somali-wide political agenda.

However, the foremost preoccupation of the new Somali government was the race for private pursuit since the individual gains expected from it was greater. As I noted in the last chapter, the impact of peripheral capitalism and the resources of the colonial state changed the communitarian Somali social relations of production to individualised private pursuit. As a result, new interest groups emerged which competed for access to modest clerical and other lowly jobs in the colonial state Administration, for their own private welfare. But now as the colonial state was withdrawing the stakes that could be inherited from it were even bigger.

Thus, it was to this end that the members of the political parties started fiercely jockeying to capture the positions that the Italian governing authority was gradually handing over to the

---

[88] See Report on the Somaliland Protectorate for the years 1950 and 1951 (London: H.M. Stationary Office, 1952).

[89] See Somaliland Protectorate: Somaliland Report for the years of 1954 and 1955 (London: H.M. Stationery Office, 1957).

Somalis.[90] Actually, the idea that this part of Somalia would soon be a sovereign state and that the Somalis would run it as directors, ministers and prime ministers had a magical effect. The expectation aroused relentless competition for spoils, consumed a lot of energy, created rivalry among the political elites and resulted in derailing the ideals of their nationalistic aims. Moreover, the very promise of granting independence for the territory within a short time frame reversed the policy priorities of the new Somali government. Domestic matters whether for personal or for other narrow pursuits gained primary priorities over national agenda and countrywide territorial unification. In 1956, the Prime Minister of the new Somali government Abdullahi Isse stated clearly that from now on, the struggle for Pan-Somali unity would not be the overriding concern of the Administration. The immediate priority of the government would be given to pressing domestic matters such as economic development, attracting foreign capital and assistance, and increasing the revenue of the government through widespread taxation (Lewis 1988:156).

Another domestic concern at the time, which also greatly preoccupied the local government, was the problem of choosing an official language for education and administration in the country. The Somali language was oral not written.[91] The government was therefore given the task of inventing an alphabet for the national language or adopting one of the foreign languages (Arabic, English, and Italian) spoken by the Somalis as the state language. Nonetheless, this language question raised intense debates among different sections of the elites and was finally left unresolved. Eventually, it was settled on October 21, 1972 when a Latin-character alphabet was adopted for the Somali language.[92]

On top of the domestic preoccupations, there were also external constraints that prevented the new government from campaigning for the unification of all Somali-inhabited territories. For instance, since southern Somalia was still under Italian trusteeship, the new local government run by the Somalis was not permitted to get involved in any political activity beyond the domestic matters of the territories. They were not even allowed to engage in the external affairs of the territory since this was the prerogative of the Italian Administration. To put it simply, with respect to the external matters of the territory only the Italian administrators had the mandate to represent and speak on behalf of the Somalis. This was indeed a blow for the aspirations of the Somali nationalists. Under the Italian Administration the Somali nationalists in the territory lost their free political expression and freedom in pursuing internationally the cause of Pan-Somali unity. This temporary suspension for the Pan-Somali aspirations had dire consequences. First, it cooled down the intensity of the struggle. Second, it loosened the cohesion of the Somali people as a nation in pursuit of a single united state.[93] Third, the

---

[90] According to Saadia Touval, "as independence was assured, the remaining goal of national unification received increased attention [by the Somali political parties]. But the political parties and the various tribal groups were mainly occupied with capturing the positions which the Italian trusteeship administration was gradually transferring to the Somalis" (Touval 1963:87).

[91] At the time the only Somali script which existed was one called Osmaniya. Yusuf Kenadid Osman invented this alphabet for the Somali language in the 1920s. Yet, although Osman was one of the early Somali nationalists, his Osmaniya script was rejected on several grounds, notably because of its distinct regional and clan identification.

[92] For more details of the language question, see B. W. Andrzejewski, `The Introduction of a National Orthography for Somalia', *African Language Studies* 15 (1974): 199-203; 'The Development of a National Orthography in Somalia and the Modernization of the Somali Language', *Horn of Africa* 1,3 (July-September 1978): 39-45.

preoccupation with domestic matters and the imposition of the Italian Administration on the territory greatly circumscribed the aspirations of a Somali-wide public pursuit between 1950-1960.

4.7.   Conclusion

In this chapter, I discussed how the colonial powers partitioned Somalia into five different territories and how the Somalis reacted to it. I also argued that the changes brought about by colonial occupation not only transformed the political economy of the Somali society as the transformationists suggested but more gravely dismembered the Somali habitat. The territorial splitting of the country and the fragmentation of the ethnic Somalis under different colonial powers was the most dramatic experience as it ruthlessly wounded the very psyche of Somali cultural nationalism. Since then, it was the healing of this psychological wound by struggling to unite the ethnic Somalis that had been the primary public pursuit of the Somali political elite. To put it differently, this Pan-Somali historical struggle is one of the underlying dynamics that largely determine the social and political conditions in contemporary Somalia.

As I explained in the main body of the chapter, the struggle for a Somali-wide public pursuit first began as a militant uprising against the colonial domination. The Dervish army led by a legendary leader Sayyid Mohamed Abdulle Hassan was the domestic social force, which started the revolt. The Dervish resistance movement was defiant and adopted a militant strategy to liberate Somalia from the foreign occupation. This early militant resistance however was traditional, conservative and conceived in the spirit of religion. In 1920, the Dervish movement collapsed when its spiritual leader, Sayyid Mohamed Abdulle Hassan passed away.

After twenty years the next struggle for a Somali-wide public pursuit emerged in the country in the 1940s. This new movement, in contrast to the early Dervish resistance, was passive, secular, and was conducted in a nationalistic orientation. It also appeared in the form of political parties, which wanted to unite Somali-inhabited territories through diplomatic and peaceful means. However, once such an occasion came at the time when Bevin proposed the unification of Somalia under British Military Administration, the political parties failed to grab the chance and support the plan. This was indeed a missed opportunity. Mohamed Omar notes that this event "has to be judged as political short-sightedness, and as a massive historic failure on the part of our politicians" (Omar 1992:52). No doubt it was the result of political immaturity on the part of the political leaders at the time but was also coupled with parochial clan, regional, and socio-economic and individualised private interests. In other words, parochial and private interests were more appealing than territorial integrity and a Somali-wide public pursuit. Furthermore, the global and regional politics were not in favour of the unification of Somalia. For example, as I mentioned earlier, the Somali political leaders were not even permitted to exercise Somalia wide political rights as long as the territory remained under Italian trusteeship. Later this changed when the period of the Italian trusteeship in the country ended.

---

[93] David Laitin and Said Samatar published a book that was entitled, Somalia: Nation in Search of a State (Boulder: Westview Press, 1987), which affirms the seriousness and the overriding importance for the struggle of the Somali-wide public pursuit.

The relevant lesson that can be drawn from this colonial period in Somalia is how the parochial tendencies towards private pursuits have constantly undermined the efforts geared towards social cohesion, nation building and state making projects. The tendency towards private pursuit provides positive impulses at sub-national levels in terms of guaranteeing security, solidarity and group survival but negatively impacts aspirations at national levels that are aimed to foster a Somali-wide interests. This is what I attempted to illustrate in this discussion. I have also shown in this chapter how during the colonial period the Somali political elite failed to reconcile the contradictory impulses emanating from the tendencies towards private and public pursuits.

In July 1960, as Somalia was granted its political independence both the northern and the southern parts of the country became united forming the Somali Republic. However, the unification of only these two parts of Somalia and the emergence of a Somali state though historic was not far-reaching. Three Somali-inhabited territories were still missing and the project of a Somali-wide public pursuit was not yet complete. Consequently, accomplishing this mission became the primary political task that the government of the new Somali Republic had to shoulder. It also explains why since independence, the principal objective in the foreign policy agenda of the Somali government(s) has been how to achieve the reunification of the missing territories.

However, in contrast to the militant and passive tactics of the Dervish movement and the political parties during the colonial era, the strategy adopted by the post-colonial elite of the Somali Republic in waging the Pan-Somali struggle was irredentism, which was pursued both by peaceful and violent means. In furtherance to the discussion in this chapter, I will examine in chapter six how the irredentist politics for the struggle of a Somali-wide public pursuit militarised the state during the Cold War era.

Nonetheless, before I conclude the discussion in this chapter, a historically informed theory worth consideration here is the lesson of how a structural problem developed in one period can continue to the next period. In other words, how an unresolved structural crisis in the past can still perpetuate a tension in the present as the case of the contemporary Somali society powerfully illustrates. For example, the dismemberment of the Somali territories was a structural problem created by colonialism. However, it was not resolved during the colonial period but was bequeathed as a deleterious legacy to the post-colonial era. Thus, the post-colonial elites of Somalia inherited a structural problem of which the seeds were already sown during colonialism. This reality urges us to search out the causes of the present in the past.

Chapter Five

Private Pursuit and Bankruptcy of the State (1960-1980)

"The only available milk camel was the state" (Ali Galaydh)

"We Somalis were not at all worried about the economic aspect of independence. We were anxious to get hold of the reins of power, taking everything else for granted" (Mohamed Omar)

5.1. Introduction

This chapter extends the discussion in chapter three. It explains further how the constraints in the material environment condemned the post-colonial state of Somalia to subsist on foreign aid and also exacerbated the negative tendency towards private pursuit that eventually bankrupted the state. As I already noted in chapter three, during the colonial period, the subsistence pastoral and agricultural production was integrated into the international markets for the benefit of export. Yet the traditional organisation of the economy and its low rate of productivity was neither improved nor upgraded. Thus, the problem of the endemic structural poverty of the economy in the country and the grinding material deprivation that this gave rise to was not resolved.

In 1960, the Somali people attained political independence in a country that had few domestic economic prospects to sustain itself, or, to be a more precise, a new country that dismally lacked a productive domestic economy to meet the costs of running a modern centralised government. Consequently, the sovereign state of Somalia had to rely heavily on foreign subsidies and grants to cover the deficits of its annual budget, the balance of payments and the financing of its development expenditures. Nonetheless, the overseas assistance was just enough for sustenance but was not enough to resolve the crisis of sustained accumulation that the political elite perennially endured. Eventually, the state and its scant foreign aid assistance became a focus for fierce competition between the political elite and this chase for private spoils derailed the agenda for a collective national project.

In this chapter, I shall first deal with the post-colonial political economy of Somalia, which roughly speaking consisted of meagre domestic revenue and massive foreign aid. I will also describe here how the poverty of the domestic resources, coupled with the failure to improve production in the traditional sectors of the economy, retarded the indigenous development in the country. This will then be followed by an examination of how the politics of private pursuit waged by the political elite drained the coffers of the state. Finally, a short conclusion is presented that ties together the themes discussed in the main body of the chapter.

5.2.   The Post – Colonial Political Economy

As I discussed in chapter three, the traditional pre-colonial economy of Somalia was mainly subsistence pastoral production, limited agriculture and some mixed simple agriculture (farming and animal husbandry). This is due to the constraints of the carrying capacity of the natural environment of which the land suitable for cultivation is very limited.[94] As a whole, the traditional domestic economy of Somalia cannot generate a surplus and that makes sustained accumulation impossible. It is in fact a meagre production, fit only for the most basic form of livelihood. The imposition of the colonial state economy during the colonial period somewhat widened the margin of the resource base of the traditional economy by means of international trade, export and revenue collection. Despite this, the domestic sources of revenue generated from the traditional economy were not enough even to cover the annual budgets of the colonial governments in the country. The rest of the cost had to be footed by their respective metropoles or the mother countries.

The scarce resources in the country also became of great concern when the United Nations was preparing Somalia for its political independence in the 1950s. During that time the United Nations, worried about the future economic prospects in the country, sent a special technical assistance team to Somalia. The team was instructed to assess the nature of the economic problems in the country and suggest ways for tackling them. After the mission, the economic report that the special technical team compiled was so disappointing that most of the delegates in the General Assembly doubted the viability of granting real statehood for Somalia (Karp 1960). The report made evident that because of the dearth of exploitable resources in the country, the post-colonial state of Somalia could not sponsor its economic development. Thus, a solution had to be found if Somalia was to survive as a fully-fledged modern state. The solution that the special technical team recommended in the report was planning - as if planning could resolve the constraints in the material environment and the economic poverty in the country![95]

5.3.   The Domestic Source of Revenue

Somalia is a land with limited natural resources. Somalia is also one of the world's poorest countries and a least developed country as measured in terms of per capita Gross National Product. At the time of independence in 1960, the Gross National Product of the country was

---

[94] For example, of all the 637,000 square kilometres of the country only 53 percent of the land is suited for livestock keeping, 8.2 percent is suited for cultivation and the remaining 34 percent of the land is mostly rocky and worthless desert of sand dunes and low scrub, suited for nothing (US, Department of Commerce, 1965). And because of the acute scarcity of the natural resources, Somalia was one of the *"two of the world's less promising deserts which Mussolini had decreed should blossom with at least an imported rose"*. The other country was Eritrea, which was also under Italian colonial rule. See further, The First to be Freed: The Record of British Military Administration in Eritrea and Somalia 1941-1943; Issued by the Ministry of Information (London: His Majesty's Stationary Office, 1944).

[95] The United Nations mission which visited East Africa in 1951 recommended that in Somalia "developmental resources are scarce; hence planning is all the more important" (U.N. Doc.T/1033, p.20.). At the time the planning model was viewed among the Third World political leaders to be the best strategy for a rapid economic development as the experience of the Soviet Union testified (Hobsbawn 1994:344-371).

put at $56 million, while the per capita income was estimated to be around $50. [96] Since independence, the economic growth of Somalia has failed to keep pace with the rise in population. In the first decade of independence, the average annual growth was only 1.3%, far below the average population growth figures of 2.6% (Mubarak 1996:11). The reason for this poor development was the negligence of the large traditional sectors of the economy, such as livestock and peasant farming. Instead, limited modern sectors, mainly of banana plantations and a few industrial establishments became the only domestic sources of revenue. However, the economic wealth that these modern sectors have generated was very limited and was largely appropriated by a few indigenous trading and urbanised class and expatriate entrepreneurs. [97] In the 1960s, to consider the traditional sectors of the economy, livestock production supported about two-thirds of the Somali population, while agriculture was a source of livelihood to another 15-20 per cent of the population. [98] Yet, the Somali government failed to improve the productive capacity of these traditional sectors, which are indeed the backbone of the economy of Somalia. In other words, the new Somali political elite continued a similar economic policy pursued earlier by the colonial Administrations that neglected to invest and develop viable internal resources in the country. [99] The notion behind the negligence of the traditional sectors of the economy, particularly the animal husbandry was that they were seen as an outmoded form of economic existence.[100] And after the independence, this negative perception is what made the two successive civilian governments of Somalia allocate few resources to develop these rural- based sectors.[101] For example, during 1963 to 1968 industry was allocated approximately 33 percent more investment than agriculture, fisheries, forestry, animal husbandry and irrigation combined. To put this in concrete figures, while industry received 214 million Somali shillings from the development

---

[96] For more accounts, see, International Bank for Reconstruction and Development, World Bank Atlas, Population, Per Capita Product and Growth Rates (Washington, D.C., 1969).

[97] For example, the industrial sector, which was only 1% of the Gross Domestic Product (GDP) was largely in the hands of Italian entrepreneurs and was dominated by Italian firms (Ahmed Samatar 1988:63).

[98] Even a very recent study estimates that the traditional subsistence sector provides the livelihood for about 80 percent of the population, and accounts for nearly 95 percent of export earnings and 65 percent of the GDP (Damooei 1997). In 1990 the population of Somalia was estimated for about 8 million of which 60 percent are still nomads - the highest percentage of any country in Africa and in the world.

[99] They continued this policy even against the warning of a study done by the World Bank in 1957. The study of the World Bank affirmed the dismal economic prospects in the country because of the fragility of the ecology. It then recommended that more must be done to improve the traditional sectors of the economy, particularly animal husbandry since it is the most vibrant sector of the national economy. For instance, the study of the World Bank emphasizes the need to improve the organisation of range management, breeding practices, veterinary health of the livestock and also to put forward mechanisms that facilitate the commercialisation and the export of the herds to overseas markets. Furthermore, the study advised the government to improve transport, communications, and services in rural areas.

[100] According to Simons, "Pastoralism was portrayed as a mode of production that was vital to Somalia's economy and foreign exchange, but one that was not yet modern enough" (Simons 1995:106). This negative view on the rural sector of the economy reflects the prescriptions of modernisation theory, which very much informed the planner of the national development programmes in the government. For a critical examination, see Gerald Braun, " The Somali Development Concept in Crisis: Pastoralism as a Strategy for Survival", *Northeast African Studies*, 11, no.3 (1989): 1-12.

[101] "Although 80 percent of the Somali people are engaged in either nomadic or agricultural life and only about 20 percent are urban residents, most of the benefits obtained under the civilian regime(s) went to the cities. The nomads were virtually ignored. They received little economic aid, and the government invested few resources in attempting to exert its authority in the bush or to put an end to clan warfare" (Laitin and Said Samatar 1987:85).

budget, the rural sectors combined were allocated 142 million shs.[102] During the early 1970s, this urban-biased economic policy of the civilian governments was reversed when the military regime of Said Barre came to power.[103] Nonetheless, the government expenditure allocated for the rural subsistence sector of the economy had only increased from 3 percent in 1963 to 14 percent in 1986.[104] Since independence in 1960 both the limited natural resources and the poor capacity for economic policy analysis have been the challenges that largely constrained the new Somali state to achieve a viable economic development. The problem of economic development was further worsened by a critical shortage of educated personnel in the country. [105] At independence, Somalia inherited an extremely rudimentary educational system and with the exception of a very small elite class, most of the population was illiterate. Historically speaking, most of the traditional rural Somalis had a very conservative attitude towards secular education. Thus, education beyond the traditional Islamic (Quranic) schools was an aspect which most Somalis had no experience with before the colonial era.[106] This was the foremost reason why during the early colonial periods Somalis scorned secular education and harshly opposed the establishment of missionary schools in the country.[107] Nevertheless, since the colonial occupation, the little secular education that existed in the country was elitist both in conception and development.[108] During the first decade after independence, school enrolments and the number of students have substantially increased but this was nowhere close to meeting the scarcity of trained personnel and the public demand.[109]

Another problem, which retarded the development of the economy in the country, was the acute lack of indigenous skilled manpower. This is how Omar lamented: "Lack of educated and skilled personnel made us dependent on foreign expertise for the daily running of the

---

[102] See further the Economic Commission for Africa, Summaries of Economic Data, Somali, Addis Ababa, compiled January 1975, M75-168, 6th year/no.9.

[103] For more discussion on this matter, see David D. Laitin, "The Political Economy of Military Rule in Somalia", The Journal of Modern African Studies, 14, 3 (1976): 449-468.

[104] See further Abdi Samatar , " Social Classes and Economic Restructuring in Pastoral Africa: Samali Notes ", African Studies Review, vol. 35 no.1 (1992): 101-127.

[105] In 1960 the population of Somalia was estimated to be 2.5 million of which the literacy rate was between 4% and 8% (Ahmed Samatar 1988).

[106] Ahmed Ashkir Bootaan, interview, April 28, 1996, Someren.

[107] Not even very long ago most Somali elders and especially the religious leaders entertained the idea that foreign education posed a threat to their religion, culture and identity. It was their duty therefore to guard the young generation against what they considered to be an "instrument of Christianisation". As Omar argued, it was because of this intense local resistance that Somalis have been latecomers to education as compared with certain other Africans in the continent (Omar 1992). In addition to this, there were also colonial reasons, which retarded the development of secular education in Somalia. For instance, of all Italian colonies in Africa, Somalia received the least financial aid for education. For this, with respect to Italian Somalia, see further Robert Hess (1966); and with respect to British Somaliland, consult further A. Castagno (1959).

[108] The Somali education system was largely elitist in conception if we consider it along the line already argued by W. A. Lewis. According to Lewis, certain kinds of education such as technical training constitute a form of social investment, while other kinds, such as studies in fine arts, are simply a form of consumption (Lewis 1955:183-84). The education in Somalia by and large was predominantly in social arts and pursued primarily as a ticket to employment in the public sector.

[109] See further, the Statistical Trends, Ministry of Education, Mogadishu, Somalia (1968). Since 1972 when Somali was adopted as a national script and was introduced as a medium of instruction into the educational system, students and school enrolments have rapidly increased (Bulhan 1980:34).

administration and economic sectors." (Omar 1992:65). In 1975 the population of Somalia was estimated to be about 3.2 million of which the total labour force was about 1.24 million. However, of this number, about 80 percent was engaged in the subsistence traditional sectors of the economy such as livestock husbandry[110] and agriculture, while only 7 percent is employed in the industrial sector and 13 percent in the services sectors.[111] As Gesheketer noted, "Somalia never developed an ample number of competent, disciplined cadres with the administrative training and technical strength necessary to manage development projects. The inability of the government to provide minimal national services undermined political stability" (Gesheketer 1997:78).

5.4. The Role of Foreign Aid on Public Finances

As Somalia progressed from a colonial to a post-colonial state, foreign aid became the main source for development projects and the largest revenue for the national economy. According to Gesheketer "Italian and British colonialism integrated Somalis into the world economy and installed government systems whose operations largely depended on external aid, not internally generated revenue" (Gesheketer 1993:19). The reason was that the country never had sufficient domestic revenue to finance its economic development.[112] Karp indicates how the material poverty in the country was the main cause for this deprivation, which perpetuated the acute dependence of Somalia on foreign beneficence in order to exist as a state (Karp 1960). And as Karp shows in Table I, the domestic sources of revenue including tax have always been a minuscule part of government fiscal resources to finance its recurrent budget. Omar also noted that in the late 1950s Italy, which was the administering authority of southern Somalia under the United Nations Trusteeship, had to pay the annual budget needed to run the country due to the shortage of domestic sources of revenue (Omar 1992). At the time, Italy paid for the Administration, salaries for civil servants and armed forces, territorial budget balancing and financed limited infrastructure. This brief account already gives a picture of how even the daily running of the new state of Somalia would not have been possible without the availability of generous foreign aid. For instance, from 950 to 1955, Italy provided an annual subsidy of over £ 3 million to Somalia (Lewis 1988:142). This external assistance was further increased in the subsequent years because of the persistent deficit in the government ordinary budget.[113] Nonetheless, most of the foreign financial aid was not invested in

---

[110] Livestock husbandry as has been scientifically and practically proved is the most suitable production for exploiting the semiarid ecology like this in Somalia. See further David Western, "The environment and ecology of pastoralists in arid savannas", *Development and Change* 13, no.2 (April 1982).

[111] For a more detailed account see the report by ILO/JASPA: Economic Transformation in a Socialist Framework: An Employment and Basic Needs Oriented Development Strategy for Somalia. Addis Ababa, 1977.

[112] In Somalia, the available domestic revenue has always been very scanty. And as the brothers Abdi and Ahmed Samatar confirmed, "the colonial welfare programme, a precursor of development aid, and the annual budgetary subsidies to British Somaliland, which amounted to more than 50 per cent of the 1958-9 budget, highlighted the underdevelopment of domestic sources of revenue" (Samatar and Samatar 1987:677). See further Abdi and Ahmed Samatar, The Material Roots of the Suspended African State: Arguments from Somalia, *The Journal of Modern African Studies*, 25, 4 (1987): 691-716.

[113] As Lewis noted, " while local revenue, derived as in the past principally from import and export dues with little help from direct taxation, rose from just over £ 1 million in 1950 to double that figure in 1956, expenditure, although decreasing from £7 million in the first year to £5 million five years later, continued to remain far in excess of receipts. By 1956 there was still a considerable and persistent adverse balance of payments, and the

development projects that would have benefited the whole economy of the country in the long run. The Italian trusteeship authority did undertake some low-cost development projects in the country, but they were so minimally implemented that they did not in anyway help to alter the structure of the economy in the country. As a result, the structure of the economy in Somalia remained more or less unchanged even after the ten years of the United Nations trusteeship authority ended in 1960. Among other reasons it was suggested that the very short time span of the Italian trusteeship Administration in the country was indeed the cause of the problem.[114] In fact, the limited time frame, domestic resource constraints and to a lesser extent the uncertainties about external finance have in conjunction prevented the undertaking of comprehensive development projects in the country that would have required a long-term investment strategy. According to Karp, "during the period of trusteeship Somalia has received a considerable amount of capital aid, but this aid, though in many ways beneficial, has not modified the country's economic structure. Nor was it intended to. Nor was it indeed possible to carry out such a tremendously difficult task within the short space of ten years. As an experiment in the feasibility of meeting nationalist aspirations in dependent areas by setting time limits for independence, trusteeship in Somalia must therefore be adjudged a failure" (Karp 1960:171).

---

general economic picture was such as to lead the World Bank mission which visited the territory in 1957 to conclude that exceptional financial assistance might be required for as many as twenty years after independence" (Lewis 1988:143-144).

[114] As Karp explained, " the major difficulty was therefore the time element, and this difficulty can be traced directly to the United Nations decision to set a deadline for the independence of Somalia" (Karp 1960:139).

Table 1

Government expenditures and revenues in Somalia
(in millions of US$)

Item	1951	1952	1953	1954	1955	1956	1957
Expenditures							
Administrative	5.1	5.7	5.9	5.8	2.5	2.7	2.9
Economic services	1.0	0.9	0.8	0.8	1.6	1.9	2.0
Social services	0.9	0.9	1.1	1.1	2.6	2.9	2.7
Security	9.5	5.0	4.0	3.3	5.0	5.0	4.3
Miscellaneous	0.4	0.4	0.2	0.4	0.8	0.7	0.7
Ordinary total	16.9	12.9	12.1	11.4	12.5	13.2	12.6
Extraordinary	1.4	1.3	0.8	0.9	1.5	1.7	1.5
Grand total	18.3	14.2	12.8	12.3	14.0	14.9	14.1
Revenues							
Income taxes	0.2	0.3	0.3	0.6	0.4	0.6	0.7
Property taxes	--	--	--	--	0.1	0.1	--
Community taxes	2.5	2.5	2.1	2.3	3.1	3.2	3.9
Government taxes and community revenues	1.9	1.9	1.7	1.8	1.9	2.0	2.2
Miscellaneous	0.2	0.1	0.2	0.5	0.3	0.3	0.1
Sub-total	4.8	4.8	4.3	5.2	5.8	6.8	6.9
Italian government Subsidies	13.5	9.4	8.5	7.1	8.2	8.7	7.2
Total	18.3	14.2	12.8	12.3	14.0	14.9	14.1

Source: Adapted from Mark Karp. 1960: 147.

Because of the precarious structure of the domestic economy in the country even after independence the Somali government did not succeed in lessening the financial dependence on foreign patrons. Before independence, the country received most of its foreign aid from Britain and Italy, the two traditional colonial powers of Somalia. However, since the 1960s, the Soviet Union and the United State became the chief financial patrons to Somalia, surpassing its former colonial powers by more than 30 percent (Mehmet 1971:37).[115] The superpower interests in Somalia developed because of the strategic location of the country, which is adjacent to the Indian Ocean and the Red Sea. During the Cold War era, this geopolitical importance made Somalia a theatre for superpower rivalry. Each superpower aspiring to have access to this strategic value provided Somalia with lavish economic assistance. In this respect, Somalia attracted superpower's attention which was out of proportion not because of its natural resources but because of its strategic domination for the

---

[115] "Turning to bilateral aid, the most striking fact is that the U.S.A. and the U.S.S.R. are the main donors. This fact underpins considerable cold-war rivalry reflecting the strategic importance of Somalia facing the Indian Ocean and dominating the entrance into the Red Sea" (Mehmet 1971:38).

entrance into the Suez Canal that could facilitate the easy access to the oil rich states in the gulf.

The smart strategy that the Somali government adopted at the time was to play the two superpowers against one another while at the same time refraining from adhering either to socialism or capitalism. This approach helped the Somali government procure more and more international aid. In the next chapter this subject will be further discussed. For the moment it suffices to say that Somalia received the highest amount of foreign aid per capita compared with other countries in sub-Saharan Africa. For instance, in the 1960s, Somalia received $90 per capita in foreign economic assistance, which was twice the average for sub-Saharan countries.[116] Yet a large share of this foreign aid was consumed as lavish salaries for the military and government officials.[117] More strikingly, in 1976 it was estimated that approximately 72,000 Somalis, out of a paid work force of 167,000, worked mostly in the government departments as office workers[118] and received government salaries (Nelson 1982:174). The educated Somalis have always preferred jobs in the civil service to any other employment field as they offered huge salaries, higher social status and better future prospects. For instance, in the 1950s as the few educated Somalis opted for administrative positions rather than teaching posts, because of the wide disparity in salaries, the development and the enlargement of secondary education in the country was extremely curtailed (Castagno 1959). In other words, private gain instead of public responsibility by the educated class has greatly hampered educational progress in the country even at this early stage. During this period, the UN Visiting Mission to Somalia warned the government that the salaries of the civil servants were too exorbitant for the budget of the country and the unnecessary expansion of the civil service sector must and should be avoided (UN Mission 1957:9-10).[119] Yet since independence, "Somalia was to become a striking example in Africa of the automatic admission of each new wave of graduates into an ever-expanding bureaucracy" (Doornbos 1993:112). It is therefore no wonder as some scholars asserted that the most important change that takes place in the first nine years of independence in Somalia is the increase in public employment, estimated at 47 percent (Laitin and Samatar 1987). Unfortunately, the enormous growth in public employment placed a heavy burden on the meagre economy of the country. Paying lavish salaries to the government staff was not a sensible policy as it wasted the meagre national budget for private appropriation. It was also a demonstration of the prevailing private pursuit culture among the Somali political elite. With the agenda of the national economic development, private interest has been overriding that of the public good. It is for this reason therefore that the limited national resources were not wisely invested in productive domestic means but privately siphoned off. Furthermore, this private oriented political behaviour of the educated elite explains their disinterest in engaging in purposeful national

---

[116] For more information, see Ozay Mehmet, "Effectiveness of Foreign Aid-the Case of Somalia", *The Journal of Modern African Studies* 9, no.1 (May 1971): 31-47.

[117] According to Omar " regarding the aid received by Somalia, there was an attitude of easy-come easy-go. No one cared to invest such funds in production. Government just relaxed and consumed these funds" (Omar 1992:69) .

[118] In the 1960s, the Somali poet Ali Ilmi Afyare perplexed the large number of the Somali clerks in the government departments who were doing nothing except chatting and sipping tea in their offices. He captured the situation in a poem: " Dawlad wada karrani ahi dunidaba ma joogtee". *[There is no government in the world that is solely composed of clerks].*

[119]At the time, salaries for the civil servants accounted for about one-half of all ordinary civil expenditure because of the sharp increases in salaries. See further, The Economy of the Trust Territory of Somaliland (1957:54)

goals and also their short term spoils politics that have been a salient figure of Somalia since independence. In the subsequent pages I shall discuss in detail how the private appropriation of the national resources by the Somali political elite increased further in the decades after independence.

As mentioned earlier, since the country lacked sufficient natural resources for economic development, planning was suggested to be the best solution to the underdevelopment problem of Somalia. Furthermore, during the 1960s, planning was a fashionable economic method in many African countries. As a result, the government of Somalia undertook its first Five Year Plan for the national economy between 1963-1967. However, putting in place a development plan in a country with limited domestic resources of revenue was no minor challenge. Fortunately, the government obtained generous foreign assistance and external grants to finance its development projects. For example, according to Ozay Mehmet between 1963-69, about 85 per cent of Somalia's total development expenditure was externally financed. Table 2 indicates the number of foreign donors who assisted in the economic development of Somalia during that period. Mehmet writes that, "this is a rare case of dependence on foreign financing among the less developed countries, where typically foreign resources account for only about 10 per cent of total investment expenditure.... Thus, Somali development in the 1960s presents a unique example of development with foreign aid" (Mehmet 1971:31-47). Nonetheless, despite this generous foreign assistance, little progress was made in the development of the economy in the first decade of independence. One can perhaps argue that the problem of the stagnation of the economy was not in any case a lack of foreign assistance. The explanations offered for the dismal success of development projects in Somalia include: poor absorptive capacity of the domestic economy, lack of explicitly stated priorities, shortage of skilled manpower in crucial occupations and fragile human resource base, domestic political squabbles and the allocation of a relatively high proportion of the recurrent budget to military build-up.[120] It is even demonstrated that the standard of living on average declined much lower at the close of the decade than at its beginning.[121]

---

[120] See the report prepared by the African Studies Centre, Somalia: A Social and Institutional Profile, (University of Boston, March 1983).

[121] For example, the estimates given in the World Bank Atlas indicate that the GNP per capita of Somalia declined at an average rate of 1.6% annually between 1961-1967.

Table 2.

Sources of Development Finance, 1963-9

Source	So.Sh.000	%
Somali	283,531	14.9
Foreign	1,691,528	85.1
U.S.S.R	388,928	20.4
U.S.A	326,489	17.2
E.E.C	245,108	12.9
World Bank	219,427	11.5
U.N.	143,567	7.5
F.R. Germany	122,951	6.5
Italy	71,339	3.7
China	39,220	2.1
Saudi Arabia	14,561	0.8
Others	47,938	2.5
Total	1,903,059	100.0

Source: German Planning and Economic Advisory Group, Reports on the Progress of Development Projects in Somali Democratic Republic (Mogadiscio and Frankfurt, 1969, mimeo.). See also Ozay Mehmet. 1971:37.

After the military regime of Siad Barre came to power in 1969, a socialist-oriented development plan was put forward. The government adopted what is called scientific socialism[122] as its ideology for economic and social development. The declared objective of the socialist government was to engineer a society based on justice and equality, and the development ideology of the regime was a greater self-reliance, which aimed to achieve economic independence. However, in spite of the rhetoric of the regime asserting that scientific socialism was the guiding principle for its economic development, mixed economy was the policy strategy adopted by the government. Furthermore, despite the declared slogans of self-reliance that the regime promulgated, the high dependence of the country on foreign grants was not reduced due to the meagre domestic sources of revenue. In fact, the important role of the foreign aid as the mainstay of the national economy has continued and even increased manifold.[123] The Soviet Union and the countries of the Eastern bloc were the chief financial patrons of the socialist military regime in Somalia at the time. Table 3 shows how the foreign funds have been the major sources of the development projects in the country between 1963-1982.

---

[122] The President of the military government of Somalia declared at the time that, "We have chosen scientific socialism because it is the only way for the rapid transformation of the country into a developed and economically advanced country" (Mohamed Said Barre, My Country and My People, Mogadishu, 1974), speech he made on October 20, 1970.

[123] For example, foreign aid grants and loans increased substantially from an average of $64 million per annum in 1970-1975 to a peak annual level of $411 million in 1986. For more, see United Nations, Somalia: Country Presentation (1990). However, Adam (1998) estimated that from 1961 onwards, 14 percent of the total national budget had been allocated to the build up of the military forces and since this period the heavy expenditure in the defence (see chapter 6) had been on increase.

Table 3
Proportion of Development Funds from local versus Foreign Sources, 1963-1982

	Local revenues		Foreign revenues	
Development plan period*	So.sh. (millions)	% of total	So.sh. (millions)	% of total
1963-1967**	0	0	1,400.0	100.0
1971-1973	118.9	16.2	615.0	83.8
1974-1978	1,260.3	32.6	2,602.9	67.4
1982-1986	3,199.0	20.0	13,050.0	80.0

Sources: Abdi Samatar. 1989:121.

* In 1963-1967 there was no tangible local revenue hence 100 percent of the country's development budget was externally funded.
** No data is found for 1968-1970 and 1979-1981.

The socialist regime of Somalia put forward the first development plan between 1971 and 1973; and the subsequent plan between 1974-1978. As Table 3 illustrates, during the period of 1974-1978 the increase of local revenue to (32.6 percent) was impressive but was not sustained.

Nonetheless, this was the time when the socialist military regime was trying to maximize and tap local resources in order to realise concretely the project of its self-reliance agenda. During that period, the military government initiated a crash economic development programme projected to increase domestic food production to a level that could achieve sustained self-sufficiency in the country. With this objective in mind, the military regime allocated more development funds to the rural sector, as shown in Table 4. Yet, with respect to the pastoral sector, most of the development expenditure was not used to improve the basic organisation of the livestock production but was mainly spent on facilitating its marketing infrastructure (Abdi Samatar 1989). All in all, the government expenditure on the pastoral sector increased only marginally, from3 percent in 1963 to 14 percent in 1986 (Abdi Samatar 1992:109). In the final analysis, the experiment of this socialist-oriented development policy hardly achieved the required domestic economic growth and its success was considered to be very dismal, as was demonstrated:

> "in terms of economic output, there was only a marginal difference between Somalia under the socialist regime and under the previous civilian regime. It would therefore be wrong to conclude that scientific socialism led Somalia out of economic poverty.... Somalia remained an economically poor state that exported animals to Arabia and bananas to Europe" (Laitin and Said Samatar 1987:118-119).[124]

---

[124] Reading the documents of the economic development in both the civilian and military governments in Somalia, I have not come across any constructive debates in the parliament and in the cabinet or coherent policy strategies in relation to the allocation of the meagre national resources for desirable and purposeful development projects. Two reasons have been proffered for the failure of the Somali government to improve and exploit the rural economy both pastoral and peasant agricultural production in the country. Abdi Samatar critically explains this dilemma as: " (1) the availability of foreign aid to lubricate the state's development machinery and (2) the state's ability, because of its colonial origin, to extract resources from the rural sector without intervening in agricultural production" (Abdi Samatar 1989:148).

Table 4. Proportion of Development Funds for Agriculture and Livestock, 1963-1986

Development Plan period	Agriculture So.Sh*	% of total	Livestock So.Sh*	% of total
Pre-coup				
1963-67	250.0	17.8	43.0	3.0
1968-70	53.0	7.7		
Post-coup				
1971-73	146.6	14.7	59.4	5.9
1974-78	1,124.5	29.1	162.1	4.2
1982-86	4,782.8	29.1	2,433.3	14.9

Sources: Abdi Samatar. 1989 : 121.

* Millions of Somali shillings.

It was also during this period that the macroeconomic imbalances, a perpetual problem in the national economy, did increase after independence. Furthermore, foreign debt figures gradually increased from 24% GDP in 1970 to 111% of GDP in 1980.[125] Somalia accumulated the highest debt to GNP ratios in the continent, which was estimated into a debt per capita figure of more than $350 (Lyons and Samatar 1995:17). The debt that the nation incurred has been huge in terms of percentage compared with a GNP per capita of less than $175.[126]

By the mid-1970s, because of two occurrences, the national development programme of the socialist military regime in Somalia encountered an acute crisis, which reversed whatever marginal progress had been made in the decade earlier. The crisis developed both as a result of natural calamity and as a consequence of a man-made historical blunder. In 1974-75, Somalia was struck by one of the worst droughts in its recent history. The drought was so severe that it affected about two-thirds of the population in the country, damaged the harvest and decimated millions of herds. This disastrous drought heavily contributed to the fall in gross domestic product and exacerbated the already critical economic condition in the country. The government was forced to react swiftly to the calamity of the drought and most of the development funds and planning resources were diverted to help the destitute pastoral nomads, disrupting the course of development planning. Moreover, because of the environmental degradation and the declining resource base in the rural areas, many destitute nomads were forced to migrate to the towns in search of livelihood and demanded government employment that hardly existed. According to the World Bank, World Development Report (1988) in 1985, 34 percent of the Somali population lived in towns. This in fact means that Somalia has a higher proportion of urban

---

[125] For more information see Jamil Abdalla Mubarak, From Bad Policy to Chaos in Somalia: How an Economy Fell Apart, (London: Praeger, 1996:14).

[126] See further "Africa's Debt profile: 1989", African Recovery, vol.4 (October- December 1990). The total debt of Somalia was calculated to be about 2.137 billion dollars, which the country largely owed to multilateral creditors and foreign governments. In 1989 the debt service payments of the country exceeded more than 124 percent of export earnings.

people as compared with Ghana or Nigeria and even much higher than its neighbours, Ethiopia and Kenya (Wisner 1994:54).[127]

The man-made occurrence, which led the development programme of the socialist military regime to further disarray, was the futile conflict of the Somali government with Ethiopia over the Ogaden region in 1977-78. The Ogaden war resulted in the terrible defeat of the Somali national army by the Ethiopian forces.[128] Furthermore, the lion's share of the scarce resources of the national economy, were wasted on the preparation of the war effort, which drained the coffers of the state and caused an acute fiscal crisis in the country (Ahmed Samatar 1988). Worse still, the political tensions that the war has raised resulted in a diplomatic row, which gravely strained the cordial relations between Somalia and its socialist allies, the Soviet Union and the countries in Eastern Europe. Consequently, the Soviet Union, which was the major source of military, technical and financial assistance to Somalia withdrew and that resulted in the termination of broad-scale development aid.[129]

However, while practically the economy of the country collapsed, the spending of the government sharply increased partly because of higher wages in the public sector employment and partly in response to a massive influx of refugees as the consequence of the war.[130] For instance, after the war more than a million refugees, mostly ethnic Somalis from Ethiopia entered Somalia. The refugees composed of ethnic Somalis, Oromos and other minority ethnic groups inhabiting the eastern part of Ethiopia were the direct victims of the war. The battles had displaced many of them, destroyed their habitat and also their local economy and this terrible condition forced them to flee to Somalia. According to estimates recorded by the United Nations High Commission for Refugees (UNCHR) and the US Census Bureau the population of Somalia swelled in 1978 and 1979 by 11.2% and 19.5% respectively because of the consequence of the war (Jamal 1988). The burden of the refugee influx on Somalia was so heavy that at the time it was viewed internationally as an unprecedented predicament in a country like Somalia which was not well-endowed with natural resources and had a poorly-developed economic structure. The high number of the refugees made Somalia a host to the largest refugee population in Africa, which the country had no capacity to cope with (see chapter 7). Indeed, the demands of the refugee population imposed a further burden on the narrowing meagre resources of the government and severely strained the country that was already suffering from acute fiscal crisis. Eventually, the government lost control over the national economy and that then gave rise to a situation in which corruption and glaring private pursuit became the order of the day.

---

[127] The large migration of the Somalis into the urban centers was also coupled with the rapid and explosive increase of the population as a whole from 2.5 million in 1960 to 7.5 million in mid-1990 (The Economist Intelligence Unit, 1991-1992:35).

[128] The death toll of the Somali military in the war was estimated to be around 25,000, which was an awesome figure for the Somali army, which in total numbered 37,000 on the eve of the Ogaden war. The death toll and the decimation of the Somali army was also an awesome figure for a population numbered about four million (Sivard 1982:15).

[129] How the departure of the Soviet Union further worsened the economic crisis in the country, see Norman Miller, "The Other Somalia; Part II: Foreign Aid and Local Politics", *Horn of Africa*, vol. 5, no.3 (1981b).

[130] According to a World Bank document, " in the second half of the 1970s, the government's finances deteriorated rapidly, mainly because of the expenditure resulting from the border conflict with Ethiopia, the cost of maintaining a large number of refugees, and a growing wage bill associated with a rapid increase in public sector employment" (The World Bank, 1989:2)

Several factors are suggested to be the causes of the malaise of the national economy and the dependence of the country on foreign assistance (even to meet its annual budget). Scholars like the brothers Abdi and Ahmed Samatar contend that it is the neglect of the subsistence traditional sectors (livestock pastoralism and peasant agriculture) which form the backbone of the national economy that stagnates the economic development in the country. As I explained above, the military regime attempted to improve the economic viability of the rural sectors especially agriculture but even that development policy did not fundamentally transform the basic structures of the rural sectors. By contrast, Mubarak argues that it is the erratic government economic policy in the urban sector (for more than two decades) that has undermined the development of the economy in the country. Others like Said Samatar and David Laitin advance the view that the economic malaise in the country is not per se due to the lack of natural resources but is also the consequence of cultural, social and political circumstances. I will argue that all the suggested factors have in conjuncture contributed to the dismal development of the economy in the country. On top of these arguments however, the policy of the foreign aid to Somalia within the environment of the Cold War politics is also a factor which we should not dismiss lightly. The easy availability of the foreign aid which underwrites a large portion of the ordinary budget in the country has indeed played a major role in perpetuating the stagnation of the domestic economy. Furthermore, the reliance on the foreign aid which the Somali political elite took for granted had a devastating effect as it gave them false development hopes and prevented them from seriously addressing the difficult task of reorganising and restructuring the domestic economy. Thus, with a long-term economic plan and development strategy in the country, the provision of the lavish foreign aid to Somalia was a plague rather than a blessing. Aid given policy created aid dependence and the economic, social and political consequences in Somalia were in this respect detrimental. The rest of the chapter discusses the background, social base and policy strategies of the Somali political elite who presided over this precarious and foreign aid cushioned national economy over the past three decades.

5.5.   The Post – Colonial "State Class"

To get a better picture, the background and the social base of the political elite in Somalia that directed and executed the political economy after independence needs to be explained. The contemporary modern political elite of Somalia was originally composed of clerical cadres and auxiliary colonial employees, soldiers, paid clan chiefs, jurists for native customary laws, petty traders and merchants. The colonial state paid salaries to those who were directly employed in the Administration while others like livestock traders and merchants in the towns have indirectly benefited the colonial economy. The educational level of the Somalis who served mostly in the lowest ranks of the colonial Administration was extremely poor. Their educational level was elementary and the colonial authority did not permit them to gain thorough professional experience or to be given promotion in the administration even in the late 1950s (Castagno 1959:367). In this respect, their early formation was humble in origin as they were recruited to serve subordinate junior office-hands under colonial officials. Thus, the genesis of the post-colonial political elite in Somalia, which eventually crystallised as merchants, intelligentsia and petty bourgeoisie, was indeed colonial since they emerged as the result of the colonial state restructuring of the Somali society.

Nonetheless, as the de-colonisation process was nearly coming to its end, members largely drawn from the clerical employees in the colonial Administration, merchants and traders gradually rose to a new social group. In 1960 this new social group took over the power of the state when the Somalis assumed the highest political and bureaucratic positions in the national government. Internally, however, as their diverse background indicates, they remained loose congeries and a bunch of individuals with contradictory political agendas and parochial interests.[131] This difference has been the decisive factor which weakened their elite unity. To put it simply, the problem was how a livestock trader, a merchant in the town and petty bureaucrat in the colonial state could overcome their internal diversity and mould a solid elite cohesion within a short period of time. As a new social group, this was the challenge that the Somali political elite confronted immediately after independence. "The Somali elite, which consisted of merchants, bureaucrats, and politicians was an unstable social stratum. The brevity of its collective social experience, and the shallowness of its material basis both as individuals and as a group, heightened individual vulnerability and intense intra-group rivalry" (Abdi Samatar 1997:698). Eventually, although they did not succeed in resolving their internal incoherence, they nevertheless managed to co-exist as a group who are mainly interested in serving their respective private pursuits. One concrete example that every analysis of the economy of Somalia has made apparent since 1950 is the lavish and disproportionate salaries that the Somali civil servants allocated to themselves, imposing a substantial drain on the limited national budget. "Somalis seldom implemented the investment or spending patterns advocated by their overlords or modern day development advisors" (Geshekter 1993: 7).

The other problem that the Somali political elite faced immediately after independence was how to blend and integrate the different colonial state traditions, structures, administrative practices, rules and procedures, as well as the preferential arrangements for civil servants in relation to benefits.[132] This predicament however was not of their own making but was bequeathed to them by the departing colonial state Administrations. Northern Somalia was under British colonial rule while southern Somalia was ruled by Italy; thus the country had inherited different colonial languages, bureaucratic procedures and cultural attitudes and heritages, daunting gulfs which could be not easily bridged.

The Somali leadership had to make these different colonial bureaucratic structures into one national Administration owned by the Somalis. This integration task was no minor feat as it resulted in considerable political strain between British- and –Italian trained Somali civil servants.[133] "Once political independence and partial reunification were achieved, Somalis began to squabble among themselves. Regional sub-cultures, aggravated by social class competition, festered over the next twenty years to eventually produce domestic conflicts as lethal as those anywhere in the world" (Geshekter 1997:72). Ultimately, the Somali leaders succeeded in integrating the two administration systems but at great cost as the discontent and

---

[131] The prevalence of different parochial interests among the Somali political elite was also what derailed the Somali-wide territorial unification during the colonial era that I have I already described in chapter four.

[132] " Italy and Britain had left them with separate administrative, legal, and education systems where affairs were conducted according to different procedures and in different languages. Police, taxes, and the exchange rates of their separate currencies were also different. The orientation of their educated elites were divergent, and economic contacts between the two regions were virtually nonexistent" (Nelson 1982:35).

[133] According to I.M. Lewis, " British exclusiveness and empiricism, the accent on quality rather than quantity in educational and social advancement, attachment to British conceptions of justice and ideals of administrative conduct, and the strict separation of politics from administration, all contrasted in northern eyes with the apparently less rigorous standards of political and public service morality in the south and with the involute Italian bureaucratic tradition (Lewis 1988:169). For a further discussion on this issue, see I. M. Lewis, A Modern History of Somalia: Nation and State in the Horn of Africa (1988).

the haggling of the amalgamation process between the northern and the southern Somalis exposed the shaky power base of the new state.[134]

With respect to a policy agenda, the new Somali political class "did not articulate a clear road map for achieving any development agenda" (Abdi Samatar 2001:110). Also, there was no clearly articulated collective national project and a lasting consensus on the fundamental issue of governance and social organisation. Moreover, the Somali political elite was lacking in commitment and conscious determination to confront the formidable task of constructing a stable political order and a viable domestic economy in the country. Furthermore, they had no competent administrative and organisational capacity, which according to their day-to-day handling of their work seemed insurmountable. Consequently, the combination of all these liabilities to a large extent incapacitated the political elite of Somalia in the pursuance of constructive economic development and meaningful social change. Cox explains this form of authority or a state class as a "political structure that tries more or less successfully to monopolize the capacity for exercising political force within the national territory but has not acquired either a firm social basis of consent or the administrative capacity to formulate and apply effective economic policies" (Cox 1987:218). Cox classifies the kind of state they lead as a 'protostate' that is capable only for predation and nothing else. [135]

In this study, the new Somali political elite is understood to be the post-colonial state class that lives off the control over the state. As Elsenhans notes,

> "Unlike the capitalists, this state class does not appropriate surplus product on the strength of its competitiveness on the market, but through the instruments of state economic policy.... I shall refer to this class as the 'State-class' because it uses its control over the state apparatus to appropriate the mass of the surplus product and decides in which form it will be employed within the framework of political conflict" (Elsenhans 1991:78).

This notion of state class fits well with the new political elite of Somalia because of their grinding material poverty and the underdevelopment of domestic resources, which made the revenues accruing to the state the only means of accumulation. Generally speaking, the Somali political elite can be described as instrumental leadership rather than societal leadership. According to Abucar,

> "The instrumental leader sees leadership as a means to an end. He often uses his position to further the interests of his family, clan or clique.... The social leader, on the other hand, sees power and influence as a means to solve human problems" (Abucar, 1995:6).

---

[134] The reason as Ahmed Samatar explained was that " there was very little understanding, particularly on the part of the new leadership and regimes, of the complexities of domestic reconstitution, let alone the difficulties inherent in profitably engaging a bi-polar international system. Within a few years, the glow of independence began to dim. In fact, as early as 1961, signs of regional discontent appeared when a group of mutinous junior military officers from the North took over major towns in Somaliland. In the same year, in a referendum, a majority of the Northerners voted against the constitution which was designed to become the basis of the new polity" (Ahmed Samatar 1998:20).

[135] According to Cox " the protostate can extract tribute but lacks the capability or incentive to reshape society, and society is neither strong enough nor coherent enough either to manage itself or to fashion a state in its own image" (ibid: 231). Furthermore, this kind of state lacks internal pacification while the state class has no ability to initiate social reforms and create political institutions imbued with a sense of national unity.

The writings of both dominant schools of Somali studies have lengthily recorded the instrumentalist politics that the Somali political elite practised since the independence 1960 (Lewis 1972, Samatar 1989). The traditionalist scholars of Somali studies writing on the politics of the civilian governments of Somalia during the first decade after independence have implicitly noted the instrumentalist leadership of the Somali elite. Their literature indicated that the major preoccupation of the political elite was how to gain access to or control the state power and apportion seats in its higher echelons. And this tendency towards instrumentalist leadership or private pursuit according to this school was prevalent even when the state was at its embryonic stage. I.M. Lewis, the doyen of the traditionalist writers, who frequently observed the debates of the elected members in the parliament during the civilian administration in the early years after the independence, confirmed how the perpetuation of this spoils politics mentality frustrated the nation-wide collective project. According to Lewis, the elected members in the parliament hardly discussed any issues of national importance be it social agenda or economic development because of their preoccupation with the politics of private pursuit. As Lewis notes,

> "The democratic parliamentary process which had seemed to combine so well with traditional Somali institutions, and had begun with such verve and promise, had turned distinctly sour. The National Assembly was no longer the symbol of free speech and fair play for all citizens. On the contrary, it had been turned into a sordid marketplace where deputies traded their votes for personal rewards with scant regard for the interests of their constituents" (Lewis 1972:399).

The transformationist scholars of Somali studies discuss explicitly and more powerfully the prevalence of the politics of private pursuit that had been the hallmark of the Somali political elite since Somalia achieved statehood in 1960. The literature of this school repeatedly use the word "competition" to denote how the politics of private pursuit and the contest among the political elite for the control of state power, as well as its resources and opportunities, gradually but progressively undermined the political stability in the country. The writers of this school also stress that one of the defining characteristics in the dynamics of Somalia during the civilian regime is that of the politics of *private pursuit*. Since the 1980s, the scholars of this school have been boldly criticising in their countless publications (Ahmed Samatar 1988,1989,1993; Abdi Samatar 1989,1992a,1992b) the private pursuit of the political elite, which gave precedence to the parochial personal interests over the public agenda.[136] According to these scholars, the Somali political elite whether they are early nationalists leaders who inherited the new-born state from the colonial rulers or the military commanders who succeeded them, their primary concern has been how to gain personal benefits. As Ahmed Samatar writes,

> "These leaders of the independence movements construed the enterprise as a rare chance to win a personally profitable place in the new structures (particularly the state) and only secondarily as an opportunity to construct new public institutions worthy of the great challenges ahead. Each segment of what was to become the power bloc (mostly traders, artisans, bureaucrats and literate-religious elements) was less concerned with the heavy structural and developmental questions facing Somalia and more preoccupied with gaining personal advantage" (Ahmed Samatar 1995:12).

---

[136] For an extensive review, see further Abdi Samatar " Leadership and Ethnicity in the Making of African State Models: Botswana versus Somalia", *Third World Quarterly*, vol.18, no 4 (1997): 687-707.

And Abdi Samatar, while linking the economic poverty of the political elite with the politics of private pursuit they ceaselessly engage in, notes that:

> "In the absence of nonpublic sources of accumulation, state revenues, including foreign assistance, became the bone of contention. This meant that those who had access to the appropriate offices could reward themselves and their clients. The competition for profitable state offices unleashed a deadly race among the petite bourgeoisie" (Abdi Samatar 1989:110).

The persistence of the politics of private pursuit in the Somali public life is what eventually destroyed the democratic establishment, ended the civilian administration and let the military take over the power of the state in the country.

For instance, in the last civilian elections of 1969, each Somali lineage had formed its own political party. The proliferation of the political parties had created an unprecedented situation in which more than sixty parties nominated more than 1,000 candidates to compete only for 123 seats. This wild competition for party seats indeed placed a high premium on private pursuit and put to an end the purported democratic politics in Somalia.[137] Private pursuit and its effect on the bankruptcy of the state continued during the military regime. In the early years of the military regime, it was the collective national agenda that prevailed over the politics of private pursuit openly practised by the civilian power-holders preceded. However, after the debacle of the Ogaden war in 1978 when the regime lost its support from the Eastern bloc, notably the Soviet Union (which was by then the chief financial patrons), and faced both an economic and political crisis because of pitfalls of the war, private pursuit had escalated. And this time the race for private pursuit was much more lethal than that waged earlier by the power-holders of the former civil regime. First, it gave rise to cut-throat competition among the political elite in the higher echelons of the government. Second, the political elite, particularly the ruling military juntas were not restrained from using any means at hand, including bullets in order to misappropriate the resources of the state. Consequently, this chase for private pursuit increasingly drained the coffers of the state on a grand scale.[138] Eventually, the dwindling national economy became the private kitchen of the President and his cohorts. At this time the President surrounded himself cronies with who were dependent on his favour. Furthermore, the President appropriated everything: the purse, the power to appoint someone, promote and also demote. It was therefore the time when the patronage system in Somalia peaked. For example, the marginalised and the impoverished urban dwellers use to joke that Siad Barre considered the state and the national economy as "parts of his tea shop" (Compagnon 1992:9).[139] In fact, since the late 1970s, it was this prevailing

---

[137] According to Davidson, "By 1969, with clientelism run riot, Somalis had achieved no fewer than 62 parliamentary parties (read: groups for dividing up the spoils of power) for an electorate far smaller than Somalia's 3 million people; and such was the uproar and corruption that a military coup d'état was carried out in 1969 without a shot being fired" (Davidson 1992:220-221). For a wider discussion with respect to spoils politics in Africa, see further Basil Davidson, "Africa: The Politics of Failure" *The Socialist Register* (1992): 212-225.

[138] For a concise historical analysis of how the political elite systematically plundered the meagre resources of the national economy from 1960 to 1991, see Abdi Samatar, "Destruction of State and Society in Somalia: Beyond the Tribal Convention", *The Journal of Modern African Studies,* vol.30, 4 (1992): 625-641

[139] For an extensive discussion on how the state has become the private fiefdom of the President and his small entourage, see Daniel Compagnon, " Political Decay in Somalia: From Personal Rule to Warlordism", *Refuge,* vol. 12, 5 (November- December 1992): 8-13.

politics of private pursuit defined and conceptualised as personal and predatory rule[140] that became the basis for the very survival of the military regime. The final mundane details of the politics of private pursuit and how the misappropriated national resources were squandered on extravagant consumption and luxury consumer goods has been described by Anna Simons.[141] Thus, further discussion is not necessary here. The only point I would like to re-emphasize before closing the discussion in this section is the apparent link between the instrumentalist leadership of the Somali elite and the perpetuation of the politics of private pursuit which eventually resulted in the bankruptcy of the state.

5.6. Conclusion

Extending the discussion in chapter three, I considered in this chapter the post-colonial political economy of Somalia. I described the constraints of the material environment in the country and the limited domestic source of revenue that could not meet even the bare costs of running a modern state system.[142] The traditional rural sectors (peasant agriculture and livestock production) cannot or perhaps were not intended to generate sufficient resources to ensure a viable economy in Somalia.[143] Firstly, the taxable capacity of these traditional sectors of the economy at their present state is not very promising. Secondly, the rural Somali population, especially the wandering pastoral nomads are no willing to pay taxes to meet state expenditures.[144] It is therefore for these reasons that the governments in the post-colonial Somalia failed to accrue enough tax revenues from these traditional sectors of the economy. Since the colonial state administration was installed in Somalia, the only domestic revenues

---

[140] In the literature on the political power and on the state in Africa both notions were extensively discussed. See Robert H. Jackson and Carl G. Rosberg, Personal Rule in Black Africa (1982); and Robert Fatton Jr., Predatory Rule: State and Civil Society in Africa (1992).

[141] Anna Simons wrote an anthropological dissertation which she later published in book form entitled: Networks of Dissolution: Somalia Undone (1995). Simons did her fieldwork in the country in the final years leading to the collapse of the state. Her dissertation is full of anecdotes and personal narrations, which lack historical grounding.

[142] I have already stated in chapter three that due to the very low productivity of the pastoral production which is the primary economy in the country the Somali social and political organisation is not able to advance beyond the kinship system. In other words, the domestic economy in Somalia cannot afford to sustain any political structure beyond the clan system.

[143] As Castagno explains, " one of the most difficult problems facing the Somali government is that of establishing the Territory's public finances on a sound basis. Ever since the beginning of the Italian colonial administration in 1905, the Territory has been plagued by chronic budgetary deficits. Expenditures always seem to outpace receipts, despite serious efforts by the various administrations to reduce the gap" (Castagno 1959:379). The persistent deficit in the budget is a lasting problem, which in Somalia may never be resolved as long as the indigenous sectors of the economy remained undeveloped.

[144] "Taxation is an unpopular subject everywhere, but in Somalia, as in probably all underveloped countries, there is an extreme reluctance to pay taxes. In part this is explained by the wretched poverty of the majority of people, but another important factor is the low level of general education. Most Somalis, according to two United Nations missions which looked closely into this matter, do not seem to understand that tax revenues are badly needed to pay for essential public services" (Karp 1960:30-31). Even today, the grinding poverty of the majority of Somali population and their dislike of the idea of paying taxes hinder the increase of the bare government revenue. It is still a puzzle how a centralised state system can be reconstituted in Somalia without a systematic and nation-wide taxation.

available were derived from import and export duties. However, these customs duties or indirect taxes were insufficient to sustain a very expensive state administration.

The easy availability of generous foreign aid meant that Somalia had no problems in getting help to sponsor the functioning of the state from its colonial inception until its collapse in 1991. This foreign financial assistance, which Somalia largely received as the Cold War dividend, underwrote a substantial part of the national domestic expenditure for more than three decades but it also created a habit of dependence. The Somali political elite relaxed and did not seriously attempt to improve the rural sectors like that of the livestock, which remains the domestic backbone of the economy. Moreover, the lavish foreign aid was not wisely used to improve the rural sectors of the economy or to invest in new domestic means of accumulation but was substantially spent on purchasing arms, military arsenals and a defence build-up.

Furthermore, the Somali political class who presided over the state were not in a position to make a difference. As I noted earlier in brief, they were a bunch of individuals of humble colonial origins, limited education and world-view who were pursuing contradictory policies and particularistic interests. They were also un-familiar with the intricacies and operations of governance and a modern state system. On top of all these they lacked vision and a constructive economic development agenda and as a result their policy interventions and responses were at best ad-hoc and erratic. However, one thing that the Somali political class attempted to resolve was the accumulation impoverishment they were enduring because of the abject poverty of the domestic economy. In other words, the foreign financial assistance accruing in the coffers of the state became the only valuable source of their private accumulation. And the intensity of the competition of this spoils politics between the state class, created fierce rivalry and hostilities, which eventually derailed the agenda for a collective national public project and bankrupted the state. In short, the constraints of the material environment in the country, the lavish provision of foreign aid and the abject poverty of the Somali state class all in conjuncture have in fact produced a dire situation, which made the chase for private spoils an overriding enterprise.

Theoretically speaking, this discussion in the chapter demonstrates how the negative impulses of the tendencies towards private and public pursuits have bankrupted the state. For stance, while the persistence of the endemic structural poverty of the economy forced the political elite to partially siphon off the very limited national resources for their own private accumulation, the territorial fragmentation of the country by the colonial intervention on the other hand compelled the political leadership to spent the rest of the meagre wealth on purchasing arms in preparation for an irredentist war. Thus, one can observe here how the contradictory impulses of the tendencies towards private and public pursuits in concurrence undermined the economic viability of the state. This analysis therefore is what the continuity and change explanations of the traditionalist and transformationist debates have failed to account. Traditionalist writers do not at all address the economic survival aspect of the tendency towards private pursuit while the transformationist proponents focus only on the chase for private spoils among the political elite at the domestic plane. In this respect, neither of the schools addresses how the externally oriented irredentist mission also contributed to the economic bankruptcy of the state.

Chapter Six

Public Pursuit and Militarisation of the State (1960-1980)

6.1.   Introduction

"Somalia has been a victim of both the Cold War and the end of he Cold War. During the Cold War the strategic value of Somalis to the superpowers was inflated. As a result the two superpowers poured armaments into that little country. When the Cold War ended, the strategic value of Somalia plunged like stock market prices on Wall Street at the start of the Great Depression. At one time it was a poor arid country but with a strategic location. In the global scheme of things, the two mighty capitals of the world --- Washington and Moscow --- were competing to make sure the country was in the "right" hands. Then suddenly the Cold War ended and that value plunged like a mighty dollar no longer mighty. Both the rise in inflated strategic value which took the form of arming it to the limit and the fall as a result of the Cold War were devastating for Somalia. No one cared enough to help prevent its disintegration" From Ali Mazrui, Crisis in Somalia: From Tyranny to Anarchy (1997).

In chapter four I discussed how the partitioning of Somalia among rival colonial powers had been the most dramatic foreign aggression that the Somali people had ever endured. Since then, the Somalis have been struggling to regain their lost territories by all means in their power. And this struggle to bring together the ethnic Somalis under one political entity has been the prime concern of the politics of public pursuit waged by the political elite. This chapter extends the discussion in chapter four and examines how the politics of public pursuit launched through an irredentist adventure militarised the state during the Cold War era.

At independence in 1960 only two of the five parts of the ethnic Somali inhabited territories merged and became the new Republic of Somalia. The two parts were British Somaliland and Italian Somalia. However, three areas which the Somali nationals inhabit were still missing and remained under foreign domination. The parts that remained under foreign occupation were the eastern regions of Ethiopia, Djibouti, and in the Northern Frontier District of Kenya. In 1977, Djibouti achieved its independence from France under a Somali President who declined to merge it with the Republic of Somalia.

As I already discussed at length in chapter four, this problem of territorial dismemberment was a terrible legacy Somalis inherited from colonialism.[145] In the closing decades of the 19th century, during the scramble for Africa, the competing imperial powers had parcelled the country into five parts. Compared with the other colonised countries in Africa, the partition of Somalia into five different colonial frontiers was indeed an exception.[146] No other country in

---

[145] Despite the existence of specified clan-inhabited geographical zones in the country, nevertheless the parcelling of the land was terrible in the minds of many Somalis since according to their world outlook the territorial integrity of Somalia exists as a social (i.e. ethnical) and emotional construct.

[146] According to Khapoya, "the Somalis are probably unique among African people in having been colonized by three different European powers and in having found themselves living in four different countries (Khapoya

Africa has been so radically fragmented into five colonial zones like Somalia. The parcelling of the country not only squeezed the grazing land of the Somali pastoral nomads but also divided family members into demarcated colonial frontiers. In fact, this was one of the most dramatic experiences that the Somalis had to confront due to the colonial partitioning of their homeland.

Immediately after independence this problem of the missing territories and how they could be regained had become the overriding political agenda of the new Republic of Somalia. Most of the Somali public were in support of the struggle in regaining the missing territories. The issue also gained a prominent position in the decision-making policy of the political class in the country early on, from the moment the Republic was established until the late 1970s. It became the salient political agenda, which dominated the foreign relations of Somalia. Furthermore, it was the sole national project that the Somali governments were prepared to pursue at all costs to the extent of neglecting the urging domestic social concerns and economic development.[147] As a result, within a few years after the country achieved statehood it was the pursuit of this Pan-Somali unity, which led Somalia to become embroiled in border clashes with Ethiopia and Kenya that presented a potential threat to the stability of the region.

After de-colonisation, Somalia was the only country in sub-Saharan Africa, which fiercely disputed and rejected the status quo of the boundaries established by the departed imperial powers. However, this blatant rejection was resented by the neighbouring countries, the Organisation of African Unity (OAU)[148], which accepted the inviolability of the inherited colonial frontiers, as well as the ex-imperial Western powers of Somalia. Yet the Somali political elite in defiance insisted that the colonial borders were artificial, unlawful and arbitrarily created, and this would not hinder them from championing the right to self-determination of their Somali nationals under foreign subjugation. Article 6 (4) of the constitution of the Somali Republic firmly states that: "the Somali Republic shall promote, by legal and peaceful means, the union of Somali territories". This political aspiration of the new Republic which was diametrically in contrast to the position taken by the OAU, calling for respect for the territorial inviolability of member states, had caused Somalia a great deal of foreign relations problems.

For instance, the territorial claims of the Somali Republic were viewed by most African leaders as a very dangerous expansionist adventure, and that brought Somalia into diplomatic isolation in the continent.[149] The quest also put the diplomatic relations between Somalia and

---

1982:29). For further discussion, see Vincent B. Khapoya, "Historical Origins of the Refugee Problem: Somalia's Colonial Experience and Irredentism", *Horn of Africa*, vol.5, no.1 (1982): 29-31.

[147] " Since independence, and the unification of British Somali-land and the Italian Somali trusteeship in 1960 to form the current state boundaries, Somali leaders have vowed to unite all Somalis. Defense and the issue of 'absent' Somali territories have always received priority in the central government budget and have dominated parliamentary debates and international diplomacy efforts" (Mubarak 1996:38).

[148] For example, in 1964 AHG /Res 16(1) was adopted by the Cairo OAU Summit which stated: that all member states pledge themselves to respect the borders existing on their achievement of independence". For further information, see the Basic Documents of the Organization of African Unity (Addis Ababa, May 1963).

[149] As Marte notes, "given the fact that most independent African countries inherited the colonial borders that were set by the former colonial powers, they were reluctant to support Somalia's irredentist ambitions and territorial claims, as they feared that this could backfire and encourage minorities in their own countries to seek reunification with their brethren on the other side of the 'colonial' border" (Marte 1994:222).

the West in jeopardy particularly those with Britain, which was one of the chief financial patrons of the country at the time. Because of the diplomatic row Britain cut its financial aid to Somalia. This then deprived the new country (whose meagre natural endowment offered few alternatives to animal husbandry and abject camel economy), the financial support needed most for its economic development. Yet, oblivious of or perhaps unconcerned with the pitfalls of these grave foreign relations problems the country was confronted with, the Somali political elite embarked early on their Pan-Somali politics with an uncompromising irredentist campaign.[150] To retreat again, a strong irredentist drive has been the marked feature, which defined the Somali Republic after independence. It was also the military preparation of this irredentist adventure that militarised the state early on. The Somali political elite justified their aggressive foreign policy as being the right strategy in the process of building a single Somali state.[151] According to their point of view, the Somali nation was fragmented beyond the Republic and without the unification of a whole nation, the Somali national identity was deemed incomplete.[152] Consequently, the politics of the Pan-Somali struggles was implicitly pursued by the political elite as a strategy of rule or a legitimisation of their power, as well as a mechanism for internal social cohesion and stability. [153] The political elite knew very well that the only sentiment, which can galvanise the lineage segmented Somali population, is the appeal for redemption of the missing Somali inhabited lands. Beyond this objective, there is little nationalist fervour to unite the population and for which Somalis are willing to be mobilised. The appeal of the Pan-Somali aspiration was that it was an emotional sentiment constructed on a cultural identity but poorly grounded in rational political calculations (Lewis 1989). More important, the ordinary Somalis were urging the leadership to struggle by any means for the unification of all the territories inhabited by the ethnic Somali population. Thus, in this respect, the general Somali public was of the opinion that unification struggle should be a very serious national preoccupation which every Somali leader must continue to advocate and fiercely campaign for.

---

[150] According to Bell, " from the beginning, Somalia pursued an irredentist policy. Even after the OAU refused to support its claim, and without significant allies or an effective army, Mogadishu was determined on the adventure. This was at the time when even the slow pace of development came to a halt" (Bell 1973:23).

[151] As has been suggested, "since independence virtually all of Somalia's foreign policy has centered around a single fact: that the entire Somali nation is not ruled by a single Somali state. This fact constitutes the Somali dilemma: Somalia remains a nation in search of a state" (David Laitin and Said Samatar 1987:129).

[152] This is the puzzle, which baffles outsiders. In Somalia, clan and national identity compete. Internally, Somalis accent clan identity while externally they prefer to project their collective national identity. In fact, for the Somalis, clan and national identity is two sides of a coin as they use them interchangeably according to the circumstance. A Somali when he is in front of another Somali will not hesitate to mention his clan name but in front of stranger he will say that he is a Somali.

[153] According to Sinclair, " internal harmony was further encouraged, at the price of external conflict, by the strong commitment of all political leaders to the nationalist struggle which aimed at extending the boundaries of the new state to include the missing Somali communities in Ethiopia, French Somaliland and Northern Kenya" (Sinclair 1980: 11). For more information, see M.R. Sinclair, The Strategic Significance of the Horn of Africa (Pretoria: Institute for Strategic Studies, University of Pretoria, 1980).

6.2.   The Somali Republic and the Cold War

The birth of the Somali Republic in the 1960s coincided with the highest peak of Cold War geopolitics between the two superpowers. Therefore, the imperatives of the Cold War made the newly emerged Republic of Somalia a pawn of the superpower politics. Thus, as Hashim notes,

> "The Cold War coming on the heels of the era of colonialism deprived Somalia, as it did many African nations, of the time required to regain an independent identity and prepare to meet the challenges of the twentieth century. Throughout her history Somalia has been a pawn in the schemes of more powerful states and coalitions of states" (Hashim 1995:219).

Somalia also became a theatre of superpower rivalry for strategic position. This means that the conflicts between Somalia and its neighbouring countries in the region, such as Ethiopia were meddled in constantly by the superpowers. And they meddled chiefly to serve and further their respective strategic interests.

In the aftermath of the Second World War II, global power struggles between the United States and the Soviet Union had emerged. Since the beginning of this Cold War rivalry till its end, the states in the Horn received the brunt of the superpowers' confrontations. Ethiopia and Somalia particularly, because of their long standing conflicts were the places in which the superpowers fought by proxy. This is how Legum and Lee expressed the vulnerable position of the Third World states during the Cold War era:

> "the political opportunities open to the major powers to pursue their interests in the Third World are mostly provided by the needs of smaller nations who are engaged less in ideological struggle than in pursuing their own conceived national interests. In their concern to strengthen their own position weak states often turn to a major power for assistance where their interests coincide - the result can turn purely local conflicts into international involvement" (Legum and Lee 1977:5-6).

This is precisely what happened in the Horn region. The rivalling states of Ethiopia and Somalia sought external assistance and that facilitated the entry of the foreign powers. The global powers in order to retain or advance their geopolitical hold in the region extended generous support in terms of military, technical and financial assistance to their respective clients. Gradually, the magnitude of the superpowers' involvement in the internal conflicts between Ethiopia and Somalia had assumed a wider dimension and became "... an integral part of East-West rivalry for the political allegiance of the grey areas of the globe, i.e. the Third World (Ayoob 1980:136).

In the case of Somalia, both superpowers and their respective allies were willing to provide generous military assistance at one time or another. The involvement of the Western countries, particularly the United States in Somalia, began within a few years after the end of World War II and continued throughout the early 1960s. The US interest in Somalia was largely motivated by the containment of Russian and Chinese influence in the country. As Schraeder writes:

"US foreign policy towards the Horn of Africa between 1945 and 1990 was guided by a series of Cold War rationales that viewed the region as a means for solving non-African problems. Specifically, U.S. policymakers did not perceive the countries and peoples of the Horn of Africa as important in their own right but, rather, as a means of preventing the further advances of Soviet communism. As a result, US relations with various regimes in the region evolved according to their perceived importance within an East-West framework" (Schraeder 1992:571).[154]

To make sure that Somalia should not fall into the Soviet Union camp, the Western countries were willing to present themselves as credible patrons and assist the new government. However, as I shall indicate below, the leadership of the Somali Republic knew that America and other Western countries were providing substantially more military assistance both to Ethiopia and Kenya (their principal adversaries) than what was offered to them. Furthermore, the new leadership of the Republic had an urgent mission. They wanted to build up the military capability of the country as speedily as possible in order to overcome the military weakness of Somalia relative to Ethiopia, its chief rival in the region. However, this military build up priority on the part of the Somali government was not what the Americans and its Western allies were willing to sponsor. Eventually, the urgency for this military project drove Somalia to the side of the Soviet Union and its Eastern allies, who were willing to help the leadership of Somalia build up a powerful army for an irredentist war.

The nature of the conflict in the Horn of Africa and the Cold War politics in the sub-region has been the subject of an academic debate. While some authors suggest a regionalist view others stress a globalist perspective. The regionalist thesis maintains that the conflict in the Horn of Africa, which is largely internal and perpetuated by historic tensions among nationalities, ethnic groups, religious differences and political dynamics, is what often invited the foreign powers to meddle in the affairs of the sub-region. The notable scholars of this tradition are Bereket Habte Selassie and Marina Ottaway.[155] By contrast, the globalist proponents contend that the prevailing conflict in the Horn of Africa is largely external and is wrought by the strategic location of the sub-region. According to this school, it is the geography and the geopolitical positioning of the countries in the Horn that attracts the foreign powers to involve in their domestic conflict. It is therefore this strategic significance, which makes the conflict in the Horn assume a global dimension. The scholars who subscribe to this globalist perspective include M.R. Sinclair and J. Bowyer Bell among others.[156] It is obvious that both debates present critical aspects of internal tensions and external geopolitical dynamics, which indeed reinforce and perpetuate the conflict in the Horn of Africa. However, the geographical location is *the* critical factor that attracted in varying degrees of superpower involvement in the Horn of Africa (see for example, Farer 1979;

---

[154] Ayoob concurs with Schraeder and notes that: " American involvement in the Horn was, however, related not so much to its interest in Africa, as to its general Cold War policy of 'containment' or pre-emption of the Soviet Union and, more specifically, to its support for Israel in the Middle East" (Ayoob 1980:164). This was because of the strategic importance to Israel of the Straits of Bal-el-Mandeb, the narrow waterway between the Horn of Africa and the Arabian Peninsula. See further, Mordechai Abir, " Red Sea Politics', Conflicts in Africa, *Adelphi Papers*, no.93 (December 1972): 25-37.

[155] For more discussion, see Bereket Habte Selassie, Conflict and Intervention in the Horn of Africa (New York: Monthly Review Press, 1980); and Marina Ottaway, Soviet and American influence in the Horn of Africa (New York: Praeger, 1982).

[156] For more information, see Sinclair (1980) and J. Bowyer Bell, The Horn of Africa: Strategic Magnet of the Seventies (New York: Crane Russak, 1973).

Sinclair 1980; Lefebvre 1991).[157] Therefore, in this study, I concur with the globalist proponents that the involvement of the superpowers in the Horn of Africa during the Cold War era is largely determined by geography and the strategic significance of the sub-region. After the Cold War ended, the strategic value of the countries in the Horn like Somalia thus plummeted. Since then there have been grave internal wars and conflicts in most of the countries in the Horn of Africa and yet no foreign power has shown an interest in meddling in it. For instance, in 1991 when the civil war broke out in the country, Somalia was left to fend for itself. This is one of the concrete examples that can be cited. In short, the external geopolitical interest in the region during the Cold War had been the overriding factor, which gave the internal conflicts a global dimension and swept the countries in the Horn into the turmoil of global politics.

6.3. The Civilian Government and the War of 1964

At the end of 1963 when the Somali Republic was only three years old, a border war between Ethiopia and Somalia broke out. There was agitation and a guerrilla uprising among the Somalis living in eastern region of Ethiopia in June 1963 after Haile Selassie rejected their demand for self-government in the Ogaden. The disturbance escalated further and when the Ethiopian army attempted to put to an end to it with a heavy hand, the Somali government felt obliged to come to the aid of its Somali kinsmen under foreign siege. Thereafter, a military confrontation between the two armed forces of Ethiopia and Somalia took place. However, although the fighting was brief it nevertheless exposed the military weakness of Somalia. During the war, the Ethiopian army, estimated at around thirty thousand troops, easily overran the Somali army, which was estimated at about four thousand fighting men. Furthermore, the Ethiopian warplanes demonstrating their superior powers, bombarded locations at the heart of the country without any risk. The defenceless situation of the new Somali Republic at the time in relation to Ethiopia and Kenya was due to the small size of its armed forces.[158] It urged the country to embark on building a large and strong army and to procure massive military armaments. For instance, while the total army of Somalia, including military, police and other security forces such as intelligence units and secret services was only 9,400, the total armed strength of Ethiopia and Kenya was 79,000 as shown in Table 1. The border war also forced the civilian government of the Republic to allocate a relatively high proportion of the budget to military purposes at the expense of economic and social development in the country.

---

[157]According to Farer, "geography is the force which has evoked varying degrees of superpower concern with the Horn. Under the terms of a mutual defense agreement signed in 1953, the United States supplied Ethiopia with over $200 million worth of military assistance, virtually one-half of all U.S. military aid to sub-Sahara Africa during the next two decades" (Farer 1979:2). For more discussion, see Tom Farer, War Clouds on the Horn of Africa: The Widening Storm (New York: Carnegie Endowment for International Peace, 1979).

[158] During the same period, the Somali government was also supporting clandestine guerrilla activity waged by ethnic Somalis living in northern Kenya, which lasted from 1963 to 1967.

Table 1

The state of the armed forces of Ethiopia, Kenya and the Somali Republic in 1965

Country	Size of armed forces	Police and other security forces	Source of external military assistance	Defence agreement with
Ethiopia	25,000 to 35,000	30,000	United States, Sweden, Norway, India, Israel, United Kingdom	Kenya
Kenya	2,500	11,500	United Kingdom	Ethiopia
Somali Republic	4,600	4,800	Italy, Soviet Union, United Arab Republic, United Kingdom	None

Source: Africa Report (January 1964), 8-18.

In 1963 the government of Somalia refused a modest offer amounting to ten million dollars in military assistance from three Western countries - USA, West Germany and Italy. The three Western countries were willing to provide this military aid to the government of Somalia in order to train an army of six thousand men which would be deployed for internal security tasks and civic action within the county. The government flatly rejected this limited military aid from the West because it was considered too little. And as Marte rightly points out:

> "But Somalia, given its irredentist agenda, was interested in more than the Western countries were ready to bargain for. Mogadishu wanted an army, and a large one, to back up its territorial claims against the neighbouring states in question" (Marte 1994:220).

During this same year, the foreign relations between Somalia and the British government dramatically worsened. The Somali government was outraged when the British government unilaterally decided to let Kenya annex the Northern Frontier District inhabited largely by Somali nationals. This then led the Somali government to break off diplomatic relations with Britain, a decision, which put to a sudden end to the budgetary aid from Britain that the country urgently needed at the time. For example, the country automatically lost substantial development aid of about £1.3 million per year from Britain, which had already been negotiated (Laitin and Samatar 1987:138). However, what worried the Somali government at the time was not the immense task of developing the extremely poor economy of the country. This issue took a secondary place to the project of the heavy investment in the military and the preparation for an irredentist war that the Somali government was deeply preoccupied with in order to unite all the ethnic Somalis in one country.[159]

Pursuing its heavy armament policy the Somali government once again made a request to the United States for huge military assistance to build up a force of twenty thousand standing

---

[159] For example, "in 1964 the average military expenditure as a percentage of GNP in Africa was 2.4; in Somalia it was 3.4. In a country with a per capita GNP of about $150, heavy military expenditures was especially hard to bear. Worse still, many avenues for economic cooperation between Somalia and its neighbours were closed off. Somalis were paying a high cost to uphold the principle of self-determination for Somalis in neighbouring countries" (Laitin and Said Samatar 1987:138-139).

troops viewed as sufficient to safeguard the sovereignty of the Republic. At the time, the Somali government was afraid of the possibility of coordinated invasions from Ethiopia and Kenya, which by then had signed a defence pact.[160] However, the United States was reluctant to sponsor the Somali desire for the establishment of a large national army and particularly for an army which would be trained for an irredentist war against its regional allies of Ethiopia and Kenya. This disappointment therefore forced the Somali government to accept a large amount of Soviet military aid estimated to be around thirty-two million dollars, which was intended to build up an army of ten thousand men and develop an air force (Africa Report, January 1964). And as expected, the decision to accept an arms offer from the Soviets opened the door for the involvement of the Soviet Union and its Eastern allies in the Somali Republic. The Soviet courtship of Somalia that had already begun was solidified when a delegation from the government in Moscow visited the country in April 1961. In contrast to the United States, the Soviet Union was not only willing to sponsor the military project of the Somali government but was also ready for an open-ended arms commitment to Somalia over a long period.[161]

For example, the Soviet Union helped the Somali government to expand its army force from a dismal number of four thousand men that was very small by absolute standards to twelve thousand well-equipped men from 1960 to 1970.[162] During that decade, a large number of Soviet military advisers arrived in Somalia in order to train the Somali army, while at the same time, a large number of high school Somali graduates went to the Soviet Union for military training. In 1969, it was suggested that more than eight hundred Somali military personnel in the national army were trained in the Soviet Union (Adam 1998:372). By the end of the decade, the heavy build-up of the military made the Somali army force the fourth largest in sub-Saharan Africa, after Nigeria, Ethiopia and Ghana, whose respective populations were much larger than that of Somalia. This means that the size of the Somali army was very large relative to the population in the country. As with respect to defence spending, Somalia ranked as number one in sub-Saharan Africa in terms of the percentage of the GNP that the country allocated to the military. For instance, in 1961 the defence spending of the Somali government amounted to 14 per cent of the national budget, which increased to 25 per cent in 1970 (Adam 1998:375).

The Soviet Union also provided the Somali government with economic aid although this was far less than the considerable military aid that the country received. The financial aid Somalia received from the Soviet Union, which began in 1962 and ended in 1977 amounted to about US$154 million (Nelson 1982:221). This financial assistance nonetheless helped to guard the anaemic Somali economy from inflation and ensured a stable foreign exchange rate that kept the Somali shilling at 6.35 to one US dollar for most of the 1960s and 1970s. Yet, despite this

---

[160] "In late 1964 Kenya's President Jomo Kenyatta and Ethiopia's Emperor Haile Selassie sgined a mutual defense agreement aimed against Somali aggression" (Nelson 1982: 233).

[161] According to Ottaway, "the decision to pursue a policy of military build-up had clearly been taken by the Somali government on its own and was not the result of outside influences. However, the Soviet Union did have a strong impact on the course of events at this time by making it possible for the Mogadishu government to implement the policy it had chosen. Somalia could not have built a large army on its own, or obtained help for such a purpose from other countries. In this respect the Soviet impact on the militarisation of Somalia was very important" (Ottaway 1982:39).

[162] The twelve thousand Somali troops consisted of ten thousand in the army, seventeen hundred and fifty in the air force, and two hundred and fifty in the navy. Furthermore, there were more than six thousand five hundred men in the police force and paramilitary corps such as the border guards (Darawishta) and the People's Militia (Victory Poineers)

close patron-client relationship, until 1969 the political influence of the Soviet Union in Somalia was negligible. Ingeniously keeping a better balance between the two power blocs and adhering publicly neither to socialism nor capitalism at the time the Somali government was able to get massive aid from both.[163] And this massive aid was what enabled the civilian government of Somalia to increase steadily its exorbitant defence expenditures as shown in Table 2. The aid also helped the government to expand the size of the army force about 500 per cent (Laitin and Said Samatar 1987:108).

Table 2

Somalia: Defence Expenditure - Pre-Revolution
(in millions of shillings)

	1967*	1968*	1969
Total Budget	272.1	281.6	301.5
Recurrent budget for defence, police and interior	98.4	106.6	117.2
% Total	36	38	38

Source: U.N. Economic Commission for Africa, Summaries of Economic Data: Somalia (Addis Ababa, compiled January 1975) pp. 10-11 and 16. See also David Laitin. 1976: 457.

* Estimates

In 1967 the last Premier of the civilian government in the country decided to moderate the uncompromisingly irredentist politics of public pursuit, which Somalia had been waging since its independence in 1960. This aggressive foreign policy approach had consumed much of the meagre resources and the energy of the nation and it could no longer be sustained either materially or politically. Therefore, a decision had to be made which could temper the current foreign policy relations of Somalia. As a result, Premier Mohamed Haji Ibrahim Egal initiated a relaxed foreign policy and a policy of détente with Ethiopia, Kenya and the French in Djibouti. What Egal wanted was to shift the attention of the government from the irredentist politics of Pan- Somali unity to the immense social and economic problems in the Republic.[164] During that period, the impact of the Suez Canal closure in June 1967 had devastating consequences on the poor economy of the Somali Republic, which worsened further the economic situation in the country. For instance, the foreign-exchange earnings from bananas and livestock, the two largest national export products, plummeted by sixty percent in the first year after the closure of the Suez Canal (See for example, Bell 1973; Marte 1994; Payton 1980).

However, the normalisation of the foreign policy, which led to the temporary abandonment of the irredentist politics of Pan-Somali pursuit and the peace treaty that Premier Egal signed

---

[163] To demonstrate the political neutrality of the Somali government with respect to the ideological rivalry between the two power blocs in November 1963 the Prime Minister of the Republic, Shermarke, visited the United States where he was welcomed at the White House by President Kennedy.

[164] This is how Mohamed Osman Omar described the situation in the country: "how could a government begin to think of liberating a territory when it could not provide food and proper medical treatment to the people it was already responsible for?" (Omar 1992:65).

with the neighbouring countries, was reacted to by most of the public with condemnation.[165] After all, since independence, the political leadership of Somalia had pursued the irredentist politics as a strategy for domestic social cohesion and also fiercely propagated it as the most important national goal. It was in this context therefore that many ordinary Somalis viewed the friendly foreign policy of the government of Egal towards the neighbouring states to be a betrayal of the Pan-Somali unity.[166] All over the country, there was widespread discontent against the détente policy of Egal and in the capital demonstrations were organised. There were also protests among members in the parliament. Yet, "although this new policy initially aroused hostility at home, with the financial resources at his disposal the new Premier was soon able to secure a favourable balance of cautious support" (Lewis 1972:396).[167]

But not every section of the society was willing to toe the line. The opponents whose view represented much of the political attitude of the public and also the military were harshly critical of the policy of détente. The military in particular that had been trained and armed for years for an irredentist war, in order to liberate all Somali-inhabited areas were badly disillusioned.[168] Thus, both the public and the military saw the Egal policy of rapprochement to be tantamount to selling out the Somali territories and the Somali people to Ethiopia and Kenya. Furthermore, domestically the public was dissatisfied with the rampant corruption, nepotism and the relentless private pursuit that largely preoccupied the elected members in the Egal government. Eventually, the displeasure with the foreign policy of Premier Egal and the sudden assassination of the President of the Republic, Abdirashiid Ali Sharmarke on 15 October 1969, precipitated the collapse of the civilian regime. Consequently, this paved the way for the military to topple the civilian government and take over the political power in the country on 21 October 1969.[169]

---

[165] " ... the most important political issue in post-independence Somali politics was the unification of all areas populated by Somalis into one country –a concept identified as pan-Somalism. It was presumed that this issue dominated popular opinion and that any government would fall if it did not demonstrate a militant attitude toward neighbouring countries that were seen as occupying Somali territory" (Nelson 1982:38).

[166] According to Marte, "the retreat from the confrontational line in the foreign policy realm also removed the aspect of having to face a common external enemy, which had been an effective unifying factor among the Somalis. When this common external threat diminished, internal divisions and clan cleavages began to resurface, exacerbating the already fragile political stability" (Marte 1994:223).

[167] For further information, see I.M. Lewis, " The Politics of the 1969 Somali Coup" *The Journal of Modern African Studies*, 10, 3 (1972): 383-408.

[168] Major-General Abdullahi Ali Omar, *Interview*, November 12, 1998, London.

[169] As Abdi put it " one of the reasons why Minister Mohamed Ibrahim Egal's government was brought down in 1969 had to do with the aggressive and often high-handed policy of 'détente' or 'entente' with Ethiopia and Kenya over the disputed territories. This policy brought Somalia no major benefits and it dashed the hopes of the Somalis living in the lost lands" (Abdi 1982:40). For a wider discussion of the politics of the military coup in Somalia in 1969, see I.M. Lewis " The Politics of the 1969 Somali Coup", *The Journal of Modern African Studies*, vol.10, no.3 (1972): 383-408.

6.4.   The Military Regime and Militarisation[170] of the State

The military takeover of the state power not only resuscitated the politics of the Pan-Somali unity or what Adam called a "Somali irredentist nationalism"[171] but also led to an aggressive military build-up in the country. To put it differently, the project of a Somali-wide public pursuit has been the foremost overriding factor which urged the militarisation of the state. Immediately after the coup, the new military regime abandoned the foreign policy stance of former civilian governments that was based on neutrality vis-à-vis the East-West power politics. Instead, the military government embarked on a different foreign policy, which began to tilt towards the Soviet Union and the Eastern bloc. This prompt change of the foreign policy in the country is what led Payton to suggest the tactic complicity of the Soviet Union behind the military coup in Somalia. In 1969 as Payton argued there was a conjuncture of events and changes which were global, regional and local as well as "'a coincidence of interests' between the Somali Army Commander [Siad Barre] and Soviet strategic planners [that] resulted in the military coup" (Payton 1980:493).

At the time of the coup, hundreds of Soviet military advisers were present in Somalia. Some of these military advisers were in Somalia for close to a decade and the intelligence apparatus they set up there during those years must have been privy to the preparations of the coup d'etat in the country.[172] A U.S. diplomat Raymond L. Thurston who served as ambassador to Somalia from 1965 to 1968, concurs somewhat with the guesswork of Payton. And this was how ambassador Thurston put it:

> "was the seizure of power by the Somali army a purely internal affairs? Bearing in mind that its cadres had been trained in the Soviet Union and that a thousand or more Soviet advisers were intermingled with it down to the small-unit level, this should be dismissed as a cold warrior's question" (Thurston 1978:16).

Yet both Marte and Ottaway disagree with the idea of complicity of the Soviet military intelligentsia behind the coup. Marte contends that despite the presence of Soviet military advisers in the country, there is no concrete evidence which implicates the Russians in the coup.[173] While according to Ottaway,

---

[170] In this study, militarisation is understood as a process whereby the expansion of the military establishment resulted in high and increased levels of military expenditure, army size and arms imports which is disproportionate to the total population of a nation and the level of its economic development. For a detailed discussion on this issue, see, The Military and Militarism in Africa, (eds.) Eboe Hutchful and Abdoulaye Bathily (Dakar: Codesria Book Series, 1998)

[171] For more discussion, see Hussein M. Adam "Somalia: Personal Rule, Military Rule and Militarism ",in The Military and Militarism in Africa, (Dakar: Codesria Book Series, 1998).

[172] According to Crozier, " the Soviet-Somali military relationship began in 1961 within about 18 months of Somalia gaining its independence. As in Egypt and other countries, the Russians gained their first foothold through Western reluctance to supply arms to a new State. Again, as in other countries, Soviet military aid enabled the Somali armed forces to enhance their power and prestige at the expense of the politicians" (Crozier 1975:4). For more insights, see Brian Crozier, "The Soviet Presence in Somalia", in *Conflict Studies*, no 54, (London: February 1975).

[173] See further Fred Marte, Political Cycles in International Relations: The Cold War and Africa 1945-1990 (Amsterdam: VU University Press, 1994).

"The impact of Soviet aid in training the army was major, but this should not be confused with influence. Not only is there no evidence that the Soviet Union influenced the policies of the Somali government, but there is no evidence either that it influenced the decision of Siad Barre and the other rebel officers to carry out a military coup d'etat. The coup, to be sure, benefited the Soviet Union in the long run" (Ottaway 1982:43).

Nonetheless, after the coup, the influence of the Soviets in the country certainly increased. More symbolically, the military regime changed the name of the Somali Republic to Somali Democratic Republic (SDR). Evidently, this new name further marked the leaning of the new regime to the left and indicated a cue or a similarity to that of the people's democracies of Eastern Europe (Nelson 1982). Moreover, the military government, after taking over the state power proclaimed that 'scientific socialism' would be the guiding principle of social orientation and of the nation's political and economic development. Furthermore, after the military coup, there was a clear sign of increased Soviet presence in the country. Crozier estimated the Russians in Somalia in the early 1970s to be about 3,600 in number (minus family dependants), of whom 1,200 to 1,400 were military personnel (Crozier 1975:4), while in the mid-1970s when the relationship between Somalia and the Soviet Union was at its height, the Russian military and civilian advisers in the country had reached between 5,000 and 6,000 in number (Ayoob 1980:145). More markedly, in the early 1970s, Soviet fleet visits became routine and frequent in Somalia.[174] According to Crozier,

"The Soviet presence in Somalia must be considered against the expected re-opening of the Suez Canal to shipping in 1975 and the steady build-up of a Russian Indian Ocean fleet since Britain's decision in 1976 to withdraw its forces east of Suez. .... In the Indian Ocean, and elsewhere, a strong Soviet fleet is an instrument of moral and material support for groups in power or seeking power and willing to work with the Russians; and of inhibition and discouragement for the independent minded. In this order of things, the new Soviet foothold in Somalia must be viewed in Moscow as a major strategic gain" (Crozier 1975:16-17).

It was during this period that high level visits between Mogadishu and Moscow took place. In November 1971, Siad Barre visited Moscow where he requested more military and economic aid. In return, Soviet Minister of Defense A.A. Grechko visited Somalia in February 1972, where he signed an agreement to improve the airstrip and the port facilities at Berbera. It was after this visit of Grechko that the real Soviet build-up of the Somali army and the transfer of sophisticated war material to Somalia actually began. On the diplomatic front, the close relationship between the military regime of the Somali Democratic Republic and the Soviet Union was further consolidated. The Soviet Union became the most important ally of the military regime in Somalia.[175] In July 1974, this close alliance finally culminated in a special relationship: the twenty years' Treaty of Friendship and Co-operation between Somalia and

---

[174] As Bell notes, "between 1970 and 1971 Soviet naval vessels made seven visits to the ports of the Persian Gulf, but twice as many to Berbera in the Somali Democratic Republic" (Bell 1975:402).

[175] The military authority granted this special alliance with the Soviets believing this Somali proverb which says that : "either be a mountain or have a mountain to lean on". This is in fact how the military regime of Somalia calculated its close relations with the Soviet Union vis-á- vis the United States who was the staunch ally of its principal adversaries in the region, Ethiopia and Kenya.

114

the Soviet Union.[176] At that time, Somalia was the first sub-Saharan country to conclude such a high-level friendship treaty with the Soviet Union. Under the treaty, the Soviets would acquire base facilities at the strategic port of Berbera, located at the littoral of the Red Sea.[177] In addition to this, the Soviets would also get full base rights and full access to all the airfields in the country that could enable the Russians to stage periodic naval reconnaissance flights over the Indian Ocean. In return, the Soviet Union guaranteed to train and arm generously the military personnel of the nation over the next ten years.

Consequently, with the help of the Russian military trainers and advisers, the Somali national army was almost doubled, from twelve thousand to twenty three thousand standing troops within a very short time from 1970 to 1975. During that same period, the Soviets poured large quantities of sophisticated weapons into the country. For example, according to International Institute for Strategic Studies (IISS) estimates, the Russians supplied to the Somali army about 250 medium tanks of which 150 were somewhat old T-34 and 100 were modern T-54/55 tanks. Furthermore, the Russians also equipped the Somali army with more than 50 Soviet-made MiG fighter aircraft.[178] This in fact made both the Somali tank force and its combat airforce the largest in the continent of Africa during that period.[179] The military regime of Somalia also diverted a great deal of the financial aid it received, which was a relatively high proportion of its budget, to arms deliveries and military purposes. For instance, between 1969 and 1978, the government expenditure on military purposes was twice that of education and health care, as shown in Table 3.

---

[176] This is how Nikolai Podgorny, President of the Presidium of the USSR Supreme Soviet, who signed the treaty in Mogadishu, 11 July 1974 formulated the special relationship: " The friendship and co-operation treaty signed today between the Soviet Union and the Somali Democratic Republic... has been prepared by the entire course of the development of relations between the Soviet Union and Somalia. In 14 years our States have travelled a great path... to the present broad, equal and mutually advantageous co-operation, which ... covers virtually all spheres of life..." (Crozier 1975:2).

[177] Subsequently, the port of Berbera became the largest Soviet base outside the Warsaw Pact states (Spencer 1978). For a more discussion, see John H. Spencer, "A Reassessment of Ethiopian-Somali conflict", *Horn of Africa* (July-September 1980): 23-30.

[178] For a more detailed account, see IISS, The Military Balance 1976-77 (London, 1977): 44

[179] According to Crozier, " to place the military development in perspective it should be remembered that only ten years ago Somalia had an army of no more than 4,000 poorly equipped men, an even smaller navy than today, and no air force at all. The military equipment provided is increasingly sophisticated and can neither be used nor maintained without Russian help and spare parts" (Crozier 1975:8).

Table 3

Somalia: Percentages of GDP Allocated for Military, Health and Education, % of GDP
($ constant, 1977)

Year	Military	Health	Education
1969	5.1	1.9	1.7
1970	5.9	1.8	1.8
1971	5.7	1.5	1.7
1972	6.2	1.8	2.4
1973	6.3	---	2.6
1974	7.5	2.0	3.5
1975	6.6	1.9	4.2
1976	6.5	1.8	4.6
1977	7.3	2.2	5.4
1978	13.8*	2.0	5.7

* Wartime figures.

Source: US Arms Control and Disarmament Agency, World Military Expenditures and Arms Transfers. 1969-1978. 1978: 66-109. See Also Ahmed Samatar. 1988: 114.

Similarly, the military expenditure of the Somali government budget rose about 10 percent per year between 1963-1973. However, this 10 percent figure per year was too high for a domestic gross national product (GNP) which grew pathetically by a little less than 3 percent annually. According to Nelson, the overall expenditure of the Somali armed forces was estimated to have amounted per year to about 27 percent of total government recurrent budget from 1972 to 1977, 37.1 percent in 1978 and 39 percent in 1979 (Nelson 1982).[180]

Indeed, the consequences of this enormous military expenditure had a further debilitating effect on the poor economy of the country and the social welfare of the nation.[181] More devastating, during the decade of 1970, the total arms deliveries that the military regime purchased, was estimated to have amounted to $960 million of the government budget, which increased to about 16 percent of GDP of the country per year (Mubarak 1996:12). In terms of the size, the military government built up a substantial national armed force that by 1976 expanded to thirty thousand military personnel, which was very high relative to the population in the country. Moreover, this huge size of the Somali armed forces that was estimated to be around one percent of the population was even higher than that of any other nation in sub-Saharan Africa (Nelson 1982 and Ricciuti 1995). Nonetheless, the military regime with the generous help of its Soviet patron continued to increase the size of the army force. On the eve of the Ethiopia-Somali war over Ogaden in 1977, the number of the Somali military personnel had grown to a 37,000-man force, which was a well-equipped force that could stand up to any

---

[180] For more discussion and a statistical account, see Harold D. Nelson (ed.) Somalia: A Country Study (Washington DC, Foreign Area Studies, American University, 1982).

[181] As Khapoya writes, " military build-ups normally do not contribute to the wellbeing of the people, they bleed the countries, they retard economic development, they tempt increased use of violence against domestic populations, and they make regional armed conflict not only more likely but also more bloody and more deadly, if it occurs" (Khapoya 1982:30).

army in the region.[182] Even after the war when the army was terribly defeated and the Soviets abandoned Somalia, the military government continued further in building up the army force, which expanded to 120,000 in 1983, and consumed more than a fifth of the national budget (Geshekter 1997 and Ricciuti 1995).[183] This staggering Somali army, which became the second largest military force in the continent of Africa, was too big in a nation of seven to eight million people.[184] In a nutshell, this is how the military government preparation of the irredentist adventure has been the single determinant which increased the levels of military expenditure, army size and arms imports in the country. It is remarkable to note that the military government in Somalia could not afford to militarise the state staggeringly without generous aid by the Cold War protagonists at one time or another. Eventually, this military might prompted the military regime to wage a war with Ethiopia over the Ogaden region in 1977-1978. In the end, the military regime of Somalia lost the war and most of its armaments were destroyed during the battle.[185]

6.5. Conclusion

Continuing the discussion in chapter four, I considered in this chapter the predicament of the colonial legacy that was bequeathed to the Somali political elite after independence in 1960. The colonial powers dismembered the country and the Somali people into different imperial frontiers in the late 19th century and that gravely impaired the collective destiny and cultural unity of the Somali society. Afterwards, the resolution of this inherited colonial problem was the primarily political preoccupation of the post-colonial Somali political leaders. It was also this dilemma that set the leadership on the course of embarking a very dangerous policy of irredentist adventure. The prevailing Cold War politics during the post-colonial era made it possible for the Somali governments to build up and sustain a well equipped and very large army force, which militarised the state. In hindsight, it was possible that the circumstances of contemporary Somalia would have been different if the Cold War global tensions had not coincided with the birth of the Somali state. According to Marte,

> "The Cold War has strongly interfered with the process of decolonisation in the region and has, to a large extent, redirected the focus of the governments from a developmental to a strictly military orientation, leading to economic stagnation, internal political imbalances between the military and civilians, and civil and regional wars" (Marte 1994:267).

---

[182] According to Marte, " by the mid-1970s, there were from one thousand to four thousand Soviet military specialists attached to the Somali army, while between one thousand and two thousand four hundred Somali military men were sent to the Soviet Union for military training. With the help of the Soviet Union, the Somalis managed to implement a large-scale military build-up, providing it with both a quantitative and qualitative military edge over its neighbors, Ethiopia and Kenya (Marte 1994:228).

[183] After the Soviet Union exited from Somalia, the United States came as a superpower patron and provided Somalia with about US $100 million of both economic and military aid from 1980 to 1988 (Adam 1998:389). For further discussion, see Ken Menkhaus, "US Foreign Assistance to Somalia: Phoenix from the Ashes?" *Middle East Policy* 5, no.2 (Janauary 1997): 126.

[184] The Somali army was indeed highly disproportionate in that it even surpassed the army of Nigeria, a nation of about 100 million people.

[185] For more information on this issue, see Colin Legum and Bill Lee, The Horn of Africa in Continuing Crisis, (New York: Africana Publishing Company, 1979).

It is nonetheless a truism to say that while the dramatic legacy of colonialism has given rise to the politics of Somali-wide public pursuit and irredentist misadventure, the deleterious overlay of the subsequent Cold War politics made the militarisation of the state possible. Thus, in this respect, both colonialism and the Cold War imperatives have gravely victimised the Somali people.[186] For instance, since 1970s, the impact of the military build-up and the militarisation of the state in Somalia had been dramatic as it diverted the meagre national resources from social and economic development issues to very expensive military purposes.[187] However, the bulk of the military expenditure did not provide benefits to the civilian population in terms of jobs or any other windfalls as it was partly used as lavish salaries for the defence personnel and was partly spent on importing arms from abroad.[188] Therefore, as I demonstrated in chapter 5 while the continuity of the material deprivation led the political elite to siphon off the scarce national resources resulting in the bankruptcy of the state, the irredentist adventure of the tendency towards public pursuit on the other hand militarised the state. In a nutshell, the continuity of the material deprivation from the pre-colonial era and the change of the territorial integrity of the country wrought about by colonialism during the colonial period have in concert deleteriously affected the stability of the post-colonial state in Somalia. In the following chapter, I will explain how the pitfalls of the politics of private and public pursuit eventually led to the collapse of the state in 1991.

---

[186] The Somalis also become victims, because of the ineptitude and the ignobility of the domestic political leadership.
General Mohamed Abshir Muse, *Interview*, July 14,1997, Addis Ababa.

[187] For a general discussion of the impact of military expenditure on the economy in Sub-saharan Africa, see Nadir A.L. Mohammed, "Trends, Determinants and the Economic Effects of Military Expenditure in Sub-Saharan Africa", The Military and Militarism in Africa, (eds.,) Eboe Hutchful and Abdoulaye Bathily, (Dakar: Codesria Book Series, 1998).

[188] " Personnel payments of the Ministry of Defence constituted on average 80 per cent of the defence budget. This part of the budget averaged 1.5 million Somali shillings during the early 1960s. It remained relatively stagnant until the end of the 1970s, thereafter rising to 3.2 billion shillings in 1982/3 and 5.1 billion in 1986/7" (Adam 1998:376).

Chapter Seven

The Pitfalls of the Politics of Private and Public Pursuits and the Collapse of the State (1980-1991)

7.1. Introduction

The chapter deals with the pitfalls of the politics of private and public pursuit that have been the marked feature of the Somali political life since Somalia achieved statehood in 1960. In fact, as I discussed in the previous two chapters, while the tendency towards private pursuit resulted in the bankruptcy of the state, that of public pursuit led to militarism. In this respect, although both pursuits represent contradictory political tendencies in a complex whole of historical processes that have been shaping the Somali society in much of its history, their current combined onslaughts have devastating effects both on the society and on the viability of the state. For example, during the 1980s, the majority of the urban inhabitant Somali population experienced the pitfalls of private pursuit as worsened living conditions, acute deprivation, high inflation and an increased financial burden on individual households. As the government revenue was privately appropriated on a grand scale, there were few national resources to be shared. Furthermore, the inflation that the dwindling national economy suffered from badly affected the purchasing power of the people and made the incomes of the government employees negligible. As a result, most of the urban households had problems in meeting their basic needs because of the acute financial burden. This, then, forced a large section of the society to withdraw from the official economy of the state. Similarly, during that same period, the regime and the state were also grappling with tremendous internal power crises because of the failure of decades of irredentist adventure and the pitfalls of that externally driven public pursuit. These challenges appeared as that of increased domestic power struggles, extreme militarisation of the state institutions, which was coupled with the growth of generalised violence, large refugee population, emergence of organised dissidence and apparent detachment of some regions in the country.

7.2. Downward Spiral of the Economy

The private embezzlement of the limited national resources on a grand scale not only bankrupted the state (see chapter 5) but also resulted in extreme impoverishment of the majority of the urban population. The period from 1980 to 1990 was the decade of rapid economic deterioration in Somalia as most people could not make both ends meet and the struggle for survival had become acute. In this respect, both the society and state were suffering from an abject material poverty.

After the Ogaden war when the Russians abandoned Somalia, the government lost its important financial patron and the economy stagnated. As I explained in chapter five, due to the meagre pastoral production in the country, the economic development of Somalia beyond subsistence level was always dependent on foreign aid. As expected, after the economic aid from the Soviet Union was cut off, the government of Somalia started looking for another foreign patron. Americans with some hesitance agreed to replace the Russians and provided

Somalia with about US$100 million of aid per year during the 1980s. Consequently, Somalia became one of the four countries in Africa, which received the most aid from the United States.[189] However, this American financial assistance was a small drop compared with the massive military, technical and economic aid that the Somali government had been accustomed to receiving from the Soviet Union. Moreover, the decade of 1980 was also the decade of the IMF structural adjustment programme and the Somali government had to implement the economic policy instructions of this institute. The government was instructed to reduce social spending, cut the employment in the public sector and devaluate the Somali shilling. The deregulation of the economy as the IMF reform policy demanded, helped the growth of an illicit trade and an informal economy in Somalia (Miller 1981). For example, the devaluation of the shilling by more than 90 percent had triggered high inflation, which resulted in the decline of purchasing power.[190] This, then, created a situation in which the monthly government wages could cover not more than three days of family expenses. This dire need forced most of the civil servants to show up at their offices every morning for only an hour and then disappear in search for an additional livelihood.[191] Gradually, this survival strategy became a widespread practice as it put the daily running of the government on hold well before the state collapsed. Finally, when the state fell apart, the bureaucratic administration existed only in name. According to Miller, the general poverty situation was also what stimulated the informal economy, which in turn encouraged widespread corruption and illegal trade in the country. For instance, as the formal economy gradually shrank and the banking system collapsed a large section of society disengaged from the official economy and resorted to elicit economy for livelihood (Miller 1981: 3-19).

Furthermore, during the early 1980s when the economy was in a downward slide, the population in Somalia was experiencing an accelerated upward growth.[192] In 1982, the population of Somalia had reached 4 million, with an alarming growth rate of about 3.1 percent per year.[193] This means that more and more people had to compete for the dwindling economic assets in the country, and that increased the tensions among the various interest groups. During that period, because of the dire poverty in the country, many Somalis migrated to the rich Gulf countries for better material well-being. In 1980, Somalis working abroad

---

[189] For this issue, see further, Nicolas van de Walle, " The Politics of Aid Effectiveness", in S. Ellis (edited), Africa Now: People, Policies and Institutions, (London: Heinmann 1996). The others countries were Kenya, Liberia and Zaire.

[190] According to David Laitin, " the consumer Price Index has averaged a 65 percent rise over the past seven years and the rate is increasing. For urban based families, getting sugar, meat, rice, charcoal, and other necessities has become a nightmarish burden" (Laitin 1982:60). See further David Laitin, "The political Crisis in Somalia", Horn of Africa, 5, no.2 (1982): 60-64.

[191] According to Omar, "for the common people in Somalia by the late eighties, the struggle for survival had become acute. A large majority of civil servants, whose average income was less than US$5.00 a month, were forced to seek additional private work to cope with the burden imposed by growing inflation. Absenteeism in Government offices increased even further. The system was on the verge of collapse" (Omar 1992:187).

[192] Two factors have helped to accelerate the growth of the population in Somalia. One was the availability of modern medicines, which reduced the death rate at birth and the other was the traditional tendency of the Somalis to have more children in order to offset the hazards of the natural climate.

[193] According to I.M. Lewis, " In a harsh environment with a high infant mortality rate and climate uncertainties, the Somalis recognise that, as with their livestock husbandry, they overproduce their human population to allow for the effects of natural hazards. Since at all levels in the population, fighting strength and political muscle are a matter of force of numbers, optimum size is the constant goal. These attitudes, widely prevalent in the population, are not conducive to birth control schemes (Lewis 1993:13).

were estimated to number around 250,000 individuals (Bradbury 1997:10). Unfortunately for the country, most of the migrated Somalis were those with skills and managerial personnel. The consequence was an acute drain on the human resources badly needed in the development of the economy.[194]

Other factors which contributed to the plummeting of the economy in Somalia in the 1980s were the collapse of the small industrial sector which constituted 20 percent of total exports, the renewed serious drought of 1979 to 1980 and the imposition of a ban on Somali livestock by Saudi Arabia after allegations that rinderpest had been detected in the Somali livestock, making them unsafe to eat (Mubarak 1996:28). Particularly banning the importation of the Somali livestock by the government of Saudi Arabia cut off by far the largest source of export earnings of Somalia.[195] This then resulted in a large budget deficit whereby arrears on debt service started to accumulate reaching up to $1billion in 1985.[196] Already, the per capita income in Somalia has been abysmally low.[197] For example, between 1979 and 1988, the real per capita GDP had decreased at 19.4 percent.[198] In 1978, the World Bank estimates, the annual income of US$130 per person ranked Somalia eighth among the world's least developed countries.

The economic and financial crisis in the 1980s resulted in the emergence of parallel economies in Somalia. While one was formal and regulated by the state, the other was informal and controlled by the businessmen in the market. The formal economy served the interest of the state class or a "state clan"[199] as Charles Geshekter preferred to call it and those interest groups allied with them. In the 1980s, the prime source of revenue to the formal economy of Somalia was largely the foreign assistance which the government annually received. During that period, Somalia received between US$300 and US$ 400 million annually of gross Official Development Assistance or about US$55 to 70 per capita.[200] And

---

[194] "The geographic location of the country makes it economically useful to oil-rich neighbors as a cheap manpower pool. Somalia's proximity to the nouveaux riches of the oil world is both blessing and curse: Somalia's main export, cattle, camels, sheep, and goats, have a ready market in the oil states, but these states entice much of the needed talent away from the homeland" (Miller 1981:4).

[195] "The Saudi Arabian market had previously absorbed more than 90% of Somalia's livestock exports. As a consequence of the ban, Somalia's total export earnings (expressed in 1980 US$) declined by 40% in 1983 and 44% in 1984, and remained low until the Saudi ban was lifted in 1989" (Mubarak 1996:28).

[196] In 1990 the foreign debt Somalia owed amounted to US$2 billion, while the inflation was estimated to have reached 600 per cent a year (Bradbury 1997). For more discussion, see Mark Bradbury, Somaliland (CIIR Country Report, 1997).

[197]Norman Miller referred to a report published by the Overseas Development Council (ODC) in London, which compared the depth of poverty with Ethiopia, Kenya, Somalia, Sudan, Tanzania, Uganda Burundi, and Rwanda. According to the report "Somalia had the *lowest* GNP, the *lowest* physical quality of life index, the *lowest* life expectancy (41 years), the *highest* infant mortality per 1,000 live births (177), the *lowest* literacy (5%), the *lowest* per capita public education expenditures ($2), and the *highest* per capita military expenditure ($7)" (Miller 1981:5). See further the article of Norman N. Miller, "The Other Somalia", *Horn of Africa*, vol. 5, no., 3 (1981): 3-19.

[198] For a further discussion, see Somalia: Country Presentation 1990 (UNCLDC II/CP. 4): 1-27.

[199] An excellent historical analysis of this issue, see Charles Geshekter, " The Death of Somalia in Historical Perspective", Mending Rips in the Sky: Options for Somali Communities in the 21st Century, (eds) Adam and Ford, (Asmara: The Red Sea Press, 1997).

despite the shaky power position of the ruling state class the availability of this foreign assistance enabled it to use the public funds for patronage purposes in order to remain in power.[201] The foreign assistance to Somalia was partly military and partly economic aid. However in 1988 the military aid to Somalia was suspended. This happened when the poor human rights record of the regime was published in the international press, resulting from the domestic political violence that the government had been perpetuating against the civilian population in the country.[202] In 1989 when the Cold War politics ended, the foreign economic aid for Somalia too was stopped. Consequently, the abrupt end of the external aid gravely diminished the wealth of the formal economy in the country.

By contrast, the largely informal remittances from abroad, a parallel economy, which was estimated to average between US $50 to 70 per capita annually in the 1980s was becoming a very important source of accumulation (Document of the World Bank 1989:2). This informal economy partly boosted by the huge wages of the Somalis working in the Gulf countries who transferred some of the earnings to their families in Somalia and partly by illicit trade practices, was growing while the formal economy was decreasing. As Mubarak writes, "Labor migration during the oil boom in the Gulf of Arabia states in the late 1970s and early 1980s produced remittances that equalled or exceeded merchandise export earnings. Most of the remittances, channelled through the black market, complemented private consumption and savings. Private investments were usually small and targeted projects with quick turnover because of the unpredictability of macroeconomic and political conditions" (Mubarak 1996:58). With respect to the illegal trade practices, smuggling of consumer goods, exchange of foreign currencies on the black market, poaching and trade in wildlife products and other hidden economic activities in the retail trade, construction, manufacturing, transportation and all types of services have developed into a booming business. [203] The big profits of this informal economy considerably enriched the business class although some of the poor sections of the society who had no access to the formal economy controlled by the state had also marginally benefited (Miller 1981). Gradually, as time passed by, the ever-widening wealth of the informal economy became attractive to the political elite whose fortune of accumulation declined as the formal economy drastically dwindled (Bradbury 1997). Consequently, since the late 1980s, the real struggle between the urbanised economic and political elite in Somalia was over the access and appropriation of the wealth both in the formal and informal economy. This struggle therefore confirms the continuity of the tendency

---

[200] See further Report and Recommendation of the President of the International Development Association to the Somali Democratic Republic, Document of the World Bank, May 2, 1989 (Report No. P-4995-S0).

[201] According to Michael Maren, " for ten years before the 1992 famine, Somalia was the largest recipient of aid in sub-Saharan Africa, in some years the third largest in the world behind perennial leaders Egypt and Israel. But most of Somalia's 6 million people never saw a penny. Much of what wasn't filtered out to pay the expenses of the relief agency was lost in the corrupt maze of the Somali government's nepotistic bureaucracy.... Aid money went to Somali bureaucrats whose primary skill was in earning money by dealing with foreign charities. And when money did drip down to the people it was used in ways designed by a government desperately trying to cling to its diminishing power" (Maren 1997:24). For a lucid historical account of the detrimental effects of foreign aid and international charity on Somalia, see Michael Maren, The Road to Hell: The Ravaging Effects of Foreign Aid and International Charity, (New York: The Free Press, 1997).

[202] For more information, see Africa Watch, Somalia: A Government at War with its Own People: Testimony about the Killings and the Conflict in the North (London: Africa Watch, 1990).

[203] "The informal economy is composed of activities mainly carried out by extensive use of family labour of not more than a few persons. It could be an unlawful activity in the sense that it circumvents state regulations such as registration, tax payments, restrictions on trading foreign exchange, snuggling of foreign goods, etc" (Mubarak 1996:128).

towards private pursuit that has prevailed over public issues since the late 1970s as this study attempts to demonstrate.[204]

7.3. Massive Influx of Refugees

In the 1980s, Somalia also had to grapple with the daunting task of hosting a massive influx of refugees, which was a crippling burden on the impoverished economy and exacerbated the crisis of the state. The refugee problem in Somalia emerged as the consequence of the failure of the irredentist politics of public pursuit that the government had been waging since 1960s. To put it more simply, the defeat of Somalia by Ethiopia over the Ogaden was what generated the influx of a substantial number of refugees to the country, making Somalia host to the largest refugee population in Africa at the time. As Ali Galaydh explains, "the cost of the war with Ethiopia was incalculable. Apart from the death of tens of thousands of combatants, the population of the contested area suffered untold death and destruction of property. Hundreds of thousands were forced to flee to the Republic and were to have eventually a great economic, political and social impact on the country" (Galaydh 1990:18). For instance, in 1981 the number of refugees in Somalia was estimated to be around 1.5 million which amounted to about 40 per cent of population in Somalia (Simons 1995:52). Other studies estimated the number of the refugees in the country to be around one-quarter of the entire population of Somalia.[205]

The refugee crisis in Somalia has a historical antecedent. Since 1950 when the British colonial administration withdrew and returned the disputed Ogaden region to Ethiopia, there had been a more or less regular influx of refugees from the area into Somalia. The main reason was the recurring political tension between the two neighbouring countries, which time and again led to border skirmishes between their respective armed forces. In the past the border refugees seeking asylum in Somalia were small in number and the international assistance that the government needed to cater for them was very limited. However, after the war in 1977-78 when the Somali military force was defeated in the Ogaden region by the Ethiopian army with the help of the Soviet and Cuban troops, a large number of refugees who fled the fighting sought refuge in Somalia. Most of the refugees were ethnic Somalis, but there were also many Oromo, an ethnic group which primarily inhabit eastern Ethiopia. The refugees entered Somalia in hordes and the government was not able to cope with the influx, which severely tested the capacity of the country. The refugee problem became a heavy burden and a serious domestic concern because of the limited financial and national resources in the country. In response, the government then declared a state of emergency in order to deal with the refugee problem. According to the official government estimation, more than one million refugees had entered the country of whom about 475 000 were in camps in late December 1979.[206] The UN Inter-Agency mission that afterwards visited the refugee camps also endorsed the estimate of the government. The report of the mission noted that:

---

[204] For a good discussion of this spoils politics since the late 1970s, see Lee V. Cassanelli, " Explaining the Somali Crisis", in Catherine Besteman and Lee V. Cassanelli (eds.) The Struggle for Land in Southern Somalia: The War Behind the War (London: Westiew Press, 1996).

[205] For further information, see the report of the UN Inter-Agency mission that visited Somalia in December 1979.

[206] Somali Democratic Republic, A Request for Assistance from the Government of the Somali Democratic Republic for the Refugees, (Mogadishu, October 1979).

"the mission visited seven of the refugee camps and held discussions with people who had visited the remainder. On the basis of these visits, and the information provided to the mission from government and other sources, the mission concluded that the Government's estimate of the number of refugees in the camps - 475 000 - was broadly correct" (UN Inter-Agency Mission to Somalia, 1979:11).

Table I illustrates the monthly influx of refugees in camps in Somalia during 1979.

Table I. Monthly Influx of Refugees in Camps in Somalia in 1979

Month	Influx	Total number of refugees
January	--	100,000
February	14,000	114,000
March	12,000	126,000
April	44,000	170,000
May	25,000	195,000
June	35,000	230,000
July	40,000	270,000
Augustus	40,000	310,000
September	21,000	331,000
October	21,000	352,000
November	39,000	391,000
December	84,000	475,000

Source: Adapted from Göran Menader, Refugees in Somalia (1980:20)

This means that at the time Somalia had the highest number of refugees in camps as compared to any other country in Africa.[207] Furthermore, the official government report estimated the refugees outside the camps to be around 650 000 in number. However, those unregistered "invisible refugees" who were living with relatives and scattered all over the country had swelled the population of some towns such as Hargeisa (Lewis 1988). Many of those "invisible refugees" had erected sprawling shelters around the outskirts of those towns. All in all the massive refugee influx into Somalia was alarming and the government appealed for help to the United Nations High Commissioner for Refugees (UNCHR) in September 1979, but UNCHR did not formally processes requests for international aid until March 1980 (Laitin and Samatar1987). The reason why the UNCHR delayed to responding to the appeal of the Somali government might be explained because of the refugee crisis in South East Asia, which the mass media was focusing on during this period.

Eventually, the Somali government received assistance from international agencies, which was budgeted on a number of 650,000 refugees. To quote a concrete figure, the Somali government received financial assistance from inter-governmental organisations,

---

[207] For further discussion, see Göran Melander, "Refugees in Somalia", Research Report No. 56 (Scandinavian Institute of African Studies, Uppsala, 1980): 1-49.

124

governmental and non-governmental agencies, which amounted to US $16 million (Melander 1980:27). However, due to the general poverty of the population in the country, this refugee aid had become a major economic source for private pursuit. Almost everyone from the top downwards who had access to it, attempted to siphon off the refugee relief economy without qualms. This wild chase for individual private pursuit then created all sources of rampant corruption, which contributed to the misuse and even the outright theft of food and medical supplies intended for refugees in the camps (Nelson 1982). Mark Bradbury writes, "as the government and many thousands of Somalis became dependent on refugees for income, humanitarian aid became a major public source of corruption" (Bradbury 1997:9). And Abdalla Manur considers this tendency of raiding the humanitarian aid intended for the refugees in a wider context. According to Abdalla Mansur:

> "It is our belief that international aid worsened the political, economic, and social situation of the country for the following reasons. First, the aid given fostered the dictatorial regime, endowing it with a new life. Secondly, it created a dependency on imported foodstuff, discouraging local food production. Last, but not least, aid made thieves of nearly all the state employees, whose salaries were not enough to support their families even for a week" (Mansur 1995:115).

The massive influx of refugees into Somalia not only placed heavy burdens on an already strained economy but also on the ecology. This is what the mission of the UN Inter-Agency observed in the country. According to the UN Inter-Agency mission report, the influx of refugees into Somalia affected the ecological balance and caused environmental deterioration, which could lead to permanent damage. For example, in some areas where the refugees were camped, firewood had been rapidly depleted and the refugees had to walk 4 to 5 miles to collect wood. More seriously, by the end of 1980, because of the lack of firewood, fuel had to be imported for domestic cooking in certain camps (Lewis 1993). Hanne Christensen who surveyed three refugee camps in 1981 on behalf of the United Nations Research Institute for Social Development noted that these areas "are slowly being transformed into stony, arid desert".[208] Furthermore, some of the refugees who were outside the camps brought with them their livestock and the crowding of this additional animal population in the countryside led to overgrazing and environmental degradation.[209]

Even more ghastly was the exploitation of the refugee population by the military regime for its own domestic political survival. The commandants in the army unscrupulously manipulated the susceptible refugees, recruiting them to defend the regime against the rebel uprising. For example, many of the male refugees were armed, illegally recruited and conscripted as a paramilitary militia into army force. Subsequently, they were forced to fight in the suppression of the growing internal dissent against the beleaguered military regime. They were also encouraged to misappropriate the property of the dissidents. This then created a deep animosity and soured the relationship between the refugees and many host groups, especially those in the north of the country that earlier received them as guests (Lewis 1989).

---

[208] See further Hanne Christensen, "Survival Strategies for the Camp Refugees in Somalia", *Horn of Africa* 5, no.4 (1982-1983).

[209] This is how Major General Jama Mohamed Ghalib, Minister of Local Government and Rural Development described the overwhelming burden of the refugees on the scarce vegetation and water in the country: "For the pressures triggered off by this influx are fast affecting the country as a whole, and especially the nomadic life of inhabitants, particularly in terms of grazing and water, for over-grazing in the countryside will automatically affect the vegetation, thereby endangering the ecological balance, which in turn threatens the existence of livestock, the main national resource, which may develop into famine" (UN Doc. A/AC.96/SR.307).

Thus, the susceptible refugees were become party to the brewing domestic social tensions and in this way their presence in the country also contributed to the political crisis of the state.

7.4. Militarisation of the State Institutions

As I discussed in the last chapter, the failure of the militarism of the state in an irredentist war, gave away to the heavy militarisation of the state institutions in the 1980s. The defeat of Somalia in the Ogaden war of 1977 to 1978 caused the collapse of the militaristic adventure of the state that was pursued for the realisation of a Pan-Somali unity or the making of a Somali-wide state.[210] This state-making project was what largely preoccupied the government of Somalia from 1960 till 1978. After this period:

> "Somalia slipped from a nation on the move to a nation adrift. Plagued by internal opposition, by lack of a reliable foreign patron, and by the threat of an Ethiopian-backed invasion, Siad Barre's chief preoccupation since 1978 seems to have been to hang on to power at whatever cost. It is therefore just to say that since then his regime has operated in a void" (Laitin and Said Samatar 1987:155).

Consequently, the failure of the Somali-wide public pursuit led the state to retreat from its external cross border venture and withdraw inward. In essence, the defeat of Somalia in the war marked a major watershed.[211] It accentuated not only the economic but also social and political problems in the country. Internally, the military regime confronted a new and difficult reality: weak social cohesion and harmony among the clan divided Somalis, fragile political institutions which should have imbued the population with a sense of national unity and lack of tangible social reforms that the government had neglected to address seriously over the past eight years.Other problems were domestic uprisings, open criticism of and dissatisfaction with the political management of the military regime. Consequently, the people, frustrated with the misery of the economic conditions they endured and the defeat of government in the war (which resulted in massive refugee influx into the country) demanded better administration and good governance. They demanded political reforms, clan equity, equal power sharing, regional equality, economic advancement, social development, etc. Furthermore, many of the political elite, particularly the generals, who were extremely demoralised by the humiliating defeat in the war, directly challenged the top ruling leadership and demanded representative government and responsible leadership (Galaydh 1990). The regime was then confronted with a crisis of political legitimacy both from within its own ranks and in the wider society. The military government however lacking prior experience of how to deal with and regulate such growing societal disenchantment employed a militaristic solution. Brutal and disproportionate repression was used to control and discipline the population. The National Security Service (NSS) created by the military regime was given the

---

[210] "The military debacle of 1978 shattered all hopes for achieving a Greater Somalia and signalled the demise of pan-Somalism. Betrayed by their socialist allies, Somalis bitterly criticised Siad Barre's leadership for bungling the 'liberation' venture and soon turned against each other" (Geshekter 1997:75).

[211] Some observers of Somali politics hold the view that the disintegration of the Somali state began with the Ogaden adventure. For a more historical analysis, see David Rawson, " Dealing with Disintegration: U.S. Assistance and the Somali State", in The Somali Challenge: From Catastrophe to Renewal, edited by Ahmed I. Samatar (London: Lynne Rienner Publishers, 1994).

absolute power to arrest and detain without trial for long periods any person suspected of being anti-government.[212] In certain regions of the country, the regime using the national army pursued a scorched earth approach against the hometowns of the dissidents. They and their sub-clan families were subjected to severe economic punishment and systematic social harassment (Lewis 1993). Many were dismissed from the government service and arbitrarily arrested. In their home areas, the constructed water wells vital for the livelihood of the wandering pastoral nomads and their livestock were poisoned and demolished.[213] And in this way their lives and their livestock economy were cruelly destroyed. In a nutshell, "the progressive popular disenchantment with Siad Barre's regime correlates closely with the progressive militarisation of government services" (Rawson 1994:158). After the 1980s, for all practical purposes, the population in those targeted regions in north and northeast was inflicted with a harsh military rule. As Ali Galaydh noted:

> "Detention and torture of members of the political elite were pathetically familiar features of the political landscape. What was new, disturbing and monstrous was the targeting of an entire clan or sub-clan as enemies of the regime. These scorched earth measures carried out by the state organs did irreparable damage to the warp and woof of the Somali society" (Galaydh 1990:21).

At the same time, as the internal power struggles among the political elite sharpened, the government reacted to those challenges by constant shuffling the cabinet, purging the top commandants of the national army and instead promoting to higher posts cadets without any professional military experience. According to Abdi Samatar:

> "The arbitrary way that the public service was managed and the uninformed and unsystematic nature of the decision-making process undermined the legitimacy of the regime. The promotion of unqualified individuals, who had connections in high places, into senior posts, displacing more seasoned and skilled employees, dealt a deathblow to the morale of public servants" (Abdi Samatar 1997:702).

The only criteria for those cadets who were promoted into senior posts in the military was loyalty to the regime of Siad Barre.[214] In fact, in Somalia, between 1978 and 1986 the rule increasingly became autocratic[215] within a narrowed political base, which

---

[212] According to Ahmed Samatar, " With the creation of the National Security Service, harassment, arbitrary arrest and imprisonment, denial of a fair public trial, and invasion of the home were common features in the life of the Somali citizen" (Samatar 1988:113).

[213] As Abdi noted, " From then on, and with the General and his aides embarking on crushing Somalia's 'domestic enemies', Somali politics seems to have completely focused on internal conflict and repression. That started with the targeting of the people of the north-eastern regions" (Abdi 1997: 54).

[214] According to Compagnon, "Colonels and generals were part of the president's patronage network; they had to remain loyal to him and his close relatives, whether they had command or were temporarily in the Cabinet.... The military apparatus offers a good example of Somali institutional decay as a result of the state's patrimonialism" (Compagnon 1992:9).

[215] Jackson and Rosberg's theoretical characterisation of personal rule in Black Africa offers categories such as Prophet, Prince, Autocrat and Tyrant. The four types represent more or less the kind of personal rule for a given country in Africa. For more discussion, see Robert H. Jackson and Carl G. Rosberg, Personal Rule in Black Africa, University of California Press, (Berkeley, 1982).

channelled power and its perquisites into the hands of the President's kin and cohorts.[216] This ruling clique then in order to survive resorted to patronage and prebends politics.[217] In this survival strategy, coercion to punish opposition groups and reward loyal cronies were both sides of the coin. Furthermore, the ruling clique extensively exploited the latent tensions between lineage groups and used the clan differences within the population as a political instrument. According to Daniel Compagnon, "by giving money and weapons to the clan segments whose goodwill he wanted to win, thereby weakening lineages hostile to his rule, Said Barre re-politicised lineage competition, deliberately breaking with the postcolonial state's long-term efforts to appear neutral"(Compagnon 1992:10). Divide and rule politics damaged the cohesion and the social fabric of the society and also weakened the very foundation and the societal infrastructure of the state. Moreover, it resulted in increasing the divisions between the segmented lineages and clans, which politicised further their social co-existence. Furthermore, the regime promoted certain sub-clans to the political and economic disadvantage of other sub-clans and lineages. This deliberate tactic of creating political and economic inequality among the clans served further as a recipe for tension and communal conflicts.

According to Lewis, the Head of the State was the very one who covertly orchestrated the deleterious segmentation of the Somali society. For instance, Siad Barre promoted three sub-clans of the Darod clan family in the process of constructing an inner power circle for himself. The three sub-clans were the Marehan, Dolbahante and Ogaden.[218] This then sewed the seeds of hatred of the members belonging to the three dominant sub-clans by other marginalised clans. Furthermore, the survival tactic of the military regime militarised the whole of Somali society. For example, the state deliberately armed the loyal clans who used the armaments to settle old scores with enemy clans. This strained the relations between the neighbouring clans and increased inter-clan feuds even among the pastoral nomads in the hinterland. Consequently, the militarism of the state institutions resulted in the extreme militarisation of Somali society. On top of the deliberate militarisation of the population in the country, there was also a dragging war of attrition across the border. Although a direct military confrontation between Ethiopia and Somalia subsided after the Ogaden war of 1977/78, sporadic border clashes continued to drag on. This war of attrition also forced the military regime of Somalia to purchase more arms and increase the number of its military force staggeringly (see chapter 6). For example, in 1981 the number of the army was 50,000-man strong and in proportion to the population of the country which at the time was 4.3 million, Somalia had the largest armed force in Africa (Nelson 1982:231).

---

[216] See the *Africa Contemporary Record* (1987-88): 393.

[217] " Promotions and postings were decided not on professional criteria and standard norms but pre-eminently on patronage, which was not determined solely by clan politics. Personal factors such as friendship, marriage, district-regional background and 'entrepreneurship' were also at play. The constant purging, selective recruitment, and the patronage system 'politicised' the army force" (Galaydh 1990:19).

[218] As I.M. Lewis noted, " It is important to emphasise that these clans (the President, his mother's brother's and his son-in-law's) all belong at a higher level of segmentary grouping to the Darod clan family. Although the regime at all times included representatives of other non-Darod clans, the magic letters MOD (Marehan, Ogaden, Dulbahante) represented the inner circle of power" (Lewis 1989:574).

128

7.5.   Emergence of Organised Violence

As the Somali-wide public pursuit project faltered after Somalia was routed in the Ogaden war, the race for control of the state intensified. The rivalling state class began to stake their claims for a more equitable distribution of the state benefits and access to its upper-echelon positions. John Markakis in his seminal book 'National and Class Conflict in the Horn of Africa' (1987) identified the centrality of the state for the emergence of the organised violence in the region. According to Markakis, "everywhere the target of the attack is the state; the custodian of wealth and protector of privilege. The state is both the goal of the contest and the primary means through which the contest is waged" (Markakis: xvi). Consequently, the already beleaguered military regime faced not only opposition within the country but was also confronted with an organised insurgent groups operating across border. This last development in fact threatened the very existence of the regime.

As the state practically became the private property of a small oligarchy hand-picked by the President himself, marginalised political elite formed dissident groups.[219] The marginalised political elite were former military generals and civilian ministers of the regime who lost their positions in the government through the internal power struggles of the state class. The first organised group which opted to wage an armed struggle against the regime was the army officers belonging to the Majeerteen clan, which inhabit mainly the central and north-east parts of the country. In April 1978, the army officers first staged a coup against the government but it was aborted. Afterwards, they left the country in order to escape arrest and formed the first organised opposition movement: the Somali Salvation Democratic Front (SSDF) and sought an operational base in Addis Ababa, Ethiopia.[220] The movement was committed to the violent overthrow of the military regime of Siad Barre and was supported financially, logistically and militarily both by Ethiopia and Libya. And from 1980s onwards the SSDF movement, which was led by Colonel Abdillahi Yusuf, had launched intermittent cross-border military operations against the government but hardly posed a real threat to the stability of the regime. Yet the response from the government to these border attacks was disproportionately ruthless. According to Said Samatar, the scorched earth policy of the military regime against the civilian sympathisers of the movement resulted in the death of more than 2,000 Majeerteen clan members in the central region of Mudug between May to June 1979.[221] In 1986, the SSDF movement collapsed when its leader Colonel Abdillahi Yusuf was arrested by the Ethiopian government, which was seeking at the time to normalise relations with the military government of Somalia. The movement was reconstituted in 1989 and is now playing a predominant role in the prevailing clan politics of Somalia.

Another clan-based uprising followed this insurgent movement. In 1981, disgruntled clan associated groups formed another armed opposition against the military regime of Siad Barre. The members of the movement largely belonged to the Isaq clan, which inhabit the north of Somalia. They named their political organisation the Somali National Movement (SNM) and like the SSDF it was granted an operational base in Ethiopia. Similarly, the SNM, like the

---

[219] As Hashim noted, " at the site of elite class formation, Barre wanted to form a hand-picked oligarchy that would serve him rather than the nation or the state" (Hashim 1995:190).

[220] Colonel Abdillahi Yusuf, the leader of the insurgent movement, *Interview*, July 11, 1997, Addis Ababa.

[221] For a more discussion, see Said Samatar, Somalia: A Nation in Turmoil, (London: Minority Rights Group, 1991): 18.

SSDF was also determined to overthrow the military regime by the force of arms. The chief grievances of this opposition group were that: they were not sufficiently represented in the economic and the political power of the state and their northern region was left underdeveloped. Moreover, they were not happy with the government interference and regulations of the livestock and the Qat[222] trade, the only economic lifeline in their region.

The emergence of the SNM as the second armed movement alongside the SSDF heavily exerted a destabilising pressure on the state. The armed rebels of the two movements started launching violent attacks and causing increased security problems both in the border areas and inside the country. Therefore, the military regime in order to survive had to find a solution that stemmed the growing armed struggles of the dissidents. Accordingly, in a bid of desperation, the military regime of Somalia signed a treaty of non-aggression and non-interference with the government of Ethiopia in April 1988.[223] In the treaty, both governments agreed to stop supporting each other's insurgent groups; and as a further step, Ethiopia closed the military bases of both the SSDF and SNM opposition groups. This unexpected peace accord between the two traditional enemies of Ethiopia and Somalia caught the leaders of the SNM by surprise. In particular, the commanders of the fighting army became confronted with a strategic military dilemma as they quickly decided to launch an all-out offensive war against the state. By sheer force, they swiftly and briefly captured the most important strategic towns in the north of the country such as Hargeysa, Berbera and Burao where the Isaq clan from which the SNM derives its main supporters, largely inhabit. The military government reacted to this surprise attack from the SNM fighters with extreme violence. The government dispatched a well-armed military force to the region in order to put down the uprising. The ensuing battles between the government forces and the SNM repels were fierce and brutal. Finally, the government forces mercilessly crushed the insurgency and took over the control of the captured towns. However, the consequences were devastating as Hargeisa, the second largest city of the country was largely destroyed and most of its inhabitants fled across the border to Ethiopia and became refugees. According to Africa Watch, an estimation of 50,000 inhabitants in the region, were killed by the government forces between May 1988 and March 1989.[224] Another dire consequence of the war was that after 1988 the government lost control of this northern region of the country as it had become ungovernable. Furthermore, the military forces stationed in that region became trapped in a protracted guerrilla war with the SNM fighters wandering in the countryside. In a nutshell, the clan-organised uprising in this northern region marked a major watershed as the central government began losing control over the provinces of the state one after another. Actually, since that uprising the state began shrinking from its provinces while clan-based insurgencies were emerging one after another in order to take over the control of the abandoned peripheries. This means that the Somali state first collapsed in the peripheries before it finally exploded at the centre.

As the north and central regions were breaking off from the centre, political turmoil also started in the south of the country. In April 1989, a third clan-organised armed opposition movement emerged in the southern port of Kismayo. This new opposition movement, which was named the Somali Patriotic Movement (SPM) was formed by a mutiny of soldiers

---

[222] Qat is mild narcotic leaves whose Latin name is (Catha Edulis Forsk), which the Somalis habitually chew as a social past time. Qat trees largely grow in the mountainous parts of Ethiopia, Kenya and Yemen.

[223] For more details, see "Somalia: Under Fire", *Africa Confidential*, (April 29, 1988).

[224] For details, see Africa Watch, Somalia: A Government at War with its People, The Africa Watch Committee, (New York, 1990); see also "Somali Government Accused in 50,000 Civilian Deaths", *Africa Report* (March-April 1990): 10.

belonging to the Ogaden clan. The main grievance of the mutinous soldiers was that the President sacked and subsequently arrested General Mohamed Gabyo, the defence minister of the national army who was also an Ogaden by clan affiliation. General Gabyo was sacked because among other matters he was not happy with the naked patronage politics of the President as Siad Barre arbitrarily appointed many of his kin-family members in the higher positions of the military. Nonetheless, the dismissal of the defence minister was a signal of how the beleaguered ruling clique was cracking from within. It was also a clearly frantic attempt of the desperate President to save his power.

However, more worrisome to the ruling clique was the domestic civil strife that was spreading unabated and this time in the southern part of the country. Within less than two months, a second Ogaden organised uprising suddenly occurred. This second opposition front was formed by an Ogaden Colonel Ahmed Omar Jess, who defected with some armed men from a military garrison based in the north of the country. The regime that was already losing both the north and the central regions of the country because of the escalating civil strife was now confronted with a serious armed uprising in the south. Both of the Ogaden-organised resistance movements were destabilising the agriculturally fertile regions closely located in the south of the capital, the seat of the ruling military clique.[225] Furthermore, the spreading civil strife was gradually moving ever closer and was engulfing the capital city from several directions. In the capital, the situation was becoming more ominous as the political power of the government was shrinking towards the city. In fact, during 1989, the authority of the government hardly existed beyond the frontiers of the capital city as the peripheral regions of the country had already been seized by clan- organised armed rebels. As the internal armed dissidents carved the outlying regions of the country from the centre, The Economist started addressing the President of Somalia as "the mayor of Mogadishu" (The Economist, September 29,1990). Therefore, Somalia represents a perfect example of a state where the peripheries of the country collapsed before the centre finally exploded. The military regime for a very short while defended Mogadishu, the only place in the country which remained under its control, but that also became a mission impossible.[226]

The emergence of a fourth armed rebel in the central regions and in the southern region where the capital city is located, has indeed precipitated the final downfall of the military regime. After the appearance of this last armed opposition movement named the United Somali Congress (USC), the military regime was in fact cornered as its defence tactics even in the capital had collapsed. The appearance of this last clan- organised dissident movement which was also a clan-based uprising was precipitated by a mutiny of Hawiye soldiers in the town of Galkaiyo, located in the central region of Mudug in October 1989. The mutiny of the armed soldiers quickly spread to the other central regions of Galgadud and Hiran. The government retaliated by bombing the towns and villages inhabited by the Hawiye clans, which resulted in

---

[225] As Ahmed Samatar noted, " the spreading of resistance to Southern Somalia had a number of critical implications. The scope of civil strife assumed truly national proportions. With the economic base ---- e.g., livestock trading ----in the North severely disrupted, Southern Somalia, the most fertile and productive part of the country, began to slide into anarchy ---- accentuating the fiscal enfeeblement of local and national institutions. In the end, unable to conceive of more positive ways to assuage this downward spiral of de-legitimacy, the Siad Barre regime deployed the same punitive tactics applied in the North to cow the peasant populations and small town communities in the South where the SPM was suspected to operate (Ahmed Samatar 1993:88).

[226] As Ali Galaydh writes, " the regions have been written off and now it is Mogadishu which is burning. The Diplomatic Corps have barricaded themselves in their compounds. The capital has imposed a voluntary 6:00 p.m. –6:00 a.m. curfew on itself, and the people are waiting anxiously for the nightmare to come to an end" (Galaydh 1990:27).

the death of many civilians. However, by that time, the clan uprising was spreading fast and the government had no military power to stop it or to put it down. Consequently, when the war finally reached the capital, the frightened red beret commandos guarding the Presidential Place turned their heavy artillery shells on the quarters of Mogadishu occupied by the supporters of the USC. [227] Finally, the centre collapsed when the rebel forces from the peripheral regions conquered Mogadishu and forced Said Barre and his cohorts to flee the city on January 26, 1991. The armed resistance which captured Mogadishu was led by General Mohamed Farah Aideed. General Aideed was the successor of Mohamed Wardhigley, the first leader of the USC movement.

Before Mogadishu collapsed, there were locally initiated peace attempts aimed at changing the course of the present history of the country. The most significant of these peace initiatives was that put forward by prominent national figures, which were later called the Manifesto Group. The group composed of more than 100 respected intellectuals and moderate politicians drafted an open manifesto. In the manifesto, they appealed to the President to start a peaceful dialogue with the insurgent groups and also put in place a provisional government. Their aim was to find a solution to the escalating political turmoil in the country and try to avert the total collapse of the state. However, the President was not ready to change the dramatic course of the political history of the country as he immediately arrested 45 of the signatories of the letter.[228] Subsequently, they were released when the mass public demonstrations in the capital coupled with international diplomatic pressure forced the President to change his mind and set them free. By that time, everything was falling apart and all the efforts of the international mediators aimed at reconciling the armed opposition groups and government had come to naught. For example, in the last hours, both Italian and Egyptian governments did their utmost to prevent the Somali state from falling apart. Unfortunately, after two months of intense fighting, the capital finally fell, resulting in the complete collapse of the state.

---

[227] Mohamed Sh. M. Guled (Gacamadheere), *Interview*, July 12, 1997, Addis Ababa. Guled was an eyewitness of this account.

[228] See further Neil Henry, "Somalia Orders Trail for Signers of Rights Letter", *Washington Post*, February 18, 1990:23

7.6.   Conclusion

As I demonstrated in this chapter, the Somali state did not collapse suddenly. The state was first plagued by multiple crises resulting from the pitfalls of the politics of private and public pursuit that the Somali political actors had been pursuing since the country achieved statehood in 1960. These accumulated crises gradually weakened the overall capacity of the state and ultimately led to its collapse. During the 1980s, the multiple crises affecting the state manifested themselves in an acute economic deterioration, refugee problems, militarised political and social institutions and finally the emergence of organised armed groups.

The acute economic deterioration which started early in the 1980s impoverished the majority of the population and depleted the coffers of the state. For example, the extremely high inflation caused by the rapid downward slide of the economy deeply affected the purchasing power of the civil servants in the administration. The monthly salaries they earned could not enable them to sustain their families. As a result, most of the civil servants started looking for private jobs in order to boost their monthly incomes. Gradually, this practice resulted in the collapse of the government administration. Worse of all the state also became abjectly poor at a time when the population of Somalia experienced a spectacular acceleration of growth rate, causing a demographic explosion. The accelerated growth rate of the population meant that many mouths had to be fed in a situation where the national resources were dwindling. The abject poverty of the state and the population explosion then led to all sorts of increased social and class tensions, mainly in urban areas such as Mogadishu.[229] Furthermore, in the 1980s, the economic collapse of the state was further exacerbated by the massive influx of refugees into the country, fleeing from the Ogaden desert as the result of the border wars between Ethiopia and Somalia. This massive influx of refugees also imposed a heavy burden on the meagre resources of the state, aggravating the already impoverished domestic economy.

To add to the problems of the extremely impoverished population and bankrupted state, the political institutions of the state also became militarised in the 1980s. The government started using violence to suppress any kind of domestic resistance. The government also brutally punished any person or a group who disagreed with its policy. Gradually, this militaristic solution to the domestic challenges became rampant and widespread. In certain regions of the country, such as the north and north-east, where about a third of the Somali population live, the government imposed a harsh military rule. Eventually, this repressive political behaviour of the government militarised the political and the social institutions of the country. Consequently, violence bred violence and that resulted in the emergence of organised armed groups. These armed dissidents also used violence to fight against the government. Subsequently, the most tragic outcomes of this vicious violence were the disintegration of the national army (the custodian of the monopoly of coercive violence) and the ruling elites. Thereafter, as the social and political institutions in the country were militarised, the domestic political violence took on its own dynamics and then developed into a fully-fledged civil war. And that civil strife kept dragging on until it dismantled the very state. Finally, the Somali state collapsed after the bureaucratic administration, the national army and the ruling elite

---

[229] A few Somali scholars in some of their respective writings, have recently made passing remarks on how the widening gap between the deprived masses, particularly the unemployed youth and the few rich in the urban centres such as Mogadishu, was also one of the causes of the civil war in the country, hidden behind the highly publicised clan conflicts. See further Ali Jimal Ahmed (ed), The Invention of Somalia, (The Red Sea Press INC, 1995); and Nuruddin Farah, Yesterday, Tomorrow: Voices from the Somali Diaspora (London: Cassell, 2000).

disintegrated completely.

A theoretical importance worth noting here is how the contradictions of the tendencies towards private and public pursuits do not lead to new synthesis in the case of Somalia but to meltdown as the collapse of the state testifies. Throughout the Somali history, the contradictory tendencies towards private and public pursuits which are the two sides of the same coin, presenting one historical rather than two separate historical processes, have negative and positive impulses in the contemporary making of the Somali society. For example, the parochial tendency towards private pursuit has positive impulses at the sub-national and sub-state levels but negatively undermines efforts geared towards wider political identity and nation building at the state levels. By contrast, the tendency towards public pursuit has positive impulses at the national and state levels as its inspired struggles against colonial occupations during the colonial period, national awakening and the state making project in the post-colonial era. However the negative effects of this tendency towards public pursuits such as a very expensive military build up, militarisation of the state and the untenable policy of irredentist adventure against the neighbouring countries have also contributed to the weakening of the state. In short, the negative effects of the contradictory tendencies towards private and public pursuits have in combination led to the meltdown of the post-colonial state in Somalia.

Chapter Eight

The Collapse of the State and its Aftermath (1991-2000)

8.1. Introduction

As the state imploded, the ruling political elite degenerated into predatory warlords and rival faction leaders that dramatically put to an end the collective public pursuit of the Somali society. Consequently, since 1991 as there was no public cause to be pursued, private pursuit became the chief preoccupation of the contending political elite. Tragically, the incessant pursuit of private spoils plunged the whole of Somalia into a vicious spiral of violence and a disastrous civil war unprecedented in the history of the country.

In this chapter I will recount the events, which took place in the aftermath of the collapse of the state in 1991 and describe how these occurrences further complicated the reconciliation process and the resolution of the political problems in the country. The major events, which followed the collapse of the state, were the post-state civil war, the international military and civil intervention, and the failure of that intervention. In this chapter, I shall argue that initially the international community assumed the responsibility for the public pursuit[230] of the Somali people during the intervention since the domestic political elite became a bunch of individuals with irreconcilable differences, totally immersed in the politics of private pursuit. However, while the international intervention was modestly successful in dealing with humanitarian exigency, its military and political operations were disastrous. The international intervention in Somalia failed ultimately because it was poorly conceived, poorly planned, poorly executed and was erroneously perceived to be a "quick fix" and a rapid exit operation. The erratic behaviour of the domestic political elite also contributed to the failure of the intervention. The warlords and faction leaders frustrated the initiatives for the Somali-wide public pursuit that the international community undertook as they were afraid that the activities geared to help the public would undermine the pursuit of their private gains.

8.2. The Post State Civil War

On 26 January 1991, as Mogadishu, the capital city of Somalia, finally collapsed, the reign of the military regime of Siad Barre came to an end. However, the clan-organized forces, the loose coalition of the United Somali Congress (USC), which defeated the military regime and celebrated that victory, then turned their guns on each other. The reason was that when Said Barre hurriedly fled the capital in a convoy of tanks, a power vacuum emerged. And this power vacuum was immediately filled when the Manifesto Group (the moderate Mogadishu intellectuals) appointed a businessman, Ali Mahdi Mohamed, as 'interim president'. During the fighting, Ali Mahdi was the leader of the civilian wing of the USC. However, the

---

[230] The public pursuit that the international community half-heartedly attempted in Somalia was limited only to humanitarian assistance, breaking the cycle of violence and restoring law and order domestically. This public pursuit is diametrically opposed to that pursued earlier by the Somali political elite which conducted an irredentist adventure aimed at achieving a Somali-wide territorial unity.

nomination of Ali Mahdi as a president annoyed General Mohamed Farah Aideed, the commander of the military wing and the chairman of the USC. Nevertheless, Aideed was not the only faction leader who rejected Ali Mahdi's leadership; the leaders of other clan factions around the country rebuffed him too. General Aideed then directly countered the leadership claims of Ali Mahdi by publicly declaring that he was the rightful person to take the mantle of the president of Somalia. Aideed unequivocally demanded to be the new president of Somalia claiming that the armed forces he was commandeering had routed the army of the military regime of Siad Barre.

This leadership dispute caused grave and irreparable damage to the fragile alliance of the USC Hawiye sub-clans. It also created personal animosity between Aideed and Ali Mahdi and hostilities between their respective sub-clans. Gradually, as the conflict was becoming quite explosive, Italian diplomats and several regional leaders attempted to diffuse the situation and reconcile the quarrelling sub-clans at two meetings in Djibouti in May and June in 1991. Yet both attempts failed to reconcile them and in November 1991, a destructive fight broke out between the armed men of the two sub-clans in Mogadishu.[231] The fighting continued for about four months and totally destroyed the public infrastructure of the capital city, from water pipelines, electrical powers to historical monuments.[232] In an eyewitness account, Mohamed Sahnoun described the appalling destruction in Mogadishu, when he visited Somalia as the head of a UN fact-finding mission in 1992. According to Sahnoun, "as our plane landed on a small strip to the north of Mogadishu—the main airport being closed— and as we drove slowly towards the city, I could not believe my eyes. I had visited Somalia before, and what I was seeing now was a total disaster" (Sahnoun 1994:viii). The four months civil war also tragically took the lives of as many as 25,000 innocent civilians (Bradbury 1997:13). Eventually, the destructive battle divided Mogadishu into two parts, and a "Green Line" was drawn between the two warring sub-clan factions. While the armed militia of Ali Mahdi controlled the north of the capital, that of General Aideed controlled the areas in the south, such as the airport and seaport. The split of the USC alliance resulted in the emergence of the Somali National Alliance (SNA). This new alliance was formed by General Aideed to counter Ali Mahdi and his forces. As a result, the two Mogadishu-controlled militias resumed fierce clashes with each other, causing further destruction and more social havoc, particularly in the southern part of the country.[233] During the last months of 1991, neutral traditional elders made repeated attempts to mediate a cease-fire and reconcile the warring militias but they also failed. Consequently, as the conflict in the south remained unabated, northern Somalia seceded. The leadership of the Somali National Movement (SNM) in the north of the country declared the political independence of the region from the rest of the country. Northern Somalia then became the Republic of Somaliland. In fact, this SNM unilateral declaration of political independence for northern Somalia also contributed further to the disintegration of the state and the country.[234]

---

[231] According to Terrence Lyons and Ahmed Samatar, " this conflict was a confused mixture of competition between factions of the USC, a personal leadership struggle between Aideed and Ali Mahdi, a fight between two subclans, the Habir Gedir and Abgal, and a desperate struggle to win public office and the financial benefits such positions promised" (Lyons and Ahmed Samatar 1995:22).

[232] See further, Jeffrey Clark, " Debacle in Somalia: Failure of the Collective Response", in Loris Fisler Damrosch, ed., Enforcing Restraint: Collective Intervention in Internal Conflicts (New York: Council of Foreign Relations, 1993): 211.

[233] See Africa Watch, "Somalia: a Fight to the Finish?" News from Africa Watch, vol 4 (February 13, 1992): 7.

Tragically, the civil war, which had been going on largely in the south of the country from December 1991 to March 1992, caused the destruction of most farms and the agricultural land and that resulted in a widespread famine in the entire region. Consequently, many innocent civilians lost their lives because of starvation and hunger-related diseases until the television screens across the globe started to show harrowing footage of extremely emaciated children, which depicted the appalling human suffering in the country. Eventually, these horrific television images finally drew the attention of the world community to the plight of the Somali people incarcerated in a self-inflicted and destructive civil war.

Yet the belated response of the international community to this human tragedy was half-hearted and timid. The UN Security Council adopted Resolution 733, on January 23, 1992, which was in fact the first resolution on Somalia since the crisis began in the country a year ago. The resolution requested the international community to provide more humanitarian aid to the country, called for the imposition of a total arms embargo on Somalia and urged the warring parties to agree to a cease-fire and to reconcile their differences through peaceful means.[235] This first resolution was followed by second and third resolutions on Somalia. However, concrete action does not automatically follow the UN resolutions as the member states and international agencies which are requested for assistance always need more time to respond because of the cumbersome bureaucratic clearances and logistical problems among other things. As a result, when the UN Security Council finally authorized the implementation of the ninety-day plan of action for emergency humanitarian assistance in Somalia as late as October, the food aid that was flown in was too little and for many hapless civilians it came too late.[236]

On the political front, the Secretary General invited the representatives of some of the conflicting parties to come to New York in February 1992, and sign what observers call "a vague cease-fire" (Lyons and Ahmed Samatar 1995:30). As a follow up, the UN Secretary General dispatched James Jonah (a Sierra Leone UN diplomat) as a special envoy to Somalia. Jonah mediated a further cease-fire, which was signed only by two rival factional leaders, General Mohamed Farah Aideed and Ali Mahdi in Mogadishu on March 3, 1992. As the cease-fire was precariously holding, the Secretary General appointed Ambassador Mohamed Sahnoun of Algeria as his special representative for Somalia in April 1992. Ambassador Sahnoun, a seasoned diplomat who had been working in the region earlier for almost a decade was indeed the right choice at the time. Moreover, the appointment of Sahnoun heralded the establishment of the United Nations Operation in Somalia (UNOSOM, which later became UNOSOM I). Sahnoun skilfully approached the political problem in Somalia by starting first a series of peace initiatives at local levels. His approach was to build the peace settlement from the "bottom up". This was the most sensible strategy since the civil war had largely broken down the social fabric of the Somali society. Sahnoun also understood the importance of the existing local social structures and networks of the clan system and used them purposefully in order to find a resolution to the political problem in the country. His focus was on the process and, in that strategy he opted for a painstaking negotiation rather than a quick fix outcome. In fact, his "bottom up" approach to the conflict helped him win trust among

---

[234] According to Lyons and Ahmed Samatar (1995:23), " the SNM's actions contributed to the dissolution of Somalia as a nation-state, the destruction of pan-Somalism, and the acceleration of the balkanisation of northeast Africa"

[235] See further, the *UN Chronicle*, (June 1992): 23.

[236] According to Mohamed Sahnoun, "Not only was the UN assistance program very limited, it was also so slowly and inadequately delivered that it became counterproductive. Fighting erupted over the meagre food supplied and introduced new elements of animosity and violence" (Sahnoun 1994:17).

many Somalis and as he explained to me, enabled him to solve many intractable problems.[237] For example, Sahnoun's sustained peace dialogue with a broad array of local actors helped him gain a diplomatic breakthrough, which made it possible for the conflicting parties to respect the cease-fire.

Sahnoun having a vision well-tuned to local realities both past and present, adopted an all-inclusive and broad-based strategy. He involved in the reconciliation process a broad spectrum of individuals representing diverse sections of the society such as military leaders, elders, religious leaders, traders and businessmen, journalists, intellectuals for peace and women's associations among others. These prominent personalities who felt that they were empowered to do so, used their social and political clout in the community to facilitate the peace dialogue and ensure that the truce remained un-violated. Unfortunately, both the process and the innovative diplomatic skills of Sahnoun were not given enough time to take their course as he was forced to resign in October 1992. Sahnoun was forced to resign because he openly criticized the obstructions and the UN Bureaucratic haggling, which in his view impeded efforts to feed the starving population in the country. Sahnoun was especially bitter because when he pleaded for more time from the UN headquarters in New York to continue his diplomatic efforts, he was told that his peace initiative had so far produced meagre results.[238] Moreover, Sahnoun held the view that the UN Administration was dragging its feet, as it did not realise the gravity of the tragedy unfolding in Somalia. Furthermore, there was a personality clash between Sahnoun and the UN Secretary-General Boutros-Ghali.[239]

Finally, as Sahnoun disappeared from the political theatre in Somalia, his "bottom up" approach to the conflict in Somalia as well as his focus on process were abandoned. The UN diplomats who replaced Sahnoun alternatively opted for a "top down" approach, which promoted the legitimacy and the political power of the warlords, and power-hungry urbanized minority elites.

After he left the UN, Sahnoun wrote a book which he entitled: *"Somalia: The Missed Opportunities" (1995)*. The central thesis of the book is that: "if the international community had intervened earlier and more effectively in Somalia, much of the catastrophe that has unfolded could have been avoided" (Sahnoun 1994:xiii). In the book, Sahnoun related three successive opportunities that the international community missed to prevent the collapse of the Somali state in 1991. The first opportunity came in 1988 when the clan-based uprising emerged in the north of the country and the military regime of Siad Barre savagely repressed the revolt. The international community failed to intervene and watched as the national military waged a war against its people. This conflict escalated into a long dragging civil war and largely contributed to the disintegration of the country. The second chance presented itself in May 1990, when a coalition of over 100 Somali politicians, intellectuals and businessmen, signed a manifesto, which called for a conference of a nation-wide political reconciliation. Again, the international community failed to support this timely initiative of the Manifesto Group and to broker a peace settlement. The third chance came immediately

---

[237] Mohamed Sahnoun, *Interview*, June 10, 1996, Addis Ababa.

[238] "A frustrated Shanoun criticised the UN officials for its bureaucratic inertia and pleaded for more time from New York to secure Aideed's consent for the deployment of the 3500 peacekeepers. But the UN leadership was getting 'very impatient' with Shanoun's meagre results. Indeed, a suspicion existed within the UN Secretariat that Sahnoun was misreading the Somali situation" (Patman 1995:92).

[239] "In October 1992 Sahnoun, frustrated with the UN's response and at odds with the secretary-general, publicly criticised the United Nations and resigned" (Bradbury 1997:15).

after the military regime of Siad Barre was overthrown in 1991. According to Sahnoun, the UN and its specialized agencies, instead of remaining in the country and attempting to promote reconciliation between the conflicting parties, left Somalia to fend for itself.

The other message in the book of Sahnoun, which is a general lesson to all of us, is that we must prevent and mediate in local crises and internal conflicts at an early stage before they become too costly and unmanageable as the tragedy in Somalia clearly exemplifies.[240] The book of Sahnoun must be recommended to anyone engaged in or concerned with early intervention and preventive diplomacy in conflict situations. In his case study on Somalia, Sahnoun strongly convinces us that adequate and timely action can possibly prevent conflict to further deterioration.

The UN, coming to Somalia too late and being itself too disorganized, failed to stop the violence in the country. In mid-1992, in addition to the ongoing political conflict, violence also erupted over the limited international food aid. The food supply was meager and inadequate and that increased the insecurity and produced even more violence. The cutthroat competition and the violence that the food scarcity unleashed made it impossible to deliver the food to those who needed it most. The violence also risked the lives of the international relief workers given the task of delivering and distributing the food aid. The 500 UN peacekeepers stationed in the country were powerless and even failed to control the seaports and secure the deliveries of the food aid. "The worsening security situation was highlighted on November 24 when a World Food Program ship carrying 10,000 tons of wheat was shelled as it tried to dock in the port capital, Mogadishu" (*Africa Report*, January-February 1993:5). As this dire situation in the country was becoming grimmer day by day, many relief agencies were forced to appeal for strong military protection for the humanitarian relief operations.

8.3.   The International Military Intervention

The constant looting of the humanitarian relief aid by warlords and gangs of bandits, prompted the UN Security Council to endorse Resolution 794, which authorized the deployment of a U.S. led Unified Task Force (UNITAF) in Somalia in December 1992. The resolution emphasized that the violent conflict in Somalia constituted a threat to international peace and mandated the UNITAF to use "all necessary means to establish as soon as possible a secure environment for humanitarian relief operations in Somalia".[241] President George Bush explaining his decision to send U.S. troops to Somalia described the intervention as a humanitarian mission to "save thousands of innocents from death".[242] The UNITAF mission to Somalia, which was codenamed *Operation Restore Hope,* had a limited and specific mandate. The goal of the mission according to Bush was to "open the supply routes, to get the

---

[240] As Sahnoun writes, " most of the time serious opportunities to mediate and check crises at an early stage have gone unheeded. Occasionally, when crises have reached important dimensions and affected large populations, hasty, and ill-prepared emergency relief operations have been put in place while a few timid attempts at reconciliation have been initiated. Even in most of the recent cases, such as Rwanda, Angola, Mozambique, Liberia, Somalia, Cambodia, Afghanistan, and Bosnia, the international community and the United Nations (UN) have begun to take serious initiatives only when large-scale civil wars have engulfed the countries and human tragedies have become overwhelming" (Sahnoun 1994:xi)

[241] UN Security Resolution 794 (December 3, 1992).

[242] "U.S. Commits Force to Somalia, But For How Long?" *Africa Report*, (January-February 1993): 5, 6, 11.

food moving, and prepare the way for a UN peace-keeping force to keep it moving".[243] At its peak, the UNITAF had 37,000 troops in the country of which 26,000 were Americans.

The UNITAF intervention in Somalia was not without critics. The troops did not intervene as traditional peacekeepers, because that would have required two preconditions: peace to keep and an invitation from a host government. In Somalia, at the time of the intervention both preconditions were missing. There was no government and no peace to keep. Consequently, according to Strobe Talbott, "once a country utterly loses its ability to govern itself, it also loses its claim to sovereignty and should become a ward of the United Nations" (*Time Magazine*, December 14, 1992:31). However, this justification was contested by observers of Somalia such as Rakiya Omaar and Alex de Waal who argued that the intervention was not properly handled because there was no prior consultation with the Somali people. Somalia is an independent and sovereign country and the Somalis are the nation whether they have a government or not. Both observers have written several reports and articles in which they strongly opposed the nature and the need of the military intervention in the country.[244] Rakiya Omaar, a Somali native who openly opposed the intervention on the media such as the CNN was fired from her consultancy position with the *Africa Watch* because she refused to temper her critical stand.

Although no one questions the humanitarian drive for the mission, the U.S.-led international force intervened in Somalia with an agenda far broader than is attested. The new agenda as spelled out by Bruce W. Nelan in *Time Magazine* is that this U.S. spearheaded military force "will be conducting an experiment in world order: armed peacekeeping, rather than peacekeeping" (Time Magazine, December 14, 1992:23). This armed peacekeeping, which was the international community's first experiment in the aftermath of the Cold War, is what Madeleine Albright, the U.S. representative to the United Nations, once called "*assertive multilateralism*". Thus, Somalia was a test case and success would have encouraged future UN military intervention in hot-spot areas elsewhere.[245] Furthermore, the operation in Somalia was easy, cheap and militarily doable as compared to Bosnia since the Somali ragtag militia could not match a determined, well-equipped, U.S. –led international force.[246] The other reason for the American troops to participate in the mission in Somalia was the conviction that the operation would be time limited while the possible casualties were assessed to be very low (Patman 1995).

---

[243] ibid: 5

[244] They co-authored an article in which they argued that: "Military humanitarian intervention has its own logic, which is difficult to reconcile with the demands of peacekeeping and reconstruction. It is never 'clean' nor quick. It cannot solve humanitarian crises; it can only alter them". They therefore pleaded that "relief and diplomatic interventions should be done earlier and better than they have been in the past, so as to make military intervention unnecessary". For further discussion, see Alex de Waal and Rakiya Omaar, Can Military Intervention Be "Humanitarian"? *Middle East Report* (March-June 1994): 3-8.

[245] According to Bruce W. Nelan, "some experts interpret going into Somalia as a test that, if it succeeds, might encourage further involvement in the jigsaw of republics that used to make up Yugoslavia" (*Time*, December 14, 1992): 25.

[246] This is the argument made by the U.S. military decision-makers such as the Defense Secretary Dick Cheney when Washington speaks about a jolt of military muscle, swift and simple job of pacification in Somalia. See further, Defense Secretary Dick Cheney and General Colin Powell, "U.S. Mission to Somalia is Necessary and Clear", USIA, *East Asia/Pacific Wireless File*, (4 December 1992): 12.

Regarding the humanitarian purpose which was to create a secure environment for the delivery of humanitarian relief, the UNITAF intervention in Somalia was positive in its short-term goal. Within a short time, the mission succeeded in getting the food moving and reaching the famished population residing in the hard-hit towns and villages without incident. In addition to that, anxiety about food scarcity diminished in the minds of the people. As a result, in the market places the food prices declined to a level at which many could afford to buy. Furthermore, security was improved and the looting of relief supplies and food convoys practically stopped. More tangibly, the UNITAF engineers did significant civic tasks by rehabilitating some of the debilitated infrastructure in the country. For example, the engineers repaired more than 1800 km of roads, refurbished 14 water wells and restored two airfields.[247]

Thus, with its short-term humanitarian focus, the UNITAF intervention was a success. But a discrepancy arose between its mandate and its long-term agenda. Both issues became a dispute between the UNITAF and UNOSOM I. Nonetheless, Bush repeatedly stated in public that the UNITAF mission would be in Somalia "only as long as necessary to establish a secure environment" for humanitarian efforts. "We believe that prolonged operations will not be necessary," (*Time Magazine*, December 21, 1992:20). But the UN Secretary General, Boutros Boutros-Ghali had a different view.[248] In the Security Council, Boutros-Ghali said in a statement to the Somali people, shortly before the first troops landed, that the UN was acting "in the cause of security, humanitarian relief and political reconciliation". It is because of this broader agenda that Boutros-Ghali insisted that the American-led intervention force must disarm the warring clans, clear the mines in the north of the country, train the Somali police force to maintain civil order, restore some kind of central authority and remain in Somalia until these missions were accomplished (*Newsweek*, December 21, 1992:8).[249] Only when these tasks were completed, would UN peacekeeping force take over the responsibility of Somalia and replace UNITAF, according to Boutros-Ghali. But the Washington Administration was adamant and argued that this broader agenda, which indeed required a long-term commitment, was beyond the narrow and limited mandate that the American troops were given in the country. The troops were there simply to provide enough security to permit the delivery of food and other relief supplies. Even President Bush when he visited Somalia and addressed the Somalis said that, "we come to your country with one reason only: to enable the starving to be fed. Once the food flows freely, the U.S. will go home" (*Time Magazine*, December 14, 1992:25).

The disagreement over the mandate and the long-term agenda of the mission between the U.N. and the policymakers in Washington was a testimony that the operation from the start was doomed to fail.[250] Broadly speaking, the mission did not work out a coherent strategy to deal with the multiple problems in Somalia. Furthermore, the agenda of the mission was not clearly defined and the agreements between the UNOSOMI and the UNITAF were vaguely formulated. In particular, the shortcoming of the UNITAF humanitarian policy was that they

---

[247] See Walter S. Clarke, "Testing the World's Resolve in Somalia," *Parameters* 23 (Winter 1993-94): 48.

[248] Boutros Boutros Ghali viewed the intervention in Somalia as a test case for the future of UN military intervention. See Boutros Boutros-Ghali, An Agenda for Peace (New York: United Nations, 1992).
[249] See further the article by Elaine Sciolino, " In Sharp Split, UN Chief Pans New U. S. Strategy in Somalia", *International Herald Tribune*, (October, 2-3, 1993).

[250] For a further discussion, see The United Nations and Somalia (1992-1996), The United Nations Blue Books Series, Volume VIII, (New York: Published by the United Nations Department of Public Information), see also Michael Maren, Somalia: Whose Failure? *Current History*, (May 1996): 201-205.

underestimated the depth of the collapse of the state structure in the country.[251] For instance, the UNITAF mission to Somalia was to tackle the humanitarian aspect of the problem but not the political crisis that produced it. As a result, they focused on the consequences rather than on the causes, which should have been addressed and attended to beforehand. Unfortunately, focusing on the humanitarian crisis without simultaneously addressing the underlying political conflict, failed to end the turmoil in the country. The important question is: how can a humanitarian catastrophe be solved in a situation where there is neither security nor political settlement?

The international military intervention in Somalia was a major opportunity for disarmament, which was an essential prerequisite for peace and political reconciliation. The large stockpiles of arms, which were dumped in the country during the Cold War era remained the main threat to the peace and security of the Somali population.[252] This is the tragic legacy that Somalia inherited from the East-West proxy wars. The superpowers left behind an enormous quantity of high-powered weaponry, which turned the entire land of Somalia into an arsenal depot. In this respect, systematic and effective disarmament was what the Somali civilians were hoping to be the foremost priority of the international forces. More optimistically, ordinary Somalis viewed disarmament "as the key to prevent another man-made famine, to facilitating political reconciliation, allowing alternative civic structures to flourish and undermine the warlords and to encouraging economic rehabilitation" (Omaar and de Waal, 1993:20). Yet, UNITAF made no real attempt to disarm the gangs, the militias and the warlords. While the UN was insisting that disarmament should be the integral part of the humanitarian operation, the UNITAF commanders on the ground were saying that such a task was not on their agenda. Eventually, the international forces confiscated some weapons but the whole exercise was sporadic and half-hearted. More detrimentally, UNITAF's chaotic disarmament efforts achieved nothing and even became counterproductive.[253] It was counterproductive for the simple reason that the random confiscation of arms left the civilian householders and shopkeepers living in the cities and towns prey to violent armed militias roving around. Even before the disarmament task began militia groups secretly moved most of their arsenals outside the cities and hid them in the countryside.[254] The result was increased insecurity among the defenceless civilians against gun-toting marauding militias. This is what one shopkeeper in Bokhara market place in Mogadishu lamented: "merchants were expecting the Americans to strength the security of the market. But this did not happen because they only

---

[251] See Kenneth Menkhaus, "International Peace-building and the Dynamics of Local and National Reconciliation in Somalia", *International Peacekeeping* 3, no.1 (Spring 1996): 42-67.

[252] " Thanks to the cold war, Somalia is awash in guns. After allowing the Soviet Union to arm them, the Somalis switched sides, allowing the Americans to arm them again. Then came two years of civil war and social collapse. Now armed robbery is just about the only trade that still offers employment to thousands of armed men. Lasting peace cannot be imposed unless most of them are disarmed" (*Newsweek*, December 21, 1992): 8.

[253] For a well analysed critique of the UNITAF failure to effectively and systematically disarm the clan factions and the bandits, see Alex de Waal and Rakiya Omaar, Somalia: Operation Restore Hope: A Preliminary Assessment (London: African Rights, May 1993): 20-27.

[254] " Nowhere were the problems caused by the American refusal to face up to the implications of its decision to intervene greater than in the area of disarmament. The U.S. had the greatest amount of military assets on the ground when the roughly thirty thousand troops landed in December 1992 and therefore the greatest capability to disarm the belligerent forces. The U.S. told the warlords, however that they could keep their weapons as long as they moved out of the city limits or to special cantonment areas controlled by warlord troops. A concentrated effort to remove or destroy the heavy arms present would have been possible and would have sent a very strong message at the beginning of the operation that the U.S. and UN were serious about restoring order" (Clarke and Herbst 1995:6-7).

disarmed merchants guarding the properties; while the thieves are still holding their guns and can still loot whenever they wish" (*African Rights*, 1993: 24).

With respect to political reconciliation, the intervention of UNITAF did not promote the peace dialogue in any significant manner. From the beginning, the UNITAF position was utterly clear: these difficult projects of political reconciliation and state building were beyond its mandate. They were regarded as the tasks of the UNOSOM II after UNITAF withdrew from the country. Yet despite this clear stand, the UN and the U.S. diplomats could not resist meddling in the political reconciliation process of the country. Their involvement in the political conflict had indeed aggravated the whole process in three respects. Firstly, their diplomacy derailed the "bottom up" political dialogue that Mohamed Sahnoun had already worked out diligently with the civic groups – clan elders, religious leaders, intellectuals, women's groups, etc. Instead, they opted for a "top down" approach and attempted to impose political solutions from above. Secondly, their peace mediation efforts deliberately promoted the warlords, which most Somalis viewed to be war criminals that should be arrested and brought to an international court of justice.[255] For instance, Ambassador Robert Oakley, the U.S. special envoy to Somalia openly reiterated that he had no intention of entering into negotiations with the warlords. Yet, Oakley sought the cooperation of the warlords as he brokered a temporary cease-fire between General Aideed and Ali Mahdi on 11 December 1992. More spectacular, during the signing of the agreement, Oakley publicly embraced the two warlords and that indeed gave them a spurious legitimacy as political leaders.[256] Furthermore, the UN diplomats sponsored a succession of peace conferences in Addis Ababa from January to March 1993, in which the self-made warlords played the predominant role. However, these costly and superimposed peace talks did not achieve anything, since after each meeting, the reconciliation points agreed to were violated by the very warlords and the clan faction leaders who signed them. One can argue that the UN diplomats hastily attempted to bring peace to Somalia through the appeasement of the warlords, albeit without success.[257] However, the immediate consequence of the re-empowerment of the warlords was that their rehabilitation badly impaired the efforts of the local civil initiatives. As Rakiya Omaar and Alex de Waal summed up, the political reconciliation had repeatedly failed in the country because it lacked (a) domestic mechanisms to enforce the implementations of the agreement, (b) the pre-existence of political structures to put pressures on the signatories to keep the agreement, and (c) economic incentives to offer the warlords concrete interests to abide by.

In short, the international intervention in Somalia helped to provide food to the starving, but failed to disarm the clan militias and/or initiate an appropriate peace dialogue and political reconciliation among the conflicting political elites.

---

[255] By contrast, the diplomatic strategy of Sahnoun was to gradually weaken the power and the political role of the warlords. He was also exploring the possibility of creating an alternative leadership.

[256] According to de Waal and Omaar, " by rushing to embrace the two warlords who had wreaked so much destruction on Mogadishu and Somalia, the US conferred an entirely spurious legitimacy on two men reviled by most Somalis as war criminals. The meeting was a boost to both of them. Both Somalis and experienced foreign aid workers expressed shock at the speed with which Ambassador Oakley embraced Aidid and Ali Mahdi" (1993:30).

[257] According to Michael Maren (1996: 202), " the UN paid massive hotel bills, flew warlords and their entourage to Addis Ababa, Nairobi, and Djibouti, and literally begged them to put their signatures on documents. Mohammed Ali Mahdi and Aideed used these meetings not to make peace with each other but as political conventions, where they lobbied and coerced other faction leaders, trying to convince them to sign on to a winning ticket".

8.4.   United Nations Operation in Somalia

On 4 May 1993, UNITAF handed over the operation of Somalia to the second United Nations Operation in Somalia (UNOSOM II). The transfer of power was authorised by the Security Council in Resolution 814 under Chapter 7 of the UN Charter, which was adopted on 26 March 1993. Under the resolution, the manpower of UNOSOM II was expanded to a multi-national force of 28,000 military personnel and 3,000 civilians from 33 different countries. The resolution also gave UNOSOM II the power to enforce peace, disarm and demobilize all the armed groups and bring all the fighting in the country to an end. Furthermore, the resolution widened the mission of UNISOM II and granted it a broad mandate to reform the economy, political and civil institutions of Somalia. In other words, the responsibility of the new mission was not only to ensure the delivery of humanitarian relief but also to help the recovery of the domestic economy, to promote peace and security, to broker reconciliation between the warring protagonists and to rebuild political institutions. Thus, while the UNITAF mission had a limited and short-term goal, the operation of UNOSOM II was unlimited and had a long-term agenda. Furthermore, while the operation of UNITAF was a peacekeeping mission, that of the UNOSOM II became a peace-enforcement mission. And as was critically argued, the expansion of the UNOSOM II mission was sweepingly ambitious and was not based on a sensible policy.[258] It was sweepingly ambitious because the UNOSOM II attempted to shoulder the responsibility of "nation building" in Somalia, which was a daunting feat. UNOSOM had neither the resources nor the organisational ability to initiate a long- term nation building programme in the country.[259] Nonetheless, the agenda behind this ambitious operation of wholesale restructuring of Somali society was not primarily dictated by the domestic conditions in Somalia but more by international global concerns. As Mark Bradbury writes, "at the end of the Cold War, and in the wake of the Gulf War, Somalia became a testing ground for the international community's response to conflict and humanitarian crisis in the 'new world order'. UNOSOM II's policies were thus driven more by international political concerns than by the situation in Somalia" (Bradbury 1997:16).

The operation with which UNOSOM II was entrusted was enormous and in reality was untenable. The mission did not have a clear political agenda, was minimally prepared and had no sufficient resources or the ability to tackle the daunting challenge of restoring order in Somalia.[260] In fact what the UNOSOM II was asked to undertake was what the UNITAF failed or had been unable to resolve during the period of its operation. UNOSOM II was asked to disarm the population and also create a stable political environment in the country. Consequently, the attempts to realize these difficult tasks created tension as warlord Aideed aggressively challenged the authority and the new, expanded mandate of UNOSOM II.
General Aideed fearing to be politically marginalized, used his radio to broadcast hostile propaganda against the UNOSOM administration in the country. This public incitement against the operations of the UNOSOM finally resulted in a showdown on 5 June 1993 when armed militias apparently associated with warlord Aideed ambushed and brutally killed 24

---

[258]See further Chester Crocker, " The Lessons of Somalia" *Foreign Affairs* 74 (May-June 1995): 5.

[259] The United Nations and Somalia (1992-1996), The United Nations Blue Books Series, Volume VIII, (New York: Published by the United Nations Department of Public Information): 85.

[260] See further, John L. Hirsch and Robert B. Oakley, Somalia and Operation Restore Hope: Reflections on Peacemaking and Peacekeeping (Washington, D.C.: Institute of Peace, 1995): 157.

Pakistani peacekeepers while they were inspecting an ammunition depot. Immediately after this outrageous killing, the Security Council adopted Resolution 837, which authorized "all necessary measures against all those responsible".[261] The resolution implicitly indicated Aideed to be the person behind the attack against the U.N. peacekeeping force. Admiral Jonathan Howe, the UN special envoy in charge of UNOSOM II, declared Aideed a wanted outlaw and ordered that he should be captured and arrested. After that warrant, Aideed became a fugitive and the target of UNOSOM II's primary mission. The manhunt to find Aideed however created more violence between the UNOSOM forces and his militiamen. In retaliation, the UNOSOM forces undertook punitive actions and staged a series of military strikes on buildings occupied by Aideed supports in south Mogadishu.[262] As a result, this escalated clashes, which developed into a continuing guerrilla war that took the lives of at least 56 UN soldiers and several hundred Somalis from June to September 1993.[263] After this battle, the credibility of UNOSOM was questioned. In the eyes of many Somalis, UNOSOM lost its neutrality in the Somali clan warfare, and as one observer put it, became perceived as "another faction and Admiral Howe as another warlord".[264]

The manhunt for Aideed bungled the purpose of the mission and totally derailed its original agenda. The mission became preoccupied with short-term exigencies and was no longer concerned with the long-term project mandated to implement it. Furthermore, UNOSOM effectively abandoned its political mission and opted for a military policy to pacify the country. UNOSOM chose for the military option rather than diplomacy in order to neutralise the violent gun-toting men loyal to the fugitive General Aideed.[265] However, the military coercion failed to tame the rag-tag militia force, which the military planners contemptuously dismissed as no match for the well-trained, well-equipped and determined U.S.-led international forces. The UNOSOM forces (with all their might) not only bogged down in their efforts to subdue the militias but also failed to capture Aideed, whose continued evasion of arrest attested to the UN's wider failures in Somalia.[266]

The UNOSOM military policy in Somalia, which was based on the concept of *making peace by making war,* was a disaster.[267] It failed to materialise into anything for the simple reason that the UN peacekeeping forces fell to squabbling among themselves.[268] The multi-national

---

[261] See, U.N. Security Council Resolution 837 (June 6, 1993).

[262] According to Lyons and Ahmed Samatar (1995: 58), " the weak, incomplete, and inconsistent U.S.-UN political strategy to encourage political reconciliation became irrelevant in the aftermath of the attack on the Pakistanis. UNOSOM and, in particular, the autonomous and U.S.-commanded Quick Reaction Force began a campaign to capture Aideed. U.S. forces bombed and strafed sections of Mogadishu and alienated much of the population".

[263] See Bradbury (1997:17).

[264] See further, Patrick Gilkes, " From Peace-Keeping to Peace Enforcement: The Somalia Precedent", *Middle East Report,* (November-December 1993): 21-24.

[265] According to Jim Hoagland, " In Somalia, the United States has been applying force without diplomacy. This is the flip side of the coin of Bosnia, where diplomacy without force is being used". See his article, Firepower Diplomacy in an Awkward African Setting, *The Washington Post,* (July 19, 1993).

[266] For a further discussion on this point, see, "Somalia: If you are not part of the solution", *Africa Confidential,* vol. 34 no.19 (24 September 1993).

[267] "Somalia: Manhunt", *The Economist* (18 September 1993): 48.

[268] "Somalia: Making monkeys of the UN", *The Economist* (10 July 1993).

troops stationed in Somalia had a difference of interests and that plagued their working relationship. For instance, some of the commanders of the international forces had even established the policy of clearing the UN orders by their respective governments before acting upon them.[269] In a nutshell, the failure of the international troops to act together in a constructive framework has completely undermined the military success of the mission.[270]

Unfortunately, the military policy even killed the top-down political reconciliation process that the UNOSOM diplomats had set in motion in the country. The UNOSOM administration proposed programmes aimed to assist in the formation of legal and judicial institutions. They also presented a blueprint to establish representative democratic government at national and regional level. Furthermore, they promised to organise free and fair elections and ensured that the international standards of human rights and justice would be promoted. On the humanitarian side, the UN Department of Humanitarian Affairs drew up a programme, which was intended to assist refugees and displaced persons to return home safely. With this proposal, UNOSOM secured donor pledges of US$130 million at a UN Conference on Humanitarian Assistance for Somalia in March 1993. However, all these political and humanitarian projects were halted because of the military policy that UNOSOM opted to pursue. This hard-line military priority continued unabated until 3 October 1993, when a battle between U.S. soldiers and gunmen loyal to Aideed resulted in carnage. In the gun-battle, 18 U.S. army rangers were killed, 73 were wounded, and hundreds of Somali lives were lost.[271] This terrible tragedy confirmed the fact that the UN's mission in Somalia had gone horribly wrong. After this debacle, president Clinton set March 31, 1994, as a deadline for the American troops to withdraw from Somalia, and UNOSOM suspended its manhunt for Aideed.

More problematic, the presence of the UNOSOM administration in the country not only enhanced the political profiles and status of the warlords and faction leaders but also enriched them financially. The UN in Somalia became an "industry". It generated revenue and wealth with which the warlords in the south, particularly General Aideed, used to finance their violent conflicts. Michael Maren's article, For Somalia's Sake, Get the UN Out has aptly made this point crystal clear. [272] According to Maren, "in the most violently contested areas, the UN presence means jobs, contracts and money. The United Nations rents houses, hires trucks and issues millions of dollars in contracts and sub-contracts to businessmen with close ties to the warlords." A good example of this was Mohammed Sheikh Osman, a former finance minister of the Siad Barre regime, who had rented out several mansions he owned to UN personnel. For one of the compounds, he received $70,000 per month in rent from the UN. Politically, Osman was aligned to the most violent faction in the south led by Aideed. But he was not the only one. There were many other war merchants who overnight turned themselves into rich businessmen for the services they provided to the UN garrison in

---

[269] Thomas G. Weiss, " Overcoming the Somalia Syndrome – 'Operation Rekindle Hope?' Global Governance: A Review of Multilateralism and International Organisations, vol.1 no. 2 (May-August 1995): 171-187.

[270] See, "The Pitfalls of Peacekeeping: United Nations: In war-torn Somalia, making a mess of things is a team effort", Newsweek, (1993): 10-11; see also Mitch McConnell, " Multilateralism's Obituary Was Written in Mogadishu", Christian Science Monitor, (October 27, 1993): 19.

[271] See Rick Atkinson, " The Raid That Went Wrong: How An Elite U.S. Force Failed in Somalia," Washington Post, (January 30, 1994).

[272] For more information, see International Herald Tribune (July 1994): 7.

Mogadishu. For these war merchants, continuation of the conflict was profit and prosperity, and financial support they provided to the warlords was what perpetuated the factional fighting. Thus, the presence of the UN administration in the country indirectly aided and prolonged the factional conflict.

The escalating factional conflicts and the military enforcement policy of the UNOSOM finally provoked an outcry. Aid agencies and relief officials began protesting that the militarised violence orchestrated by the international troops derailed the original mandate of the intervention – humanitarian aid. UNOSOM's excessive force hampered the humanitarian activities of the relief workers. Furthermore, the UNOSOM military approach was widely condemned while some of the international forces were reported to have committed serious violations against human rights.[273] These scathing accusations then prompted the UNOSOM administration to abandon its military strategy and focus on political and humanitarian objectives. But it was already too late. The Security Council decided in early November 1994 to withdraw all the UN troops from Somalia by 31 March 1995. Despite its heavy military cost the U.S. and UN mission in Somalia was a total failure. Regrettably, the UN departed from Somalia in a situation which in fact was not better than the conditions which urged its intervention in the first place.[274] As the UN left Somalia, Somalis started debating the consequence. Some argued that the clan civil war would resume again, while others maintained that the conflict would drastically reduce since the presence of the UN in the country contributed to fuelling the violence rather than extinguishing it.[275]

In retrospect, the presence of the UN in the country was a plague rather than a blessing. After the UN abandoned Somalia, the violent conflict in the south of the country subsided as faction leaders and warlords lost both of their political clout and the financial resources they needed to wage wars.[276] The new situation then forced some faction leaders and warlords to ensure that peace and security prevailed in the areas they controlled. The domestic tranquillity, which they created, permitted reconciliation at the local and at the regional levels to be initiated. A bottom up peace dialogue and reconciliation process was revived and pursued. This gradual community building process eventually resulted in the formation of the Puntland regional autonomy in the northeast of the country in August 1998. The formation of the Puntland Administration, although it is not yet effective, is a development of building Somalia from locality and regional levels; and there are attempts to be replicated in other areas of the country. Already, certain parts of the country such as in the Bay and Bakol areas in the south are also in the process of forming regionally based local autonomy along the lines of the Puntland Administration. However, the fear is that the newly established Transitional National Government (TNG) constituted at the centre in August 2000, which was imposed at the top, may disturb or slow down these important regional initiatives aimed at building the state from below. It remains to be seen how the two processes can be reconciled.[277]

---

[273] See, "Somalia: Human Rights Abuses by the UN Forces," *African Rights Report* (London, July 1993): 33-34.

[274] As Michael Maren (1996: 205) writes, " there is almost no evidence that the United States and UN were ever there, little trace of the $4 billion that was spent".

[275] Dr. Omar Ma'alim Mohamed, *Interview*, June 9, 1996 Addis Ababa.

[276] See Ali A. Jama, Country File: Somalia: 'Outside involvement risks perpetuating the Somali conflict' *Humanitarian Affairs Review*, no.11 (Autumn 2000): 44-50.

[277] See Martin Doornbos, "Somalië: botsende scenario's voor politieke reconstructie", *Internationale Spectator*, jaargang 55, nr 4,(april 2001): 192-198.

8.5. Conclusion: The Lessons Learned from the Somalia Experience

"The new world order was born in Somalia, and quickly died there" (Jeffrey Bartholot, Newsweek International, January 29, 2001).

The intervention in Somalia was the first mission that the international community had undertaken after the end of the Cold War in 1989. UN Secretary General Boutros Boutros-Ghali personally initiated the intervention in order to revitalise the organisation and upgrade its capability.[278] He wanted to prepare the organisation for a new global role and it was presumed that the success in Somalia would invigorate the UN for future global policing. Thus, in a broader global context, Somalia was an experiment for building the new world order that the Administration of President Bush envisioned in the early 1990's. Unfortunately, the UN intervention in Somalia had failed terribly and disappointed not only the Secretary General but also many other international and regional policy makers.[279] Boutros-Ghali, badly shaken by the UN fiasco in Somalia, tempered his optimistic agenda for peace that he had outlined earlier.[280] Perhaps the UN intervention in Somalia could have been a success if the intervention had taken place before the political crises shattered the state structures into a state of 'worst-case scenario'.[281] There are lessons that can be learned from the failure of the UN intervention in Somalia for future peacekeeping operations elsewhere.

First, the UN intervention in Somalia failed because the operation was launched too late. Although the international community was aware of the impending disaster in Somalia, they neglected to prevent it. They also failed to employ timely diplomatic intervention and missed serious opportunities, which time and again presented themselves as that Mohamed Sahnoun outlined in his book [282] that would perhaps have defused the violence and limited the political disaster. In this respect, the international community let the conflict in Somalia drag on till it fragmented the central authority and the state disintegrated entirely. In other words, the enduring violence destroyed all the vestiges of state institutions. Eventually, when the international community hesitantly and half-heartedly intervened in Somalia, the situation in the country was beyond repair and so grave that the operation became counterproductive. The international community should have intervened in Somalia at an earlier stage in order to avert the conflict. The lesson we can learn from this vain last minute attempt is the overriding importance of *early intervention* and *preventive diplomacy* if an internal conflict is to be effectively checked before it becomes endemic and unmanageable. This is a daunting challenge for the UN as there are nowadays many simmering and even erupting internal conflicts around the world which the UN as an institution can hardly do anything about without the commitment and cooperation of its member countries. Nonetheless, a good

---

[278] See his visionary first publication, An Agenda for Peace (1992).

[279] This is what Robert G. Patman writes " the UN operation in Somalia has been a bitter disappointment to those in the international community who saw it as a model for dealing with the disorder and conflicts of the post-Cold War world" (Patman 1995:101).

[280] See his second publication, An Agenda for Peace, 2d ed. (New York: UN Department of Public Information, 1995).

[281] For a further discussion, see Kenneth Menkhaus and Louis Ortmayer, "Somalia: Misread Crises and Missed Opprtunities", Opportunities Missed, Opportunities Seized: Preventive Diplomacy in the Post-Cold War World, (ed.) Bruce W. Jentleson (New York: Rowman &Littlefield Publishers, 2000): 211-237.

[282] Mohamed Sahnoun (1994).

example of preventive diplomacy is the current mediation effort by Nelson Mandela in the conflict in Burundi. This timely mediation has so far served to manage the conflict in Burundi and prevent a full-blown civil war in that country.

Second, the UN intervention in Somalia was a fiasco because the international community underestimated the depth of the state collapse in Somalia. They failed to comprehend that the political disorder in Somalia was not only the absence of a government but was also a failed state.[283] It was because of this conceptual shortcoming that the intervention of the international community focused on the consequences rather than on the real political crises that caused the catastrophic collapse of the state. For instance, although the international community modestly attended to the humanitarian exigencies of the situation, it hardly addressed seriously the underlying political problem concerning the disintegration of the institutions of the state in the country. A sensible approach would have been to attend first to the political problems in order to stabilise the political environment the country. Thus, in retrospect, the experience in Somalia challenges the conventional belief that humanitarian intervention without involvement in the domestic politics is the best appropriate response to a collapsed political system. According to Walter Clarke and Jeffrey Herbst, "Where people are dying in large numbers because of civilian conflict, the illusion should be discarded of a type of intervention that does not immediately interfere with the domestic politics of a country and does not include a nation-building component. Where famine is man-made, stopping the famine means rebuilding political institutions to create order" (Clarke and Herbst 1995:10). Finally, even the modest success of the humanitarian intervention was not sustained because of the rampant violence and the chaos that the prevailing political crises in the country perpetuated. In short, the international community underestimated not only the profound political disaster in Somalia but also failed to formulate an appropriate resolution. This is an important lesson for future operations.

Third, the UN intervention in Somalia failed because the mission was perceived to be a quick fix and a rapid exit operation. And it was behind this premise that the international community hastily intervened in Somalia. The mission, however, because of its "quick fix" nature was poorly conceived, poorly planned and poorly executed. There was no clear political agenda to establish what the mission entails and the realistic means to achieve the goals. In other words, the details of the operation were not spelled out in advance. There was also no sufficient preparation for the intervention. Everything was hurriedly decided and put together. Furthermore, the mandate of the mission was vaguely formulated and was not even adhered to accordingly. Prior to the intervention, the situation on the ground was not thoroughly assessed and was not intelligently understood since the international community was absent from Somalia for a long period of time. More simplistically, the intervention in Somalia was thought to be an easy operation since the political problem there was perceived to be a marginal quarrel between rival warlords and ragtag militias. As a result, the whole policy of the intervention was dictated by short-term exigencies since what the international community wanted in Somalia was a quick fix, rapid exit and a declaration of success.

---

[283] " It is evident that both government and the state have collapsed in Somalia. Yet, most political actors both inside and outside the country act as if the regime is the only institution, which collapsed. They never question the total demise of the state. It is under this wrong assumption that they have been attempting to re-establish a government in Somalia since 1991. But so far this has failed to materialise because it is not possible to restore a government prior to a state" (Mohamoud, 2001:6). For more discussion, see Somalia: The Pitfalls of Drain of Human Resources (Mohamoud 2001).

A good example of a quick fix solution is how the international community approached the national political reconciliation. The UN administration attempted to resolve the political conflict in the country by focusing too much on quickly imposed outcomes and too little on the process. In fact, it was the disregard for the *process - which painstakingly builds up towards a possible negotiated outcome* that has made the resolution of Somalia's conflict so problematic over the past 10 years.

Another example is how the international community put more emphasis on track I diplomacy and far less on track II diplomacy. Track I diplomacy is an official channel which the international diplomats formally use while dealing with politicians and governing authorities in any given country. By contrast, track II diplomacy is an informal channel where the local level civic groups and organisations are the major players.[284] However, by focusing too much on track I diplomacy and a quick fix solution, the UN diplomats sought out the warlords who presided over the collapse of the state as interlocutors in the political reconciliation.[285] This means that the UN diplomats dangerously promoted the political interests of the capricious warlords at the expense of informal civic groups. It may even be a truism to state that the international intervention in Somalia was flawed both in design and execution. Eventually, the short-term exigency that dictated the UN policy in Somalia became a disaster in itself since the complexity of the political crisis in the country was awesome and could not be fixed quickly. In fact, the dynamics of the political conflict in the country presented daunting challenges, which can only be tackled on a long-term basis. The lesson we can learn from this experience in Somalia is that quick fix intervention hardly solves anything. It can even be a recipe for failure as the diplomatic blunders in Somalia demonstrate.

Fourth, the UN intervention in Somalia failed because diplomacy was not seriously tried during attempts to resolve the political conflict in the country. For instance, before the intervention took place, half-hearted diplomacy was attempted to address the problem. But even this limited diplomatic effort, although undertaken too late, was not allowed to take its course. The international community was in a hurry and was not patient enough to wait for the ongoing "bottom up" diplomatic initiatives to materialise. As a result, diplomacy was abandoned immediately and instead a huge military intervention was launched to restore the political order in the country. Yet, the military option was not a sensible alternative.[286] With a sensible policy and an appropriate strategy, the military intervention should have been a last resort. At the time of the intervention, the appalling human suffering that the fighting of the unscrupulous rival warlords had caused was a challenge to our collective conscience and that precipitated the military intervention. Thus, seen from this humanitarian angle, the military intervention was a necessity and understandable. But what was not understandable and was fundamentally wrong was when the intervention mission launched for humanitarian operation was altered to a military operation. A mission in which violence and frequent military

---

[284] For more information, see Sagaren Naidoo, " The Role of Track Two Diplomacy in the Democratic Republic of Congo Conflict", *African Journal on Conflict Resolution (ACCORD)*, 1. no. 2 (2000).

[285] As Matt Bryden writes, "after so many setbacks, what the UN bureaucracy needs from Somalia is a quick fix that will allow a rapid exit and a declaration of victory. The UN wants only to stick the signatures of the Somalia's warlords at the bottom of a tidy peace agreement, greased along with promises of fat bankrolls for reconstruction. That they are recreating the same corrupt donor-driven system that fuelled Somalia's implosion in the first place is of a little concern to the international bureaucrats. Since this is the only solution the UN can come up with, it seems that Somalia's misery is just beginning", *Africa Report*, (May/June 1994): 23.

[286] According to Alex de Waal and Rakiya Omaar, " military intervention does not solve diplomatic problems; it merely changes the diplomatic agenda" (de Waal and Omaar, 1994): 8.

engagements between the foreign forces and Somali militias prevailed. Eventually, the primacy of the military operation compromised the political impartiality of the UN administration, made it an actor in the conflict and finally derailed the original humanitarian purpose of the mission. The most sensible winning strategy of the UN administration in Somalia should have been diplomatically aggressive and militarily passive. In hindsight, the UN military intervention in Somalia aggravated the complexity of the political problems and prolonged the conflict.[287] The lesson we can learn from the disaster of this military policy in Somalia is that diplomatic mediation must be given ample time and must be exhausted before military intervention is ever considered to resolve a domestic conflict for any future operation. This however depends on the effectiveness of the diplomatic mediation in helping to manage the conflict.

Fifth, the UN intervention in Somalia failed because it attempted to build the state from above. In fact, as I mentioned earlier, the international administration endeavoured to take the political role in the country that the fragmented Somali political elites failed to undertake. For instance, the Administration, particularly in its early stages took public responsibility for feeding the hungry Somalis (which saved thousands of lives), restored some public services, rehabilitated debilitated social infrastructures and attempted to establish a central authority. However, whatever public pursuit the international administration had tried to embark on, the warlords and the faction leaders systematically worked against it.[288] And warlord Aideed was the most stubborn among them as he frustrated every initiative with regard to the wider public pursuit of the whole Somali nation that the UN administration undertook. Aideed even challenged the very presence of the international administration in the country, as he feared that their presence would hinder his scheme for private pursuit. Thus, the extremely fragmented political elites in Somalia were neither supportive nor interested in the public pursuit project that the UN administration undertook as this would compromise their private pursuit agenda.

In a nutshell, the failure of the UN intervention in Somalia was not only caused by the political and military blunders of the Administration but much more so by the private pursuit that the Somali political elites pursued as a zero-sum game. During the intervention, the most serious question that the international administration failed to ask is: how can a state be built from above when the domestic elites are in disarray and are immersed in the struggle for private pursuit? This is in fact the chief reason why we failed to reconstitute the state over the past ten years. It is also a critical factor, which is still making the restoration of the state very difficult.

Another daunting problem that the state collapse in Somalia raises is the challenge of transforming families and clan-families into a cohesive community. The making of a community of citizens is the prerequisite for the making of a viable state. A society divided into feuding lineages and clan-families like that of Somalia cannot form a viable state. More simply, a house divided cannot stand. Yet, the international community attempted to build a

---

[287] According to Dennis Dijkzeul, " Interventions aimed at fostering peace and rebuilding societies sometimes back-fired, and instead served to fuel and thus prolong conflicts, as was the case with Somalia". See further his article, " The Rise and Fall of Emergency Relief", *Humanitarian Affairs Review* (Autumn 2000): 26-31.

[288] According to Robert G. Patman, " In the final analysis, however, while the UN 'humanitarian' intervention in Somalia was poorly conceived and mistake-ridden, it failed ultimately because of the truculent and myopic leadership of a dozen or so Somali warlords. Having started a civil war which ravaged the country and the lives of so many of its people, these power-hungry faction leaders spurned the opportunity to make peace under UN auspices" (Patman, 1995:104).

state in Somalia where there was neither a moral community – or, to put it simply, a community of collective concerns and belonging - nor a corporate political elite with a common and a well-defined national goal. In this respect, the effort of the international community can be described as putting the cart before the horse; or in other words, attempting to restore a state without a moral community. The building of a community and the state has always been the task of the domestic elites. Unfortunately, the domestic political elites in Somalia are preoccupied with the race for private pursuit. Only a cohesive political elite with a public pursuit agenda can engineer a community of citizens and build a viable state. Transforming clan-families and ethnic groups into a community of citizens and the building of a cohesive political elite will be the greatest challenges for the Somalis and for other Africans both in academia and those with political power for the foreseeable future. The construction of these underlying political cultures, without which a viable state cannot be build, must be the primary agenda for Africa in the twenty-first century.

Chapter Nine

Conclusions
Somalia: Beyond the Collapse of the State

9.1. Introduction

It is now time to try to bring together the threads of the study. Firstly, in this chapter, I summarise what I modestly hope will contribute to the understanding of why the Somali state collapsed, to the research in the field of Somali studies and also to the search for a ways of rebuilding a viable political order in the country. The primary aim of this study is to present a comprehensive historical processes which advance continuity and change explanations that offer different interpretations for the collapse of the state to those hitherto available.

Secondly, after the summary, I shall give a brief account of the attempts that the Somalis have so far made to restore a political order in the country. Since the Somali state collapsed in 1991, both "top down" and "bottom up" efforts have been undertaken in order to reconstitute the state. Thirdly, I describe the serious political tensions between the regional and the centralised-based attempts in establishing a viable political system in Somalia. Finally, I delineate the political uncertainty that confronts Somalia at the present and which is likely to prevail in the foreseeable future.

9.2. Alternative Propositions

In this study, taking a cue from a historically informed theory, I have attempted to advance alternative explanations for the collapse of the state. I have explained how the constraints in the material environment and the misfortunes in the Somali history across time have set in motion the destructive turn of events in the present Somalia.[289] I also attempted to construct a coherent explanation of the cumulative structural crises that the pitfalls of the triple history - pre-colonial, colonial and post-colonial dynamics - have produced. In this long-term view, I considered how the impact of the harsh ecological conditions, extreme poverty of the pastoral economy, colonial partitioning of the country, Cold War imperatives, decades of armed struggles and crisis of governance have all contributed to the collapse of the state.

The constraints in the material environment in the country had been a source of conflict and struggle for survival among the Somalis in much of their history. The Somali livestock husbandry that is the dominant means of economic existence even today is fit only for the most basic of subsistence and does not generate a surplus which can be used in building local administrations and a governing authority. Historically speaking, this precarious material existence among other factors has largely condemned the Somali people to develop a rudimentary political organisation that does not advance beyond lineage and kinship relations. To put it simply, the pre-colonial Somali social formation had a weak social stratification, lacked a class of political leadership and was stateless in the very sense of the word. Furthermore, as I demonstrated in this dissertation, the limited nature of the domestic

---

[289] Both aspects are paramount to this study because of their centrality for the purpose of clarifying the narratives of the collapse of the state.

economy is what aggravates the crisis of accumulation that the colonial and post-colonial Somali political elite perennially endure. In reality, this grinding material deprivation forced the political elite to become rivals for the control of state power as well as its resources and opportunities. Also the meagre pastoral economic existence, which hardly grows beyond bare subsistence level, was what condemned the modern state of Somalia to survive on foreign aid handouts from its colonial inception until its implosion in 1991. The Somali state collapsed after the external financial aid was cut off.[290] In short, as I argued in this study, examining historically the poverty of the domestic economy provides better insights as to why the state collapsed after the Cold War ended in 1989 and the domestic elites consequently became embroiled in a survivalist civil war. This political economy approach is superior to the explanations based on primordial clan animosity and other essentialist explanations.

As I described in this study, Somalis have also been unfortunate victims of the predicaments they have been placed in through the ages. The history of the Somalis has always been a history of struggles against foreign aggressions, conquests and occupations. For instance, the Somali people have been struggling against the expansion of the neighbouring feudal Ethiopian state, the colonial occupation and the partitioning of the country among colonial powers in much of its recorded history. Furthermore, since the colonial state was imposed, the struggle of liberating the country from foreign occupation and re-uniting all the territories inhabited by the ethnic Somalis had become the overriding priority in the agenda of the Somali political elite and governments. In fact, this Pan-Somali agenda was the most salient political project that defined the policy priority of the post-colonial Somali leadership over domestic social concerns and economic development. More markedly, the struggle to regain the missing territories led the subsequent Somali governments to pursue a very risky and untenable policy of irredentist adventure against the neighbouring countries. Unfortunately, the failure of the irredentist liberation struggle was what gradually militarised the institutions of the state and precipitated the crisis of governance in the 1980s. The militarisation of the state apparatus and the crisis of the governance have had grave results as they led to domestic social tensions, elite conflicts and to a civil war that ultimately resulted in the implosion of the state.

In essence, the contribution of this study in the field of Somali studies is to show how the constraints of the material environment and predicaments in the history of the Somali people across time, have largely determined the present social and political condition in Somalia. The central argument of this thesis is that the deleterious effects of both misfortunes – the poverty of the domestic economy on the one hand and the pitfalls of the colonial intervention and the division of the country on the other hand - have generated cumulative structural crises over time, which led to perennial conflicts and struggles that eventually destroyed the state. Presumably, if the domestic economy has had a sufficient surplus and colonial powers had not partitioned the country, the Somali state would probably not have withered away by now.

Theoretically, in this study, I examined the problematic nature of the collapse of the state both within the premises of the general theories (both modernisation and dependency) of state in Africa and within the specific debates in the Somali studies. In other words, I have adopted

---

[290] " Somalia in the Cold War era received a higher level of foreign aid per capita than any other country save Israel; the Somali state was literally run on external assistance and collapsed soon after that aid was withdrawn. Somalia earned a reputation as a `graveyard' of failed foreign assistance projects. Both the sheer quantity of aid and the politicised and poorly conceived quality of external assistance during the 1960 –1990 period left an indelible mark on Somali society and its response to foreign aid agencies" (Menkhaus 2001:311). Perhaps an indelible trait worth noting here is that the availability of massive foreign assistance is what by and large fostered a political culture of dependence and opportunism among the ruling Somali political elite (see chapter 5).

both the universal and the local levels of analysis to seek to understand how and why the state collapsed. However, the existing grand theories of the state in Africa, despite their divergent insights and concerns hardly shed enough light on clues that point to the processes leading to the fragmentation of the state, simply because the proponents of these universal approaches have taken for granted the permanence of the state world-wide. It is because of this certainty that the survival and the future existence of the state is not considered as a unit of analysis. The substantial issues these general theories of state mainly deal with regarding the state in Africa since the 1960s affirm this shortcoming. For instance, while the modernisation theory focused on the idiosyncrasy of the political system, the dependency alternative emphasised the external exploitation and the statist writers stressed the instrumentalist and the patrimonialist nature of the state in Africa. Thus, none of the approaches seriously questioned and/or addressed the basic structural crisis of the state in Africa, a subject which requires rigorous research elsewhere since it is not the aim of this study to pursue it any further. This weakness therefore certainly prevented those grand perspectives from foreseeing the implosion of states like that of Somalia during the 1990s.

The theoretical proposition of this study in contrast to the highly abstract universal level of analysis advanced by grand theories is that the crisis and in some cases the collapse (i.e. of Somalia) of the state in Africa can better be explained if we examine each respective state against its own historical conjuncture and specificity. In other words, the problematics of each state in Africa must be analysed within the dynamics of its own concrete historical trajectories and specific formation. In this instance I have analysed the collapse of the state in Somalia in the light of its own long-term historical trajectories through which the political institutions of the Somali people have evolved. The explanatory value of this approach is that it provides us better insights into both the specificity and the process of the legitimate normative evolution of the state.

With respect to the national and domestic level of analysis, the study takes cues from the existing debates of the Somali studies. I have tried to construct in a coherent manner a continuity and change explanations as to why the state collapsed. This is the point of departure of this study since the continuity and change debates link together internal and external dynamics that have been shaping the Somali social formations over a long period of time. For instance, the traditionalist scholarship of Somali studies claims that it is the *continuity* of the primordial socio-cultural aspects in the society, which is the fundamental source of the contemporary predicament in Somalia. By contrast, the transformationist writers of Somali studies alternatively contend that is the *change* of the political economy and power relations of the production wrought by the external dynamics (e.g. the colonial intervention), which exacerbated the domestic conflict that set the course for the fragmentation process of the state.

The theoretical proposition of this study in contrast to the traditionalist scholarship of Somali studies is that the causes of the state collapse in Somalia are determined internally by the continuity of private pursuit (understood here as spoils politics) rather than primordial clan animosity. This study also contests the theoretical proposition of the transformationist scholarship of Somali studies as it argues that the causes of the state collapse were wrought by the tendency towards public pursuit which the change brought about by the external colonial imposition and the partitioning of the country has given rise to. Thereafter, the grave consequences of the colonial divisions were later exacerbated by the imperatives of the Cold War politics in the Horn of Africa and by the militaristic policy of the Somali state that opted for an irredentist adventure. As I explained in the main body of the dissertation, the premises concerning private and public pursuit that I have developed advance alternative explanations to the collapse of the state to those hitherto available. In a nutshell, this alternative proposition is the essence that this thesis contributes to the theoretical debates in the field of Somali studies.

The added value of this study in the field of Somali studies and particularly the part dealing with the formation and the fragmentation of the state is that it attempts to present a continuity and change explanations that offer different interpretations for the collapse of the state. I have formulated these new interpretations after examining critically the history and the political economy of the Somali society across time. For instance, the continuity of the tendency towards private pursuit given rise to by the extreme material deprivation in the country helped to accentuate the persistence of narrow clan identity, kinship-based polity, wild chase for private spoils as well as all sorts of parochial interests. In this respect, the tendency towards private pursuit has positive impulses at the sub-national and sub-state levels but negatively affected the aspiration geared to promote the pursuit of the public good at the national and state levels. By contrast, the tendency towards public pursuit which the colonial fragmentation of the country awakened, inspired Somali-wide struggles against foreign aggressions and conquest and also fostered the idea of collective identity. In this sense, the positive impulses of the tendency towards public pursuit pushed the process of the social formation towards wider political identity, unity and nationhood while its negative repercussions (notably the militarisation of the state and the very risk irredentist adventure), undermined the viability of the post-colonial state of Somalia.

In a nutshell, the tendencies towards private and public pursuit which are indeed the two sides of the same coin, group certain decisive dimensions (including those elements already advanced by the dominant schools of Somali studies) that led to the historical demise of the Somali state project. Furthermore, in this study I tried to demonstrate how dialectic does not always lead to a new synthesis but sometimes to meltdown as the negative impulses of both historical dynamics have eventually fragmented the state. This study thus attempts to construct a mode of analysis and interpretation in the hope of shedding a new light on our understanding of the current political upheavals in Somalia. More importantly, this research contributes to practical policy approaches and proposals of post-conflict reconstruction in Somalia. The challenge that Somalia now faces is the development of institutional mechanisms that facilitates peace and development at the local and national levels. In this respect, the present post-conflict political development in Somalia demands innovative, strategic and systematic approach as well as a high level of creativity.

With respect to the general debate on the state in Africa, the contradictory tendencies towards private and public pursuit affirm the incompleteness of state making in the continent. For example, in a wider context, the tendency towards private pursuit demonstrates the persistence of parochial ties and sentiments based on kinship, ethnic loyalty, religion, language, regional, cultural identity and a host of other ascriptive criteria that still hinder the project of state building in Africa. By contrast, the tendency towards public pursuit is denoted by the diverse policy strategies adopted by the most ruling elites in the continent that were aimed to foster social reforms, embark on programmes for economic development and build viable state systems in the continent following independence. Thus, these concrete manifestations demonstrate how the working of the opposing tendencies towards private and public pursuit can also be observed on the continental plane. Let me make one point clear: I am not introducing here new definitions of these phenomena since these contradictory dynamics are discernible, albeit as different facets, in any given country in Africa. In this study I have only considered the workings of these frameworks within the context of Somalia. For example, with respect to public pursuit while most of the post-colonial African elites attempted to foster social coherence with the aim of building nations within the borders of their respective countries, the Somali elites by contrast embarked on the task of enlarging the boundaries of the state by irredentist adventure since according to their view Somalis are already a nation.[291] Eventually in Somalia the contradictory dynamics of these processes reinforced the total collapse of the state while in many countries in Africa these tendencies remain the underlying causes for the crisis of the state. The challenge confronting most states in Africa is how to develop economic resources and construct effective social institutions that promote the pursuit of the public good, which in the long run restrains the tendency of the politics of private pursuit.

9.3. Post –Conflict Development in Somalia

Somalia is the only country in the world, which has remained stateless over the past ten years. In this respect, Somalia has achieved the longest record of a withered state in the modern world, where the state system is the only internationally accepted mechanism for human organisation.[292] Since 1991 after the state collapsed, the social landscape of Somalia has completely changed. Somalia as a country has broken down into a series of clan-based fiefdoms that frequently clash over territory. This means that the country disintegrated into its traditional clan geography, which was the case before Somalia achieved the title of statehood in 1960.[293] The Somalis, wherever they were in the country before the conflict exploded, returned to their traditional homelands. The clan-based civil war that broke out in the aftermath of the state collapse forced them to seek safe havens in their respective clan areas. Consequently, Somalia now is a place where there is hardly a national state but numerous clan-based localities. The civil war in 1991 particularly created an atmosphere of deep mistrust and fear and badly damaged the social harmony among the Somali clans. Furthermore, the civil war caused a lot of grievances that many people will not easily forget. Today, ten years have passed since the state collapsed yet the social fabric of the society is still in tatters while the political authority at all levels is up for grabs.

Since the state collapsed, two parallel peace and reconciliation processes were initiated. One was a "top down" approach launched to restore a fully-fledged national government in the country. This traditional diplomatic "top down" approach was the strategy preferred and adopted by the UN, regional organisations, governments and the Somali political elite such as faction leaders to achieve national reconciliation. The external actors have initiated this high-level national process without understanding the complexity of Somali society.[294] They also failed to envision the collapse of the external economic backing and the ideological and

---

[291] For further information, see David D. Laitin and Said S. Samatar, Somalia: Nation in Search of a State, op. cit: 129-152.

[292] See Abdullah Mohamoud, " Somalia: The `Ungovernable' Country? *West Africa*, (4-10 August 1997): 1257-1258.

[293] Traditional clan-based geographical zones had existed in the country throughout Somali history (see chapter 3).

[294] For more information, see I.M. Lewis, " Misunderstanding the Somali Crisis", *Anthropology Today* 9 (August 1993): 2.

political underpinnings that sustained the survival of the crumbled centralised authority after the global history changed course at the end of the Cold War. Furthermore, they did not at all realise that the local social forces and the political leadership, which represented the collapsed central government, were in disarray and had fragmented into a bunch of individuals of irreconcilable political differences. Through this "top down" approach, twelve national reconciliation conferences (between 1991 and 1997) were convened with the goal of restoring a central authority in Somalia yet no success was achieved. The immediate reason for this was that the faction leaders and warlords who sign the peace deal and agreed to form a national government frequently failed to honour their promises.[295]

However, more fundamental reasons can be cited as to why the "top down" approach to restore a central authority in the country faltered dozens of times. First, the faction leaders and warlords who played the dominant role in the process of national reconciliation had neither legitimacy nor a real social base in the country. The only power they had was the barrel of the gun and the threat of this means of violence enabled them to keep the population hostage. No one nominated them to attend those conferences, which were held abroad. The ordinary people knew that those self-styled leaders were concerned only with their private vanity rather than the public good. Second, the civil war created a deep hatred and distrust among the Somali clans and no clan desires to be ruled by a leader(s) from other clans. Somalis in general feel wary of the establishment of a centralised political authority in the country, at least in the present situation, where power has become increasingly unrestrained due to degeneration of the social fabric and the normative social values of the society. Furthermore, "it is part of the Somali culture to care about the specific part of the country where one lives. With local identity and a sense of community among kinsmen narrowly conceived, rebellious clan factions were unwilling to accept a singular rule of law from any central authority" (Geshekter 1997:66).[296] Third, the people had a terrible experience of centralised government under the military regime of Said Barre. The central authority of Somalia was oppressive and brutal and many people became victims because of its arbitrary misrule. It is for this reason therefore that many people are unwilling to risk this oppressive system of rule for the second time.[297]

Even if the external actors had succeeded in establishing a central government in the country through a "top down" approach, its survival could not have been guaranteed because of the lack of domestic resources. As I discussed in chapter three and chapter five, the *camel economy* in the country is very limited and cannot afford to sustain a centralised system of authority. The experience of the vanished Somali state is a clear testimony for this. The post-colonial Somali state in fact survived through foreign assistance from its birth in 1960 till its demise in 1991. The concrete proof is that the Somali state collapsed immediately after the Cold War ended. As the foreign assistance was stopped the state tumbled. Thus, those who are in favour of the restoration of a central authority must not underestimate the depth of the

---

[295] Mark Bradbury notes that, "there was little incentive for military leaders and their militias, who were profiting from an economy of plunder and extortion, to implement any peace accord. With the peace conferences held outside Somalia there was little pressure on the factional leaders to adhere to the agreements" (Bradbury 1997:42).

[296] This quotation appears to contradict the irredentist politics of the Somali state over the past decades. But this is not the case. As the experience of past Somali history demonstrates, it is easier to mobilise the fragmented Somali clans against foreign threats and aggressions across borders than to appeal to them cooperate together in the domestic affairs of the country.

[297] Dr. Omar Ma'alim Mohamed, *Interview*, June 9, 1996, Addis Ababa.

poverty of the domestic economy in the country.[298] This is an aspect which both the external actors and the Somali political elites overlook or perhaps are not sufficiently interested to address in diplomatic official circles. The other crucial issue that I have attempted to highlight in this search study is the societal aspect of making a central authority in Somalia. As I asserted in chapter three, because of the low productivity of the camel economy, which is still the primary source of livelihood in Somalia, the social organisation of Somali society cannot advance beyond the kinship system. In other words, the prevalence of this kin-ordered mode not only prevents the institutionalisation of political power but also perpetuates the tendency of lineage or clan loyalty rather than a Somali-wide solidarity. Thus, the important question is: Is it realistic or even possible to establish a viable central authority in Somalia without a cohesive community? This is a daunting challenge, which the Somali political elite must ponder and deliberate on before taking a hasty decision that may not produce a durable political structure.

The other reconciliation process was a "bottom up" or a building block approach.[299] This peace initiative hardly received any media publicity and was neither encouraged nor supported externally. It was basically an internal affair and a locally driven peace process. The dominant players were the local-level leadership such as the traditional elders, religious leaders, locality and community leaders, local traders and networks of grass-roots civic associations such as women, intellectuals, etc. The local-level leadership initiated the reconciliation procedures as a gradual process and attempted to build the peace step by step. They took time and they had the patience to realise a durable peace settlement in their respective localities. They were also committed and had a strong resolve to secure lasting peace agreements between the different interest groups. The reconciliation process was gradual and measured and the conflicting parties had to negotiate for weeks and in some cases months in order to reach a consensus on a given issue. However, this time-consuming process was not what the external actors and the rivalling Somali faction leaders and warlords were prepared to endure since what they wanted was a quick convention and the declaration of a quick victory.

This initiative of building peace painstakingly at grass-root levels began in the north-west and north-east areas of the country after the central authority collapsed in 1991. The local-level leadership in both areas has done its utmost to save this part of the country from the civil war. They have greatly succeeded. The civil war that started in 1991 remained confined mainly to the south of the country. But, they have done more than preventing the civil strife in their respective regions. They have also set in motion a local level or grassroots peace process whereby the clans and sub-clans inhabiting those areas have to settle their differences through dialogue rather than through the barrel of a gun. The communities in both zones have to negotiate everything starting from the basics such as security matters, sharing resources all the

---

[298] According to Kenneth Menkhaus and Louis Ormayer, "this disjoint between the country's internal capacity to finance a government and the actual costs of an even-minimalist state structure was laid bare by UNOSOM efforts in 1993-1995 to assist in the rebuilding of a `sustainable' government in Somalia. Reviewing the actual size of the prewar Somali GNP and the country's likely tax revenues, UN officials concluded that even a bare-bones national police force would cost more than the entire annual budget of a future Somali state. All of the rest of the trappings of the contemporary state were well beyond the means of this impoverished country. Sustainability, as it turned out, was never an operative principle during the rise and expansion of the Somali state" (Menkhaus and Ormayer 2000:392).

[299] Since 1991 limited studies have been published which examine the significance of the building block approach in the contemporary post-conflict Somalia. See for instance, M. Bryden, `New Hope for Somalia?' The Building Block Approach', *Review of African Political Economy*, vol.26, no.79 (March 1999): 134-40; K. Menkhaus, Somalia: Political Order in a Stateless Society, *Current History*, vol. 97, no.619, (May 1998): 220-4.

way to the establishment of district and regional administrations.[300] The reconciliation dialogue was not without difficulties since the peace process was sometimes one step forward and two steps back. Nevertheless, the process was democratic as every interest group was allowed to participate in it. The local-level leadership peace platform helped the communities in both areas to tolerate their differences, created a culture of compromise, concession and discussion through which the interest groups can settle disagreements without recourse to violent means.

In 1993, the political leadership in the north-west (or what is now called the Somaliland Republic), because of the race chase for private spoils, failed to restore peace and stability among the clans and the sub-clans in the area. After that the traditional elders and the religious figures stepped in and took the initiative of building the peace painstakingly at grass-root levels.[301] The peace dialogue of the Council of Elders (Guurti)[302] has taken four months to iron out the differences among the rivalling groups but finally helped to restore a relatively viable stability in Somaliland. According to Bradbury,

> "The 1993 Borama conference was an impressive example of an indigenous Somali reconciliation process, in which the role of lineage elders as mediators in the internal affairs of the communities were clearly displayed. It provided an alternative model to the reconciliation process promoted by the United Nations in Somalia after the resignation of Ambassador Sahnoun" (Bradbury 1997:29).

The success of the peace initiatives of the traditional elders was that they first approached the settlement of disputes at the local level and then tried to build up to the sub-clan, clan and inter-clan levels. In short, the clan elders have succeeded where the political leaders have failed. In the Somali context, the elders and the religious leaders are the embodiment of tradition and moral order. They are seen as peacemakers who are also knowledgeable in cultural techniques of conflict-mediation and resolution (see chapter 3). For instance, during the Borama conference, the chairman of the Council of Elders, sheikh Ibrahim, stated that: "our task is to ensure security and reconciliation. The government's responsibility is management, administration and development" (Omaar, 1993:48).

The other success story of a post-conflict peace settlement in Somalia, initiated at the local levels, was that promoted in the north-east regions of the country. In December 1993, a peace conference was held in the city of Growe. The participants were mainly traditional elders, community leaders, representatives of various interest groups, intellectuals and religious figures. In this conference, the armed faction leaders attended only as observers. The main objectives of the conference were to find ways and means of achieving peace and cooperation among sub-clans and larger clan-families living in the adjoining regions of Bari, Sanaag, Nugaal, Sool and Mudug in the north-east. The conference adopted far-reaching resolutions that included implementation of security, economic development, social policies and

---

[300] Hussein Ali Dualeh, *Interview*, June 13, 1996, Addis Ababa.

[301] Rakiya Omaar writes that, "the betrayal of the hopes for Somaliland by some power-hungry politicians and military officers has pushed traditional elders to take matters into their own hands. Conflict resolution within clans and between clans has always been the responsibility of elders" (Omaar 1993:46-48).

[302] The success of the Guurti in bringing peace and stability in Somaliland has been widely publicised. A very good and concise article is that of Rakiya Omaar, "The Best Chance for Peace", *Africa Report*, (May/June 1993): 45-48.

cooperation among the five regions.[303] Since then, peace and security have prevailed all over those regions.

The peace and tranquillity that the regions in the north-east and in the north-west of the country have enjoyed over the past ten years also enabled the local population to experiment with local administrations and authorities. The north-west regions of Somaliland had a head-start. After 1991 Somaliland had a regional authority and even succeeded in holding three local elections. Furthermore, the regional authority succeeded in achieving relatively a functioning administration although they did not get any help from the outside world. Likewise, in the north-east regions a protracted process of negotiation between the political leaders and the local level leadership finally resulted in the formation of Puntland Administration in 1998. [304]

In both areas, the process of establishing local-level authorities has received little publicity and even little interest outside Somalia although it has been going on over the past ten years. In hindsight the intervention of the local-level leadership in the peace and the reconciliation process in both areas has been extremely important. They have not only helped to spare this part of the country from the civil war that destroyed southern Somalia but they also greatly contributed to the painstaking formation of local authorities from the "bottom up" approach, which is the best way to reconstruct a viable authority in Somalia at the present. Unfortunately, in southern Somalia, the local-level leadership was not allowed to emerge and reconcile the local communities as the armed faction leaders and warlords suppressed them and prevented them from doing so.[305] The tragedy is that now ten years have passed since the civil war broke out and still southern Somalia remains in the grip of a vicious and unending violence. It has also become an area where lawlessness and banditry are rampant compared with those peaceful regions in the northern parts of the country. Worse still, the dragging on of the violent conflict in the area tore asunder the fabric of the social order.

The success of the post-conflict local government experiment in these northern regions of the country could be a model or a catalyst for Somalia as a whole and also for others elsewhere who are trying their best to reconstitute their lives at the local levels. The war-torn communities in Sierra Leone, Congo, Kosovo and others could perhaps draw relevant lessons from this Somali experience. Furthermore, this Somali experiment of building peace, communal reconciliation and local level authorities from the "bottom up" approach needs to be studied and scrutinised in order to ascertain its long-term viability. Over the past ten years, Somalis have repeatedly failed to restore a central authority but succeeded in establishing locally and regionally based authorities. The reason is that the existing material environment and the social and political capacity of the contemporary Somali society cannot support any governing system beyond that of localised authorities. As Bradbury writes,

---

[303] See Abdullah Mohamoud, "Somalia: Aideed's homecoming" *West Africa*, (20-26 June 1994): 1084-1085.

[304] See further the publication of the War-torn Societies Project, Rebuilding Somalia: Issues and Possibilities for Puntland (London: Haan, 2000).

[305] The reason is that in southern Somalia there are productive resources that can still be plundered. Southern Somalia possesses rich agricultural resources that the factional leaders and the warlords are still jockeying to capture and control for their zero-sum game private pursuits. Anyone interested in knowing more about this war hidden beneath southern Somalia's seemingly perennial clan conflicts must read the book edited by Besteman and Cassanelli, The Struggle for Land in Southern Somalia: The War Behind the War, op.cit.

"The political constitution of Somali society lies not in the centralised political institutions of a European model, but in a particular social system where the notion of a 'social contract' has more to do with regulating political and economic relationships between pastoral kinship groups, than with delegating responsibility to a central polity" (Bradbury 1997:43).

9.4. Regional Versus Central Authority

In August 2000, a reconciliation conference that was held in Djibouti resulted in the formation of a "top down" centralised transitional national government in Mogadishu. Since then political tension has been simmering between the already existing local and regional authorities and the newly created centralised authority. Both the regionally based authorities of Puntland and Somaliland were the first domestic powers to reject the formation of the central government in the country. They do not want to recognise it and they do not want to deal with it at any level. In fact, they see the Mogadishu-based transitional national authority both as a threat to their political power and as a challenge to the regional administrations they have been building gradually from the scratch since 1991. Their main concern is that the peace and the political stability they have diligently realised in their respective regions may be at stake if they join southern Somalia, which is still in the grip of anarchy. They therefore argue that the so-called central authority in Mogadishu must first bring under their control the violent situation in Mogadishu and the southern regions. And only after they succeed in normalising the political situation in the south, restoring peace and order and establishing effective local control in the southern regions will they enter into a dialogue with them. Otherwise, they are not going to have anything to do with them. In short, what the regional authorities in Puntland and Somaliland are saying is: we have already put our houses in order, let the authorities in Mogadishu do the same thing in the south of Somalia before they start dreaming of a Somali-wide government.

Since the "top down" authority was established in Mogadishu, Somalis were debating the pros and cons of both regional and central administration. The establishment of the central administration "has inspired considerable debate and commentary inside and outside Somalia.... These debates are very important in the battle for public opinion inside Somalia, and hence important for external actors to understand. At this point in time, the debate is fairly evenly divided" (Menkhaus 2000:10).[306] The supporters of local and regional-level authorities argue that building Somalia from the bottom up is the most sensible since this approach offers the best hope for the future. The local communities own the "bottom up" process and what they have built so far at the local levels they achieved because they diligently utilised their own cultural and political resources and societal capacity. This "bottom up" approach of building the social fabric of the Somali society will take longer to achieve tangible results, but at the same time it has the potential to realise a society built on a culture of peace and democracy. It can also help to lay the foundation of a tradition for viable governance. This is how one of the Somali regionalists summed up the argument:

"In the best case scenario, the country will be de-centralised into smaller manageable units. Each unit will need to develop its own economic base and modern institutions, including all levels of education, to allow it to exist as viable entity. The sum of the

---

[306] See further Ken Menkhaus, "Somalia: A Situation Analysis", *WRITENET Paper* No. (07/2000): 1-21.

decentralised units will make up a strong nation with many functioning elements" (Jama, 2000:48).

The supporters of the top-imposed central authority by contrast contend that Somalia is in dire need of a national government. Over the past ten years Somalia remained without a central government. The situation cannot and must not remain like this any longer. To survive as a Somali nation we urgently need a country-wide national government. Thus, the establishment of a central authority in the country is not only the best option but it is an utmost necessity, as this will restore the unity and the nationhood of the Somali people. In brief, keeping in mind the local political situation in Somalia at present, the essence of the debate centres on which system of governance is viable in the long run. The supporters for the "bottom up" local and regional administrations forcefully argue that the building block approach is the most sensible strategy in the process of establishing a viable system of governance in the country. By contrast, the advocates of the "top down" central authority on the other hand, claim that what is now urgently needed is a nation-wide administration acceptable to the outside world and one which also rehabilitates the tattered international relations image of Somalia.

In this discussion, I.M. Lewis, the traditionalist proponent of Somali study is in favour of building the country from the "bottom up" levels. Lewis admires the achievements that the local level leadership in Puntland and Somaliland regions have so far made by putting in place locality-based political units, which are formed organically and according to him must be considered exemplary examples of the post-conflict political development in the country. By contrast, Lewis is very critical with the newly created and top-imposed central government in Mogadishu and the role of the UN in this process. [307] According to Lewis, the international community and the UN are attempting to re-impose on Somalia, "an archaic colonial structure that failed conspicuously to deliver 'good government' in the past. All those who have the interests of the Somali people at heart (and by no means all Somali politicians have that) should endeavour to understand how progress in Somaliland and Puntland has been achieved and how their successes might be replicated in the troubled south" (Lewis, 2001).[308] Abdi Samatar, one of the transformationist critics, contests this view of Lewis as he supports the transitional government formed in Djibouti in 2000. Samatar argues that the political reconciliation process, which resulted in the formation of this new transitional government in Somalia is not an outcome dictated or imposed by the UN on the Somali people but it is a realisation made possible by the collective efforts of the Somalis themselves. This outcome of the political process was negotiated by all groups of civil associations and leaders of different communities and thus was indeed inclusive. Therefore, the new government is legitimately elected and chosen by the Somalis and in this respect the scathing critics of Lewis are misplaced (Abdi Samatar, 2001). The dynamics of the present political tensions between the local, regional and central authorities in Somalia are very important processes that need to be observed very closely in the following years.

On top of the power struggles between the regional and central authorities, the other issues which remain a source of tension in the foreseeable future is the fear of one clan domination over others and the sharing of the limited resources in the country. Generally speaking the

---

[307] I.M. Lewis, New UN Adventures in Somalia, *Horn of Africa Bulletin*, No. 3, (2000): 19-20.

[308] See also this recent article of Lewis, "Why the Warlords Won: How the United States and the United Nations misunderstood the clan politics of Somalia", *TLS* (June 8, 2001).

peace and political reconciliation in Somalia is still a very fragile process. In this respect, what the people now need is a committed leadership that build up the governing institutions in the country both at the "bottom up" and at the "top down" levels diligently and in complementary spirit. Yet, we must not forget one aspect and that is the domestic economy in the country is the most important single parameter of what institution of governance is and is not possible or viable in Somalia. As I repeatedly discussed in the dissertation, the lack of a viable economic existence from which to generate sufficient tax revenue will be the greatest obstacle in sustaining a central authority in Somalia. The existing meagre domestic tax revenue can only support the most minimal system of governance. This must be obvious to anyone who has being following the political development in Somalia over the past decade. According to Menkhaus, "since the only subnational polities that have really worked effectively in Somalia in the 1990s are municipalities, this scenario would be roughly akin to the league of commercial city-states. This scenario would in some ways be more 'organic' in the Somali context. Such a polity would develop very gradually, over years and even decades. Given Somalia's weak tax revenues, this scenario is the only economically viable one, but this vision of a minimalist state runs deeply counter to the political instincts and habits of the current political class in Somalia, whose formative years were spent in large civil services supported by foreign aid and expansive government mandate" (Menkhaus 2000:19).

Establishing a central state with a minimum functional task will constitute a greater challenge and requires serious negotiations among all the political actors in the country. Perhaps the political power in the country can be reconstituted in a new alternative arrangement if the central authority is willing to delegate more political power to the local and regional authorities. However, the most difficult aspect is that the Somali power elite has to create and practise a new political habit which will not a minor feat. Still, as this saying goes: old habits die-hard. In the meantime, my position on this local, regional versus central debate will not differ from the statement that an old Somali made when the country was under the British Military Administration in the 1940s. A British officer once asked an old Somali man, "What do you want the most?" and the old man replied, "to be well governed, but to be left alone" (Hanley 1993:57). Keeping in mind this fundamental political wish of many ordinary Somalis and also their decentralised traditional polity down the ages the challenge of the contemporary Somali power elite will be how to put in place a system of governance that realises the equilibrium of this political desire.

9.5. Uncertain Political Future

After ten years of statelessness, Somalia still charts an uncertain political future. This political predicament is discernible at all levels – local, regional and national.[309] One thing however is certain: that the Somali population yearns for a stable political environment, which is free from fear, civil disturbances and violent conflict at all levels. Political stability is a prerequisite for the inhabitants in the country to rebuild their lives, economic livelihood and also engage in all types of social activities without undue concern. Uncertain economic prospects that the population faces also compound with the political crisis in the country.

For instance, over the past ten years, most of the Somalis who remained in the country have been primarily concerned with one thing and that was how to survive and remain alive in the midst of turmoil. On top of the civil war and the political violence that prevailed in Somalia, the people also become victims of natural calamities. In the last few years Somalia was plagued by alternating and frequent droughts and floods.[310] This year the rain has again failed and the farmers in the southern parts of Somalia have been badly affected. Moreover, since last year the economic hardship of the inhabitants in the country has been dire because of the ban on Somali livestock by the Saudi Arabia and other Gulf states. After a fatal Rift Valley fever broke out in Saudi Arabia and Yemen, which are the main markets, the import of the Somali livestock was banned (Menkhaus 2000). As a result, the livestock business which is the mainstay of the domestic economy and remains the only lifeline to most of the Somalis both urban and rural inhabitants particularly (the north and the north-eastern parts) of the country has been on hold since then. Furthermore, since the September 11, 2000 attacks on the World Trade Center and the Pentagon, the USA has put Somalia on the list of the countries, which harbour terrorists. And immediately after the September 11 attacks the humanitarian NGO's and UN organisations working in the country withdrew their staff from Somalia under the pretext that they are taking security precautions.[311]

Nonetheless, despite all these hardships and problems if there had been viable, responsible public institutions and accountable leadership in the country, the appalling situation that the Somalis are now undergoing perhaps might have been less tragic. Unfortunately, since the state collapse in 1991, the politics in Somalia has become the business of a few political entrepreneurs. These political entrepreneurs who are largely the relics of the past regimes in Somalia are only interested in acquiring absolute power. They are also immersed in the

---

[309] "Attempts to rebuild the Somali state have floundered and conventional international strategies seem not to produce meaningful results. Warlords' and faction leaders' machinations to create homeland-like mini-states in the provinces, akin to apartheid in South Africa, have also failed to gain the public's respect and the international community's recognition. Two of the more 'advanced' clan-states have succeeded in restoring peace in most areas of their provinces, but have yet to establish legitimate, functioning, inclusive institutions" (Abdi Samatar 2001:114).

[310] "A decade of civil war and massive population displacement has worsened living conditions in a country already impoverished and suffering annually from cycles of drought and floods" (UNHCR Country Report: Somalia, October 2, 2001: 3).

[311] " The United Nations pulled its international staff out of Somalia after being told flights to and from Mogadishu could no longer be insured after the suicide attacks on the United States. The European Union withdrew its expatriate staff last week because of 'general tension and uncertainty there' following the attacks on the US" (BBC News: UN pulls out of Somalia, September 24, 2001:1), http://news.bbc.uk/hi/english/world/africa/newsid_1560000/1560822.shtml [accessed 12 October 2001].

politics of private pursuit. Thus, these old relics have neither the vision/strategy nor the interest to salvage the Somali society from its present predicament.

In Somalia, the absolute power and the concentration of power in one hand or in the hands of a few is the kern of the problem since the concept of institutionalised power is an alien phenomenon with respect to the social organisation of the Somali society. As I discussed in dissertation, in the pre-colonial Somali social formation, power was diffuse in the political arrangement and was exercised by consensus. No on had absolute power and there was no leadership in which the power concentrated. During the colonial period, this decentralised political power had come to an end (see chapter 3). The colonial state was the embodiment of power and had absolute power. Furthermore, the colonial state conferred political power on certain selected Somalis who eventually inherited this absolute power after the decolonisation process was completed. But sadly, over the past four decades, this colonially created and empowered Somali leadership misused their political power as they employed it to oppress their powerless countrymen and also to plunder the limited national resources for their own private gains.[312] As a result, the population is wary of the establishment of any sort of a political power at any level. This is indeed an aspect that the Somalis must ponder if they want to realise a viable political environment in the country in the future.

Another problem is the long-term dependence on foreign help that Somalia grew accustomed to during the past four decades. This sowed the habit of expecting that outsiders would come to aid Somalia. In fact, since independence and even before (see chapter 5and 6), Somalis have been living beyond their means. But if this help was something that the Somalis had taken for granted during the Cold War era, the world reality of today is totally different. No foreign power or a country is now prepared to assist Somalia on a grand scale as before. This is the reality that the Somali power elite must understand. Furthermore, if the Somalis want to stand on their own feet this habit of dependence must be lessened or abandoned totally. Instead, they should rely on and use what they have in the country and not what they expect from the outside world. For instance, they should exploit creatively the meagre material resources in the country dominated by the camel economy as well as their socio-cultural, ethical, ideological and political institutions and out of these create a polity that suits their world reality and can be sustained.

This leads me to the aspect of the narrow political identity that has been the hallmark of Somali social organisation throughout its political history. In this respect, Somalis hardly acted or cooperated together as a single and a stable political unit and if they did on occasions when they collectively faced foreign threats that solidarity was always short-lived (see chapter 3). As a result, corporate responsibility and political solidarity had always existed in the smallest units of Somali lineages. Thus, among the Somalis, viable community cooperation is possible but this can only be initiated at local levels. All in all, the findings of this dissertation demonstrate that the meagre economic existence and the restricted political development which the domination of the kinship relations perpetuate can only support the establishment of minimal political institutions in Somalia. And this minimal political arrangement begins when the people first start to cooperate at the lowest level of political identity and at the local levels in matters of specific community services such as constructing water reservoir, schools and all

---

[312] " Somalia's social and political balance sheet since independence is dominated by liabilities that have significantly diminished the nation's sense of a common destiny. The murderous and illegal uses of state power and the sectarian exploitation of national resources figure prominently in the population's collective memory of the last three decades" (Abdi Samatar 2001:114).

other kinds of basic infrastructures. Fortunately, in certain parts of the country, this locality-based communal corporate responsibility is already being experimented with.[313]

More importantly, this local level factional cooperation that brings the co-residents together can also foster dialogue, building of trust, confidence and partnership and help to strengthen the local capacity. Moreover, it can empower the community to take self-help initiatives and not wait for others to come and help them. Furthermore, local infrastructures that the community owns will not be easily destroyed, as has been the fate of the government owned property during the civil war in 1991. Thus, a renewed public pursuit that is inward-oriented in contrast to the past irredentist adventure and wherein locality-based cooperative civic duty is the cornerstone is perhaps the most sensible policy strategy by which a future Somalia can be gradually reconstructed.

---

[313] For more information, see Abdi Samatar, "Somali Reconstruction and Local Initiative: Amoud University", Bildhaan, 1, (2001), pp.107-131. In this article Abdi Samatar describes how community members in the town of Borama, which is located in the northwest of Somalia have succeeded in realising cooperative civic schemes in their locality beneficial to all the inhabitants. According to Samatar, " the discussion about Amoud University shows that building people's confidence that they can work together for the common good and establishing their trust in public institutions are not necessarily long-term propositions. I argue that there is one critical factor to reversing the trends of the last three decades in Somalia. That key is to create institutions that constrain sectarian entrepreneurs while strengthening shared values and hopes. The community-owned Amoud University may signal a new type of public effort in Somalia, one that will enhance accountability, rebuild public trust, and advance a common agenda" (Samatar 2001:109).

References

Abdi, Ali A. 1997: The Rise and Fall of Somali Nationalism: From Traditional Society to Fragile 'Nationhood ' to Post-State Fiefdoms. *Horn of Africa Journal*, Vol. 3 (4), 35-72.

Abdi, Sheikh Abdi.1982: Somalia: A Litmus Paper for U.S. Foreign Policy in the 1980s? *Horn of Africa Journal*, Vol.3 (2), 34-43.

Abdi, Sheik Abdi. 1993: Divine Madness: Mohamed Abdulle Hassan (1856-1920). London: Zed Books.

Abir, Mordechai. 1972: Red Sea Politics. Conflicts in Africa. *Adelphi Papers*, no.93: 25-37.

Abucar , Mohamed H. 1995: Mass Politics, Elections and African Social Structures: Botswana andOther African Countries. *International Sociology*, Vol.10 (1), 5-22.

Adam, F. 1900: *Handbook of Somaliland*. London

Adam, Hussein. 1994: Formation and Recognition of New States: Somaliland in Contrast to Eritrea. *Review of African Political Economy*, Vol.21 (59), 21-38.

Adam , Hussein and Ford, Richard.1997: *Mending Rips in the Sky: Options for Somali Communities in the 21st Century*. Lawrencville and Asmara: The Red Sea Press.

Adam, Hussein M. 1998: Somalia: Personal Rule, Military Rule and Militarism. In Hutchful and Bathily (eds).

Africa Confidential. 1988: "Somalia: Under Fire". April 29: 6

Africa Confidential. 1993: "Somalia: If you are not part of the solution". Vol. 34 (19).

Africa Contemporary Record. 1987 - 1988: 393.

African Recovery. 1989: Africa's Debt Profile. Vol. 4 (October – December).

Africa Report. 1993: U.S. Commits Force to Somalia, But For How Long? January – February: 5, 6, 11.

African Rights Report. 1993: Somalia: Human Rights Abuses by the UN Forces. July, 33-34.

Africa Watch. 1990: *Somalia: A government at war with its people*. The Africa Watch Committee: New York.

Africa Watch. 1992: "Somalia: a Fight to the Finish?" News from Africa Watch, Vol. 4, February 13:7.

Ahmed, Ali J. 1995: *The Invention of Somalia*. Lawrenceville: The Red Sea Press.

Ahmed, Ali J. 1996: *Daybreak is Near: Literature, Clans and the Nation-State in Somalia*. Lawrenceville and Asmara: The Red Sea Press.

Almond, Gabriel and Coleman, James S. (eds.). 1960: *The Politics of Developing Areas*. Princeton: Princeton University Press.

Allen, Chris. 1995: Understanding African Politics. *Review of African Political Economy*, No. 65, 301-320.

Amin, Samir. 1976: *Unequal Development*. Sussex: Harvester.

Amin, Samir. 1980: *Class and Nation: Historically and in the Current Crisis*. Translated by Susan Kaplow, New York and London: Monthly Review Press.

Anderson, Lisa. 1986: *The State and Social Transformation in Tunisia and Libya (1830 – 1980)*. New Jersey: Princeton University Press.

Andrzejewski, B.W. and Lewis I.M. 1964: Somali Poetry: An Introduction. Oxford: Clarendon Press.

Andrzejewski, B.W. 1974: The Introduction of a National Orthography for Somalia. *African Language Studies*. No.15, 199-203;

Andrzejewski, B.W. 1978: The Development of a National Orthography in Somalia and the Modernization of the Somali Language. *Horn of Africa Journal*. July-September, 39-45.

Apter, David E. 1965: *The Politics of Modernization*. Chicago: University of Chicago Press.

Askar, Ahmed O. 1992: *Sharks and Soldiers* .London: Haan Publishing.

Atkinson, Rick.1994: The Raid That Went Wrong: How An Elite U.S. Force Failed in Somalia. *Washington Post*. January 30.

Ayoob, Mohammed. 1980: The Horn of Africa. In *Conflict and Intervention in the Third World*. Ayoob, Mohammed (ed). London: Croom Helm.

Barre, Mohamed S. 1974: *My Country and My People*. Mogadishu.

Barth, Fredrik. 1982: General Perspective on Nomad-Sedentary Relations. In Nelson (ed.).

Batuta, Ibn. 1975: *Ibn Batuta in Black Africa: Selections Translated by Said Hamdun and Noel King*. London: Collings.

Bartholot, Jeffrey. 2001: The new world order was born in Somalia, and quickly died there. *Newsweek International*. January 29.

Bayart, Jean-Francois. 1991: Finishing with the Idea of the third World: The Concept of the Political Trajectory. In Manor, James (ed.) *Rethinking Third World Politics*. London: Longman, 51-71.

Bayart, Jean-Francois. 1993: *The State in Africa: The Politics of the Belly*. New York: Longman.

BBC News. 2001: UN Pulls Out of Somalia. September 24 (http://news.bbc.uk/hi/english/world/africa/newsid_1560000/1560822.shtml)

Beachy, Ray. 1990: *The Warrior Mullah: The Horn Aflame, 1892-1920*. London: Bellew Publishing.

Bell, Bowyer J. 1973: *The Horn of Africa: Strategic Magnet of the Seventies*. New York: Crane Russak.

Bell, Bowyer J. 1975: The Strategic Implications of the Soviet Presence in Somalia. *Orbis*. Vol.19, no.2. (Summer): 402-411.

Bestman, Catherine and Cassanelli, Lee V. (eds).1996: *The Struggle for Land in Southern Somalia: The War Behind the War*. Boulder: Westview Press.

Bildhaan. 2001: *An International Journal of Somali Studies*. Vol.1.

Blomstrom , Magnus and Hettne, Bjorn. 1984: *Development Theory in Transition: the Dependency Debate and Beyond-Third World Responses*. London: Zed Books.

Boutros-Ghali, Boutros. 1992: *An Agenda for Peace*. New York: United Nations.

Boutros-Ghali, Boutros. 1995: *Supplement to An Agenda for Peace: Position Paper of the Secretary General on the Occasion of the Fiftieth Anniversary of the United Nations*. New York: United Nations.

Bradbury, Mark. 1997: *Somaliland CIIR Country Report*. London: Catholic Institute for International Relations.

Bradbury, Mark. 1999: New Hope for Somalia? The Building Block Approach. *Review of African Political Economy,* vol.26, no.79 (March): 134-40.

Braudel, Fernand. 1980: *On History. Translated by Sarah Matthews*. Chicago: The University of Chicago Press.

Braun , Gerald. 1989: The Somali Development Concept in Crisis. *Northeast African Studies*. Vol. 11, 1-12.

Brons, H. Maria. 2001: *Society, Security, Sovereignty and the State: From Statelessness to Statelessness?* Utrecht: International Books.

Bryden, Matt. 1994. Somalia: Status Quo Ante? *Africa Report*. May-June, 23.

Bulhan, Hussein A. 1980:The Captive Intelligentsia of Somalia. *Horn of Africa Journal*. Vol.3 (1),25-37.

Burton, Richard F. 1894: *First Footsteps in East Africa*. Two volumes. London: Tylston and Edwards.

Compagnon, Daniel. 1992: Political Decay in Somalia: From Personal Rule to Warlordism. *Refuge*. Vol. 12 (5), 8-13.

Callagy, Thomas. 1984: *The State-Society Struggle: Zaire in Comparative Perspective*. New York: Columbia University Press.

Cardoso, Feranndo H. and Enzo, Faletto. 1979: *Dependency and Development in Latin America*. Berkeley: University of California Press.

Cassanelli, Lee V. 1982: *The Shaping of Somali Society: Reconstruction of the History of a Pastoral People, 1600-1900*. Philadelphia: University of Pennsylvania Press.

Castagno, A.A., 1959: *Somalia. International Conciliation Series, no.522*. New York: Carnegie Endowment for International Peace.

Chazan, Naomi. Mortimer, Robert. Ravenhill, John. and Rothchild, Donald.1992: *Politics and Society in contemporary Africa*. Boulder: Lynne Rienner Publishers

Cheney, Dick and Powell, Colin. 1992: U.S. Mission to Somalia is Necessary and Clear. *USIA, East Asia/Pacific Wireless File*. December 4, 12.

Christensen, Hanne. 1982-1983: Survival Strategies for the Camp Refugees in Somalia. *Horn of Africa Journal*. Vol. 5 (4).

Clark, Jeffrey. 1993: Debacle in Somalia: Failure of the Collective Response. In Loris F. Damrosch (ed). *Enforcing Restraint: Collective Intervention in Internal Conflicts*. New York: Council of Foreign Relations.

Clarke, Walter S. 1993-1994: Testing the World's Resolve in Somalia. *Parameters*. Vol. 23 (Winter 1993-94).

Clarke. Walter and Herbst, Jeffrey.1995: *Somalia and the Future of Humanitarian Intervention*.Center of International Studies, Monograph Series, No. 9 (Princeton: Princeton University

Clarke, Walter and Herbst, Jeffrey (eds.). 1997: *Learning from Somalia: The Lessons of Armed Humanitarian Intervention*. Boulder: Westview Press.

Clapham, Christopher. 1985: *Third World Politics: An Introduction*. Madison: University of Wisconsin Press.

Collins, Douglas. 1960: *A Tear for Somalia*. London: The Adventures Club.

Cox, Robert W. 1987: *Production, Power, and World Order: Social Forces in the Making of History (Vol.1)*, New York: Columbia University Press.

Crocker, Chester. 1995. The Lessons of Somalia. *Foreign Affairs*. Vol. 74 (May-June).

Crozier, Brian.1975: The Soviet Presence in Somalia. *Conflict Studies*. No. 54.

Damooei, Jamshid. 1997: Analyzing Somalia's Past and Present Economic Constraints and Opportunities for Creating a Conducive Economic Environment. In Adam and Ford (eds.).

Davidson, Basi 1992: Africa: The Politics of Failure. *The Socialist Register*. 212-225.

De Waal, Alex, and Omaar, Rakiya. 1993: Somalia: Operation Restore Hope: A Preliminary Assessment. *African Rights*. London: African Rights. May, 20-27.

De Waal, Alex, and Omaar, Rakiya. 1994: "Can Military Intervention Be "Humanitarian?" *Middle East Report*. March-June, 3-8.

De Waal, Alex. 1995: Africa: Hope not Restored. *TLS*. December 29.

Dexter, Lewis A. 1970: *Elite and Specialized Interviewing*. Evanston: Northwestern University Press.

Doornbos, Martin. 1990: The African State in Academic Debate: Retrospect and Prospect. *The Journal of Modern African Studies*. Vol. 28 (2), 177-198.

Doornbos, Martin. 1993: " Pasture and Polis: The Roots of Political Marginalization of Somali Pastoralism. In Markakis, John (ed.). *Conflict and the Decline of Pastoralism in the Horn of Africa*. The Hague: Institute of Social Studies.

Doornbos, Martin. 2001. Somalië:botsende scenario's voor politieke reconstructie. *Internationale Spectator*. Jaargang 55 (4), 192-198.

Dos Santos, Theotonio. 1973: The Crisis of Development Theory and the Problems of Dependency. in Latin America. In Bernstein, H. (ed). *Underdevelopment and Development*. Harmondsworth: Penguin.

Drake-Brockman and Ralph E. 1912: *British Somaliland*. London: Hurst & Blackett, Ltd.

Dualeh, Hussein A. 1994: *From Barre to Aideed: Somalia the Agony of a Nation*. Nairobi: Stellagraphics.

Dijkzeul, Dennis. 2000: The Rise and Fall of Emergency Relief. *Humanitarian Affairs Review*. Autumn, 26-31.

Economist, The. 1990: September 29, 47. "The Mayor of Mogadishu".

Economist, The. 1993: July 10. "Somalia: Making Monkeys of the UN".

Economist, The, 1993: September 18, 48. "Somalia: Manhunt".

Economist, The. 1995: September 16, 55-58. "Somalia: A Society Without the State".

Economist, The, 2000: October 21, 56. "Somalia: Not yet reborn".

Ellen, Chris. 1995: Understanding African Politics. *Review of African Political Economy*, 65: 301-320.

Ellis, Stephen, 1996: Africa after the Cold War: New Patterns of Government and Politics. *Development and Change*. 1-25.

Ellis, Stephen. 1999: Staatsinriching in Africa: Import of eigen kweek? *Internationale Spectator*.Jaargang 53 (5), 294-298.

Elsenhans, Hartmut. 1991: *Development and Underdevelopment: The History, Economics and Politics of North-South Relations*. London: Sage Publications.

Evans-Pritchard, E.E. 1940/1978: *The Nuer: A Description of the Modes of Livelihood and Political Institutions of a Nilotic People*. New York: Oxford University Press.

Farah, Nuruddin. 2000. *Yesterday, Tomorrow: Voices from the Somali Diaspora*. London: Cassell.

Farer, J. Tom. 1979: *War Clouds on the Horn of Africa: The Widening Storm*. New York: Carnegie Endowment for International Peace.

Fatton, Robert Jr. 1992: *Predatory Rule: State and Civil Society in Africa*. Boulder:Lynne Rienner Publishers.

Frank, Andre G. 1967: *Capitalism and Underdevelopment in Latin America*. New York: Monthly Review Press.

Frank, Andre G. 1969: *Latin America: Underdevelopment or Revolution*, New York: Monthly Review Press.

Frank, Andre G. 1975: *On Capitalist Development*. Bombay: Oxford University Press.

Freund, Bill. 1984: *The Making of Contemporary Africa: The Development of African Society Since 1800*. London: Macmillan.

Galaydh, Ali K. 1990: Notes on the State of the Somali State. *Horn of Africa Journal*. Vol. XIII,1-28.

Gendzier, Irene. 1985: *Managing Political Change: Social Scientists and the Third World*. Boulder: Westview Press.

Geshekter, Charles. 1993: *Somali Maritime History and Regional Sub-Cultures: A Neglected Theme of the Somali Crisis*. The European Association of Somali Studies First Conference, September 23-25.

Geshekter, Charles. 1997: The Death of Somalia in Historical Perspective. In Adam and Ford (eds).

Ghalib, Jama M. 1995: *The Cost of Dictatorship: The Somali experience*. New York: Lilian Barbar Press.

Gilkes, Patrick. 1993: From Peace-Keeping to Peace Enforcement: The Somalia Precedent. *Middle East Report*. November-December, 21-24.

Hamilton, Angus. 1911/1970: *Somaliland*. Westport, Connecticut: Negro Universities Press.

Hanley, Gerald. 1993: *Warriors: Life and Death among the Somalis*. London: Eland.

Hashim, Alice Bettis. 1995: *The Fallen State: Dictatorship, Social Cleavage and Dissonance in Somalia*. University of Virginia: UMI Dissertation Services.

Henry, Neil. 1990: Somalia Orders Trail for Signers of Rights Letter. *Washington Post*. February 18.

Hess, Robert. 1966: *Italian Colonialism in Somalia*. Chicago: University of Chicago.

Hirsch, John L. and Oakley, Robert B. 1995: *Somalia and Operation Restore Hope: Reflections on Peacemaking and Peacekeeping*. Washington DC: United States Institute of Peace.

Hoagland, Jim.1993. Firepower Diplomacy in an Awkward African Setting. *The Washington Post*. July 19.

Hobsbawm, Eric. 1994: *Age of Extremes: The Short Twentieth Century 1914-1991*. London: Abacus.

Hutchful, Eboe and Bathily, Abdoulaye (eds). 1998: *The Military and Militarism in Africa*. Dakar: Codesria Book Series.

Heyden, Goran. 1983: *No Shortcuts to Progress*. London: Heinemann.

Hyden, Goran.1996: Rethinking Theories of the State: An Africanist Perspective. *Africa Insight*. Vol. 26 (1), 26-35.

Ibn Khaldun. 1967: *The Muqaddimah: An Introduction to History*. London: RKP *International Herald Tribune* (July 1994): 7.

Issa-Salwe, Abdisalam M. 1994: *The Collapse of the Somali State: The Impact of the Colonial Legacy*. London: Haan Associates.

Jackson, Robert H. and Rosberg, Carl G. 1982: *Personal Rule in Black Africa*. Berkeley: University of California Press.

Jackson, Robert H. 1986: Negative Sovereignty in Sub-Saharan Africa. *Review of International Studies*. Vol. 12, October, 247-64.

Jama, Ali A. 2000: Country File: Somalia: Outside involvement risks perpetuating the Somali conflict. *Humanitarian Affairs Review*. No.11, Autumn, 44-50.

Jamal, Vali. 1988: Somalia: Economics for an Unconventional Economy. *World Employment Programme*. Research Working Paper WEP10-6/WP. Geneva: International Labour Office.

James, F. L. 1888: *The Unknown Horn of Africa*. London: George Philip & Son.

James, Lawrence L. 1985: *The Savage Wars: British Campaigns in Africa, 1870-1920*. London: Robert Hale.

Jardine, Douglas. 1926/1969: *The Mad Mullah of Somaliland*. New York: Negro Universities Press.

Kapeteijns, Lidwien. 1994: Women and the Crisis of Communal Identity: The Cultural Construction of Gender in Somali History. In Ahmed Samatar (ed).

Khapoya, Vincent B.1982: Historical Origins of the Refugee Problem: Somalia's Colonial Experience and Irredentism. *Horn of Africa*. Vol.5 (1), 29-31.

Karp, Mark. 1960: *The Economics of Trusteeship in Somalia*. Boston: Boston University Press.

Khazanov, A.M. 1983: *Nomads and the outside world, Translated from Russian by J. Crookenden*. Cambridge: Cambridge University Press.

Lacoste, Yves. 1984: *Ibn Khaldun: The Birth of History and the Past of the Third World*. London: Verso.

Laitin, David D. 1976: The Political Economy of Military Rule in Somalia. *Journal of Modern African Studies*. Vol. 14 (3), 449-468.

Laitin, David, D. 1982: The Political Crisis in Somalia. *Horn of Africa Journal*. Vol. 5 (2), 60-64.

Laitin, David D. and Samatar, Said S.1987: *Somalia: Nation in Search of a State*. Boulder: Westview Press.

Lapalombara, Joseph and Weiner, Myron (eds). 1966: *Political Parties and Political Development*.Princeton: Princeton University Press.

Lawrence L. James. 1985: *The Savage Wars: British Campaigns in Africa, 1870-1920*. London: Robert Hale.

Leeuwen, van Carel, Emeljanenko, Tatjana, and Popova, Larisa. 1994: *Nomads in Central Asia: Animal Husbandry and Culture in transition (19th-20th century)*. Amsterdam: Royal Tropical Institute.

Lefebvre, Jeffrey A. 1991: *Arms for the Horn: U.S. Security Policy in Ethiopia and Somalia 1953-1991*. Pittsburgh: University of Pittsburgh Press.

Legum, Colin and Lee, Bill. 1979: *The Horn of Africa in Continuing Crisis*. New York: Africana Publishing Company.

Levy, Marion. 1966: *Modernization and the Structure of Societies: A Setting for International Affairs*. Princeton: Princeton University Press.

Lewis, I.M. 1955: Sufism in Somaliland: A Study in Tribal Islam. *Bulletin of the School of Oriental and African Studies*. Vol. XVII, 581-602.

Lewis, I.M. 1957: *The Somali Lineage System and the Total Genealogy*. London: Crown Agents (mimeo).

Lewis, I.M. 1958: Modern Political Movements in Somaliland. *International African Institute, Memorandum XXX*. Oxford: Oxford University Press.

Lewis, I.M. 1959: Clanship and Contract in Northern Somaliland. *Africa*. Vol. XXIX, 274-293.

Lewis, I.M. 1960: The Somali Conquest of the Horn of Africa. *Journal of African History*. Vol. I, 213-30.

Lewis, I.M. 1961: *A Pastoral Democracy: A Study of Pastoralism and Politics Among the Northern Somali of the Horn of Africa*. Oxford: Oxford University Press.

Lewis, I.M. 1955/1969: *Peoples of the Horn of Africa: Somali Afar and Saho*. London: International African Institute.

Lewis, I.M. 1969: From Nomadism to Cultivation: The Expansion of Political Solidarity in Southern Somalia. In Douglas, M. and Kaberry P. (eds). *Man in Africa*. London: Tavistock, 59-78.

Lewis, I.M. 1972: The Politics of the 1969 Somali Coup. *Journal of Modern African Studies*. Vol. 10 (3), 383-408.

Lewis, I.M. 1988: *A Modern History of Somalia: Nation and State in the Horn of* Africa *(Revised, Updated, and Expanded Edition)*. Boulder: Westview Press.

Lewis, I.M. 1989: The Ogaden and the Fragility of Somali Segmentary Nationalism. *Journal of the Royal African Society*. Vol.88 (353), 573-579.

Lewis, I.M. 1993: *Understanding Somalia: Guide to Culture, History and Social Institutions*. London: Haan Associates.

Lewis, I.M. 1993: Misunderstanding the Somali Crisis. *Anthropology Today* 9 (August), 2.

Lewis, I.M. 1994: *Blood and Bone: The Call of Kinship in Somali Society*. Lawrenceville, NJ: The Red Sea Press.

Lewis, I.M. 2000: New UN Adventures in Somalia. *Horn of Africa Bulletin*, no.3: 19-20.

Lewis, I.M. 2001: *UN Paperclips for Somalia*. www.hiiraan.com (Somali news site), January 18.

Lewis, I.M. 2001: Why the Warlords Won: How the United States and the United Nations Misunderstood the Clan Politics of Somalia. *TLS*, June 8.

Lewis, W. A. 1955: The Theory of Economic Growth. Illinois: Homewood.

Leys, Colin. 1975: *Underdevelopment in Kenya*. Berkeley: University of California Press.

Leys, Colin. 1980: Kenya: What Does 'Dependency' Explain?, *Review of African Political Economy*. Vol.17 (January-April), 108-113.

Leys, Collin. 1996: *The Rise & Fall of Development Theory*. Nairobi: EAEP.

London Gazette, The. 1946: June 5.

Lilius, Suzanne Muddle. 2001: Variations of the Theme of Somaliness (Proceedings of the EASS/SSIA International Congress of Somali Studies). Turku: Centre for Continuing Education, Åbo Akademi University

Loughran, K, Loughran, J, Johnson, J.W. and Samatar S.S. 1986. *Somalia in Word and Image*. Washington DC: Foundation for Cross Cultural Understanding.

Luling, Virginia.1997: Come Back Somalia? Questioning a Collapsed State. *Third World Quarterly*. Vol. 18 (2), 287-300.

Lyons, Terrence and Samatar, Ahmed I. 1995: *Somalia: State Collapse, Multilateral Intervention, and Strategies for Political Reconstruction*. Washington D.C: The Brookings Institution

Mamdani, Mahmood. 1996: *Citizen and Subject: Contemporary Africa and the Legacy of Late Colonialism*. Princeton: Princeton University Press.

Mansur , Abdalla Omar. 1995 : Contrary to a Nation: The Cancer of the Somali State. In Ahmed, Ali J. *The Invention of Somalia*. Lawrenceville: The Red Sea Press.

Maren, Michael. 1993: How the Culture of Aid Gave Us the Tragedy of Somalia. *The Village Voice*. January 19.

Maren, Michael. 1994: For Somalia's Sake, Get the UN Out. *International Herald Tribune*. July 7.

Maren, Michael. 1996: Somalia: Whose Failure. *Current History*. May, 201-205.

Maren, Michael. 1997: *The Road to Hell: The Ravaging Effects of Foreign Aid and International Charity*. New York: The Free Press.

Markakis, John. 1987: *National and Class Conflict in the Horn of Africa*. Cambridge: Cambridge University Press.

Marte, Fred. 1994: *Political Cycles in International Relations: The Cold War and Africa 1945-1990*. Amsterdam: VU University Press.

Martin, Bradford G. 1976. *Muslim Brotherhoods in Nineteenth Century Africa*. Cambridge: Cambridge University Press.

Marx, Karl. 1964: *Pre-Capitalist Economic Formations*. Translated by Jack Cohen. London: Lawrence & Wishart.

Marx, Karl, and Engels, F.1970: *The German Ideology: Part One*. New York: International Publishers.

Max, Emanuel. 1981: The Ecology and Politics of Nomadic Pastoralists in the Middle East. In Wolfgang Weissleder (ed). *The Nomadic Alternative: Modes and Models of Interaction in the African-Asian Deserts and Steppes*. The Hague and Paris: Mouton Publishers.

Mazrui, Ali A. 1997: Crisis in Somalia: From Tyranny to Anarchy. In Adam and Ford (eds).

McConnell, Mitch. 1993: Multilateralism's Obituary Was Written in Mogadishu. *Christian Science Monitor*. October 27.

Mehmet, Ozay. 1971: Effectiveness of Foreign Aid-the Case of Somalia. *The Journal of Modern African Studies*. Vol. 9 (1), 31-47.

Melander, Göran. 1980. *Refugees in Somalia. Research Report No. 56*. Uppsala: Scandinavian Institute of African Studies.

Menkhaus, Kenneth. 1996. International Peace-building and the Dynamics of Local and NationalReconciliation in Somalia. *International Peacekeeping*. Vol. 3 (1), 42-67.

Menkhaus, Kenneth. 1997: US Foreign Assistance to Somalia: Phoenix from the Ashes? *Middle East Policy*, Vol. 5, No. 2 (January): 126.

Menkhaus, Kenneth. 1998: Somalia: Political Order in a Stateless Society. *Current History*, vol.97, no 619, (May):220-4.

Menkhaus, Kenneth. 2000: Somalia: A Situation Analysis. UNHCR Centre for Documentation and Research. *Writenet Paper* No. 07 (November): 1-21.

Menkhaus, Kenneth and Ortmayer, Louis. 2000. Somalia: Misread Crises and Missed Opportunities. In Bruce W. Jentleson (ed). *Opportunities Missed, Opportunities Seized: Preventive Diplomacy in the Post-Cold War World*. New York: Rowman & Littlefield Publishers, 211-237.

Menkhaus, Kenneth. 2001: Evaluation of the War-torn Societies Project in Puntland. In *WSP Somali Programme. Rebuilding Somalia: Issues and Possibilities for Puntland*. London: Haan Associates

Migdal, Joel S.. 1988: *Strong Societies and weak States: State-Society Relations and State Capabilities in the Third World*. New Jersey: Princeton University Press.

Miller, Norman N. 1981: *The Other Somalia*. Hanover: N.H. American Universities Field Staff.

Miller, Norman N. 1981b: The Other Somalia; Part II: Foreign Aid and Local Politics. *Horn ofAfrica*. Vol. 5 (3).

Moghadam, F. E. 1988. Nomadic Invasion and the Development of Productive Forces: An Historical Study of Iran (1000-1800). *Science and Society*. Vol. 52 (4), 389-412.

Mohamoud, Abdullah A.1994: Somalia: Aideed's Homecoming. *West Africa*. (20-26 June): 1084-1085.

Mohamoud, Abdullah A. 1997: Somalia: The 'Ungovernable' Country?. *West Africa*. August 4-10, 1257-1258.

Mohamoud, Abdullah A. 2001: Somalia: The Pitfalls of Drain of Human Resources. In Lilius, Suzanne Muddle (ed.) *Variations of the Theme of Somaliness* (Proceedings of the EASS/SSIA International Congress of Somali Studies). Turku: Centre for Continuing Education, Åbo Akademi University.

Mohammed, Nadir A.L. 1998: Trends, Determinants and the Economic Effects of Military Expenditure in Sub-Saharan Africa. In Hutchful and Bathily (eds).

Morse, A.H.E. 1913: *My Somali Book*. London.

Mubarak, Jamil A. 1996: *From Bad Policy to Chaos in Somalia: How an Economy Fell Apart*. Westport: Praeger Publishers.

Naidoo, Sagaren. 2000: The Role of Track Two Diplomacy in the Democratic Republic of Congo Conflict. *African Journal on Conflict Resolution (ACCORD)*, Vol. 1, No. 2: 1-17.

Nelson, Harold D. (ed). 1982: *Somalia: A Country Study, American University Foreign Area Studies Area Handbook Series*. Washington D.C.: Headquarters of the Department of Army, 3rd edition.

Newsweek. 1992: December 21, 8.

Newsweek. 1993: 10-11.

Newsweek International. 2001: January 29.

Oliver, Roland and Atmore, Anthony. 1977: *Africa Since 1800*. Cambridge: Cambridge University Press.

Omaar, Rakiya. 1993: The Best Chance for Peace. *Africa Report*. (May/June): 45-48.

Omar, Mohamed O. 1992: *The Road to Zero: Somalia's Self-Destruction*. London: Haan Associates.

Ottaway, Marina. 1982: *Soviet and American Influence in the Horn of Africa*. New York: Praeger.

Pankhurst, Estelle Sylvia. 1951: *Ex-Italian Somaliland: How it was acquired and how it was ruled its future*. London: Watts and Co.

Pankhurst, Richard. 1965: The Trade of the Gulf of Aden Ports of Africa in the Nineteenth and Early Twentieth Centuries. *Journal of Ethiopian Studies*. Vol. 3 (1), 36-82.

Parsons, Talcott. 1952: *The Social System*. London: Tavistock Publications.

Patman, Robert G. 1995: The UN Operation in Somalia. In Thakur, Ramesh and Thayer Carlyle A.(eds.). *A Crisis of Expectations: UN Peacekeeping in the 1990s*. Boulder: Westview Press

Payton, D. Gary. 1980: The Somali Coup of 1969: The Case for Soviet Complicity. *Journal of Modern African Studies*. Vol.18 (3), 493-508.

Petras, James F. 1978: *Critical Perspectives on Imperialism and Social Classes in the Third World*. New York: Monthly Review Press.

Polanyi, Karl. 1944: *The Great Transformation: the Political and Economic origins of our Time*. Boston: Beacon Press.

Polanyi, Karl. 1966: *Dahomey and the Slave Trade*. Seattle: University of Washington Press.

Putnam, Robert D. 1993: *Making Democracy Work: Civic Transitions in Northern Somalia, 1886-1986*. Madison, Wisconsin: The University of Wisconsin Press.

Pye, Lucien W. and Verba, Sidney (eds). 1965: *Political and Political Development*. Princeton, NJ: Princeton University Press.

Rawson, David.1994: Dealing with Disintegration: U.S. Assistance and the Somali State. In Samatar, Ahmed. (ed.).

Rayne, Major H. Sun. 1921: *Sand and Somalis: Leaves from the Notebook of a District Commissioner in British Somaliland*. London: H.F. & G. Witherby.

Rirash, A.M. 1988: Camel Herding and its Effects on Somali Literature. *Northeast African Studies*. Vol. 2.

Ricciiuti, Edward R. 1995: *Somalia: A Crisis of Famine and War*. London: Evans Brothers Limited.

Rodd, J.R. 1923: *Social and Diplomatic Memories*. London.

Rodney, Walter. 1972: *How Europe Underdeveloped Africa*. Dar es Salaam: Tanzania publishing House.

Rostow, Walt.W. 1967: *The Stages of Economic Growth*. Cambridge: Cambridge University Press.

Sahlins, M. 1968: *Tribesmen*. Englewood Cliffs. New Jersey: Prentice-Hall.

Sahnoun, Mohamed. 1994: *The Missed Opportunities*. Washington DC: United States Institute of Peace Press.

Samatar, Abdi I. And Samatar, Ahmed I. 1987: The Material Roots of the Suspended African State: Arguments from Somalia. *The Journal of Modern African Studies*. Vol. 25 (4), 669-690.

Samatar, Abdi I. 1989: *The State and Rural Transformation in Northern Somalia, 1886-1986*. Madison, Wisconsin: The University of Wisconsin Press.

Samatar, Abdi I. 1989b: Somali Tradition, Peripheral Capitalism, and the Politics of Development. *Northeast African Studies*. Vol. 11 (1), 39-52.

Samatar, Abdi I. 1992: Social Classes and Economic Restructuring in Pastoral Africa: Somali Notes. *African Studies Review*. Vol. 35 (1), 101-127.

Samatar, Abdi I. 1992b: Destruction of State and Society in Somalia: Beyond the Tribal Convention. *The Journal of Modern African Studies*. Vol. 30 (4), 625-641.

Samatar, Abdi I. 1993: Dictators and Warlords are a Modern Invention. *Africa News*. December 21.

Samatar, Abdi I. 1997: Leadership and Ethnicity in the making of African State Models: Botswana versus Somalia. *Third World Quarterly*. Vol. 18 (4), 687-707.

Samatar, Abdi I. 1999: *An African Miracle: State and Class Leadership and Colonial Legacy In Botswana Development*. Portsmouth: Heinemann.

Samatar, Abdi I. 2001: *I.M. Lewis's Retired Ideas and Somalia*. www.hiiraan.com (Somali news site).

Samatar, Abdi I. 2001: Somali Reconstruction and Local Initiative: Amoud University, *Bildhaan*, 1, 107-131.

Samatar, Ahmed I. 1988: *Socialist Somalia: Rhetoric and Reality*. London and New Jersey: Institute of African Alternatives and Zed Books.

Samatar, Ahmed I. 1989: Somali Studies: Towards an Alternative Epistemology. *Northeast AfricanStudies*. Vol. 11 (1), 3-17.

Samatar, Ahmed I. 1993: Under Siege: Blood, Power, and the Somali State. In Anyang'Nyong'o.P (ed) *Arms and Daggers in the Heart of Africa: Studies on Internal Conflicts*. Nairobi: Academy Science Publishers.

Samatar, Ahmed I. (ed) 1994: *The Somali Challenge: From Catastrophe to Renewal?*. Boulder: Lynne Rienner Publisher.

Samatar, Ahmed I. 1995: *Somalia: State Collapse, Multilateral Intervention, and Strategies for Political Reconstruction*. Washington D C: The Brookings Institution.

Samatar, Ahmed I.1996: The Death of a State, and Other Reflections. Paper presented at the University of Otago in Dunedin, New Zealand.

Samatar, Ahmed I. 2001: The Somali Catastrophe: Explanations and Implications. In Lilius, Suzanne Muddle (ed.) *Variations of the Theme of Somaliness* (Proceedings of the EASS/SSIA International Congress of Somali Studies). Turku: Centre for Continuing Education, Åbo Akademi University.

Samatar, Ahmed I. (ed): 2001: *Bildhaan: An International Journal of Somali Studies*, Vol.1. 1-131.

Samatar, Said S. 1982: *Oral Poetry and Somali Nationalism: The Case of Sayyid Mohammed' Abdulle Hassan*. Cambridge: Cambridge University Press.

Samatar, Said S. 1991: *Somalia: A Nation in Turmoil*. London: Minority Rights Group.

Samatar, Said S. 1993: The Politics of Poetry. *Africa Report*. September/October, 16-17.

Sandbrook, Richard. 1976: The Crisis in Political Development Theory, *The Journal of Development Studies* 12, No. 2: 165-185.

Sandbrook, Richard. 1985: *The Politics of Africa's Economic Stagnation*. Cambridge: Cambridge University Press.

Schraeder, Peter. 1992: The Horn of Africa : US Foreign Policy in an Altered Cold War Environment. *Middle East Journal*. Vol. 46 (4), 571-593.

Sciolino, Elaine.1993: In Sharp Split, UN Chief Pans New U. S. Strategy in Somalia. *International Herald Tribune*. October, 2-3.

Selassie, Bereket Habte. 1980: *Conflict and Intervention in the Horn of Africa*. New York: Monthly Review Press.

Shivaji, Issa G. 1975: *Class Struggles in Tanzania*. London: Heinemann Educational Books.

Simons, Anna. 1995: *Networks of Dissolution: Somalia Undone*. Boulder: Westview Press.

Sinclair, M.R. 1980: *The Strategic Significance of the Horn of Africa*. Pretoria. Pretoria: Institute for Strategic Studies, University of Pretoria.

Sivard, Ruth L. 1982: *World Military and Social Expenditures, 1978*. Leesburg: World Priorities.

Smith, Tony. 1979: The Underdevelopment of Development Literature. *World Politics* 31, No. 2 .

Smith, Tony. 1985: Requiem or New Agenda for Third World Studies? *World Politics*, 532-651.

So, Alvin Y. 1990: *Social Change and Development: Modernisation, Dependency, and World-System Theories*. London: Sage Publications.

Spencer, H. John. 1978: A Reassessment of Ethiopian-Somali Conflict. *Horn of Africa*. Vol. 1 (3), 23-30.

Stevenson, Jonathan. 1995: *Losing Mogadishu: Testing U.S. Policy in Somalia*. Annapolis: Naval Institute Press.

Swayne, Major H.G.C. 1900: *Seventeen Trips through Somaliland and a Visit to Abyssinia*. London: Rowland Ward, Ltd.

Swift, J. 1977: Sahelian Pastoralists: Underdevelopment, Desertification and Famine. *Annual Review of Anthropology*. Vol. 6, 457-478.

Time Magazine. 1992: December 14, 31.

Time Magazine. 1992: December 21, 20.

Thurston, Raymond L. 1978: The United States, Somalia and the Crisis in the Horn. *Horn of Africa Journal*. April-June, 11-20.

Touval, Saadia. 1963: *International Politics and the Drive for 'Unity in the Horn of Africa' Somali Nationalism*. Cambridge: Cambridge University Press.

USIA, East Asia/Pacific Wireless File, 4 December 1992: 12.

Van de Walle, Nicolas. 1996: The Politics of Aid Effectiveness. In Ellis, Stephen (ed.). *Africa Now: People, Politics and Institutions*. London: Heinmann.

War-torn Societies Project. *Rebuilding Somalia: Issues and Possibilities for Puntland*. London: Haan Associates, 2000.

Washington Post, The. 1993: July 19.

Weber, Max. 1984: *The Theory of Social and Economic Organisation*. (Edited and with an introduction by Talcott Parsons). Massachutes: Cambridge University Press.

Weeks, George. 1964: The Armies of Africa. *Africa Report* (January 19): 8-18.

Weiss, Thomas G. 1995: Overcoming the Somalia Syndrome - Operation Rekindle Hope? *Global Governance: A Review of Multilateralism and International Organisations*. Vol.1 (2), 171-187.

Western, David.1982: The environment and ecology of pastoralists in arid savannas. *Development and Change*. Vol. 13 (2).

Wisner, Ben.1994: "Jilaal, Gu, Hagaa, and Der: Living with the Somali Land, and Living Well. In Samatar, Ahmed (ed).

Wilson, Henry S. 1994: *Contemporary History: African Decolonisation*. London: Edward Arnold,A Member of the Hodder Headline Group.

Wolf, Eric R. 1982: *Europe and the People Without History*. Berkeley: University of California Press.

Zartman, I. (ed.), 1995: *Collapsed States: The Disintegration and Restoration of Legitimate Authority*. Boulder: Lynne Rienner Publishers.

Documents

African studies Centre. 1983: *Somalia A Social and Institutional Profile*. Boston: University of Boston.

Four-Power Commission. 1959: *Reports of Investigation for Former Italian Colonies/Council of Foreign Ministers (Deputies)*, Vol. 1, Part 2, 3.

German Planning and Economic Advisory Group. 1969: *Reports on the progress of Development Projects in Somali Democratic Republic*. Mogadishu and Frankfurt, mimeo.

Great Britain, Colonial Office. 1944: *The First to be Freed: The Record of British Military Administration in Eritrea and Somalia 1941-1943*. Issued by the Ministry of Information. London: His Majesty's Stationery Office.

 1952: *Report on the Somaliland Protectorate for the years 1950 and 1951*. London: H.M. Stationary Office.

-.1957: *Report on the Somaliland Protectorate for the years of 1954 and 1955*. London: H.M. Stationery Office.

ILO/JASPA: 1977: *Economic Transformation in a Socialist Framework: An Employment and Basic Needs Oriented Development Strategy for Somalia*. Addis Ababa.

International Institute for Strategic Studies (IISS) 1977: *The Military Balance 1976-77*. London.

Organisation of African Unity. 1963: *Basic Documents of the Organisation of African Unity*. Addis Ababa.

-. 1975: *Economic Commission for Africa, Summaries of Economic Data, Somalia*. Addis

Ababa, M75-168, 6th year/ No. 9.

Refugee Policy Group. 1994: *Hope Restored? Humanitarian Aid in Somalia 1990-1994*. Washington DC: Refugee Policy Group, 114.

Report of a Mission Organized by the IBRD at the Request of the Government of Italy. 1957: *The Economy of the Trust Territory of Somaliland*.

United Nations. 1952: *Report on Somaliland Under Italian Administration*. (T/1033), 1-38.

-. 1970: *Social and Economic Council, Economic Commission for Africa. Summaries of Economic Data: Somalia 1968-69*. (070-702), No. 9.

-. 1975: *UN Economic Commission for Africa, Summaries of Economic Data: Somalia* (Addis Ababa), 10-11, 16.

-. 1979: *Report of the UN Inter-Agency Mission*. December.

-. 1979: *UN Inter-Agency Mission to Somalia. Report of the Mission to Somalia*, December 10-16 1979, 11.

-. 1990: *Somalia: Country Presentation* (UNCLDC II/CP.4), 1-27.

-. 1992: *The United Nations and Somalia (1992-1996): The United Nations Blue Books Series, Volume VIII*. New York: United Nations Department of Public Information.

-. 1992: *UN Chronicle*. June, 23.

-. 1992: *UN Security Council Resolution 794*. December 3.

-. 1993: *UN Security Council Resolution 837*. June 6.

-. 1996: *UN Document. UN A/AC.96 /SR.037*

-. 2001: *UNHCR Country Report: Somalia*. October 2.

The Economist Intelligent Unit. 1991: *Somalia Country Profile 1991 - 1992*. London.

Somali Democratic Republic. Ministry of Foreign Affairs 1959: *The Somali Peoples' Quest for Unity. An explanation of the issues involved in the Somali/Ethiopian, Somali/Kenyan disputes and the liberation of French Somaliland.* Mogadishu.

-. 1960: *The Constitution of the Somali Republic.* 31st June.

-. Ministry of Education 1968: *Statistical Trends.* Mogadishu.

-. 1979: A Request for Assistance from the Government of the Somali Democratic Republic for the Refugees. Mogadishu, October.

United States. Department of Commerce, Bureau of International Commerce. 1965: *Basic Data on the Economy of the Somali Republic*, prepared by Joseph Eblan.

-. 1978: *Arms Control and Disarmament Agency- World Military Expenditures and Arms Transfers 1969-1978.* 66-109.

World Bank. 1968: *International Bank for Reconstruction and Development, World Bank Atlas, Population, Per Capita Product and Growth Rates.* Washington DC.

-. 1988: *World Development Report.*

-. 1989: *Report and Recommendation of the President of the International development Association to the Somali Democratic Republic.* Report No. P-4995-S0. May 2.

-. 1991: Report No. 8727-SO, Volume 2.

Lightning Source UK Ltd.
Milton Keynes UK
UKHW021939281020
372395UK00014B/177